Jerry Lawler Record Book: 1970-1996

Mark James

Jerry Lawler
Record Book:
1970-1996

Copyright @ 2018 by Mark James

Published by Mark James www.markjamesbooks.com

Book layout by Mark James
Cover layout by Mark James
Content Editing by Mark James
Cover Photo taken by Jim Cornette

James, Mark
Jerry Lawler Record Book: 1970-1996/by Mark James – 1st ed.

Printed in the United States of America

ISBN-13: 978-1722119423
ISBN-10: 172211942X

Table of Contents

Introduction:

Jerry Lawler is a legend in Memphis, TN. While his wrestling career started in 1970, it still continues to this day, forty-eight years later. With a career so extensive and one that covers such a long period of time, I get multiple requests each week asking, "Did Jerry ever go against...?" There's even an occasional phone call from Jerry Lawler himself, asking, "Hey, when did I originally fight...?". That is the reasoning behind this book. I wanted the young and old wrestling fans to share in the knowledge of Jerry's amazing career. This information needs to be available instead of it being kept hidden on a computer somewhere. Regardless of the decade, Pro Wrestling was always for the fans. That's what my books continue to be about, getting the info to the fans. As a kid I ALWAYS wondered who had already fought, where they had fought, etc. The wrestling promotions made money back then by selling tickets for the matches that were happening that day, not five years ago. Video tape libraries were decades away. If it didn't make the promotion money, then they didn't care about it. That's why there's hardly any original wrestling TV recordings saved from the 1970s and 1980s. With over thirty active wrestling territories in the United States back then, can you imagine if each one had kept their video tape libraries? Nope, they promotions usually just taped over the previous week's show, to save the cost of a new tape. That's why I put my books out, to make sure the history is preserved and not forgotten about.

After forty-four books, I can't tell you how happy I am to finally be able to do a book that focuses solely on Jerry Lawler. During my youth, (which spanned from the mid-1970s through the mid-1980s), Jerry Lawler was my hero. He was my quarterback, he was my Superman. You name it, he was it. He was that for many kids in the Memphis/West TN area during that time. As happens, in the late 1980s, the 1990s, etc, new kids came along and Jerry was the same thing for them. Then it repeated again, etc. New kids, but the same old King, though with new feuds. Jerry Lawler stood the test of time and was a hero to many of us. Which era of Jerry Lawler was the best? The truth is that statement is completely subjective and can only be answered by each person in their own way. With that in mind, ask an older fan and they might mention Lawler vs. Jackie Fargo or Lawler vs. Dundee as their favorite feud, another fan might mention Lawler vs. Andy Kaufman or Lawler vs. Jimmy Hart. Younger ones might mention Lawler & Jeff Jarrett and their war with the Moondogs, or when the WWF invaded Memphis. To each era, that version of Jerry Lawler was their hero and the greatest wrestler alive.

I hope this book helps you look back on fond memories of Jerry's matches. By the same token, I hope it also enlightens your appreciation for Jerry's amazing career in the ring. Ask an older fan and they might mention Lawler vs. Jackie Fargo or Lawler vs. Dundee as their favorite feud, another fan might mention Lawler vs. Andy Kaufman or Lawler vs. Jimmy Hart. Later still they might mention Lawler & Jeff Jarrett and their war with the Moondogs, or when the WWF invaded Memphis. To each era, that version of Jerry Lawler was their hero and the greatest wrestler alive.

As far as what's here, I've looked for all the match listings and results for Jerry Lawler, from 1970 through 1996. There's somewhere around 4,000 of them in this book. Eventually there will be a second collection featuring 1997 through today. The depth of research for this book took forever. I do want to take a second and thank my friend David Baker for his large contribution of Lawler results and listings. David is a great guy and definitely shares my desire to document the old days as much as we can. If you have any more matches, that aren't included in this book, please send them to me.

I wanted to take a second to thank Jim Blake for writing the Foreword to this book. I am honored he'd take the time and effort to be included in this book. Jim has know Jerry Lawler for almost as long as I've been alive and I couldn't think of anyone better to give us insight into the King. Jim's been a good friend to me for the past several years and I am thankful for his help.

I always make a point to give thanks to the people in my world who help make this crazy thing possible. So many people to list: Gayle James, Chris James, Dave Millican, Jim Cornette, Jerry Lawler, Bill Dundee, Jimmy Hart, Jerry Jarrett, Jimmy Valiant, Austin Idol, Rick Morton, Shane Russell, Dave Brown, Mike Shields, David Hileman, Tommy Musso, Chris Swisher, Reggie Bernard, Bert Prentice, Scott Teal, George Schire, David Baker, Coach Phil Thompson, Alvin Minnick, Conrad Thompson, Paula & Brian Carpenter, Eddie Austin, Randy Hales, Brandon Owen Harber, Glenn Moore and a ton of people I will regret not remembering to list here. People inside and outside the wrestling business have been extremely good to me. I can't thank you guys enough and my appreciation for you is more than you will ever know, thank you all.

Lastly, I want to dedicate this book to a guy I didn't know, and actually never met. One of my best friends, David Hileman, would tell me about the endless conventions he was going to, mostly with his younger niece, Amanda Redfoot and her boyfriend, Mikey Lewis. I was so jealous because where I live, we get none of these cons. Whatever the convention was centered around, (movies, comic books, horror, wrestling, pop culture, etc), I would get to hear all the great stories. I looked forward to hearing the amazing details of who they got to meet that weekend. Sadly, in July 2017, Michael Lewis (Mikey), took his own life. Mikey's actions, and hearing what many others struggle with on a daily basis, made me do my own research. It made me realize the people who commit suicide aren't weak but are in pain. Real, never ending, pain. By this I mean they can't make the voices, or the pain stop. Weakness isn't in the equation, the struggle is real and they are beaten down every single day. This is an illness. Mikey, through David, helped me look deeper, to gain a better perspective of these people's situations. There's no helping Mikey now. The good news is there are people who care. People who are trying to understand and give the support to those who need it. If there's anyone out there who needs help right now, please call the national suicide prevention hotline at (800) 273-8255. People do care and you don't have to go through this alone. They may be able to help you. So Mikey Lewis, this book is dedicated to you, in hopes someone else may find a way to get help and discover a way through their pain.

Mark James
MarkJamesBooks.com

Foreword:

I first met Jerry when I was managing Pop-i's, a record store/pinball arcade on the Highland Strip near Memphis State University. He would hang out at my shop after his classes and one day we struck up a conversation where we learned we were both Beatles fans and devotees of the great artist, Frank Frazetta. Jerry had earned a full art scholarship MSU (now known as the UofM, University of Memphis) and while discussing his body of artwork, Jerry bragged he was as good as Frazetta. I pronounced him nuts and a blasphemer.

He asked me if he were to bring in a painting of his, and it was that good, would I buy pay $30 for it? I laughed and said, "Go away kid. You're bothering me." He was serious and showed up the next day with my first Jerry Lawler painting. I didn't say a word, I just dug $30 out of my pocket and laid it on the counter. That was the beginning of a long relationship regarding art, on many different levels.

Jerry Drawing At The Memphis Comic Expo.

Jerry's family consisted of a married brother and a hard working, widowed mother. Mrs. Lawler hard and brought up her children to be well mannered and respectful. Jerry was lucky. They lived in a modest house near Treadwell High School in Memphis. This is important in Jerry's development, because it was there he became a pupil of the late Helen Stahl. She would become not only his art teacher but more importantly, his mentor. She was responsible for Jerry's full art scholarship to Memphis State University. He eventually dropped out of college because his art teachers were nowhere near as talented as he was.

Over the years I continued to buy Jerry's art whenever he needed money. He was a remarkable talent. He was so good that I had friends who would have him paint a picture and then sign their names to it. Even at that young age, he was a bundle of energy and a tireless self-promoter. I had several underground newspapers (Atlantis, Strawberry Fields, Tennessee Roc and Nashville Skyline). Jerry's art was featured in every issue, which covered art, music & humor. I was a hippie and Jerry was the All-American boy. He was so clean-cut that he never smoked, drank liquor or did any drugs. He still hasn't till this day.

I was friends with Scott Shannon, the #1 top forty disc jockey in Memphis. Jerry was a huge fan of his and felt he could be as good on the radio as "SuperShan". I got them together and Scott cut an audition tape on Jerry. This allowed Jerry to take the tape around and eventually got a job as night DJ at KWAM, a middling Country & Western radio station. Jerry was good but was unsatisfied with the playlist he was provided. The list included some of the stalest, old dissonant country caterwauling around. Jerry called me to get his some progressive country. I carried a stack of records that personified the direction of country music. Jerry played them with the gusto of a renegade disc jockey trying to attract a younger, more vital audience. He was cut off at the transmitter and fired over the phone. He had been too far ahead of the curve.

Jerry went back to his art for money. He painted 2, 8'x8' murals for my record store, The Yellow Submarine. He also painted the Beatles and Nowhere Man on the wooden counters. One mural was so outstanding that it was stolen in the dead of night by some ambitious thieves with bolt cutters.

Meanwhile, Jerry had made his first appearance on Memphis Studio Wrestling. He had sent several drawings of prominent wrestlers to the TV station. The host, Lance Russell, was so impressed with the art; that he had Jerry on the show to highlight him. It was also at this time that Jerry started painting billboards for Eddie Bond's and Jackie Fargo's sign company. Jerry credits Fargo with giving him the opportunity to become a professional wrestler. There was a long period where Jerry was beaten black and blue. As his new career progressed, he bulked up; gained confidence; and became the cocky anti-hero to the Memphis audience. His rise and fame became a remarkable story.

Jerry Lawler was outrageous, smug, snarky, contemptible and everything your mama wanted you to have nothing to do with. Jerry even did a publicity photo of himself, nude on a bearskin rug, with only his crown discretely positioned over the "crown jewels", he continued to provoke audiences with his audacity and insulting arrogance. All this controversy ignited record sell-out crowds at the Mid-South Coliseum and unparalleled ratings for the television station.

During this period, I, along with my mentor, the late Jim Dickinson, made the first record with Jerry. It was a perfect vehicle for the bad-boy persona of the King. The song boasted about Jerry's ruggedness, good looks, macho-ness and all-around invincibility. The song was "Bad News", a perfect description the Lawler image.

The next record was "Cadillac Man". It was cut at Sam Phillips Studios with Knox Phillips handling the engineering. Jerry was a true son of Memphis. The song had originally been released in the 1960s on a Yellow Sun record by the Jesters. Jerry respected all the traditional achievements of Memphis music. By now, the sessions had become legendary; and all the elite musicians in Memphis were flocking to be a part of it, and meet Jerry. The musicians were always surprised to meet a nice guy, who was personable, intelligent and affable. They were entertained when Jerry recorded in character, singing shirtless with his crown on his head. "Cadillac Man" was another song tailored to Lawler's reputation. The public knew that Jerry only drove Cadillac's. The song revels in the King's love of these cars and disdain for anyone who could not afford one. The flipside was his homage to Chuck Berry's "Memphis, Tennessee", wanting his version to be punk and underground, Lawler gave it a straightforward vocal atop a cacophony of steel drums.

The third record was cut at Allied Studios with the late Lewis Willis engineering. It was especially written for the King and entitled, "The Ballad of Jerry Lawler". This audacious song lauded Jerry as the handsomest, best singer (since Elvis), Best guitar player, best piano player, best athlete, etc. The flip side, "90 Pound Weakling" extols Lawler's emergence as a he-man who'd kick sand in your face if you crossed his path... All his records personified Lawler's character as the baddest man in town and a braggart who's ego knew no bounds.

The records were a huge success at the wrestling matches. The audience bought them to break. Jerry had the bright idea of becoming enraged when anyone disrespected his artistic achievement. This caused countless Lawler-haters to flock to the merchandise table and buy the record. As the records were smashed and stomped, Jerry would rage like a madman. This incited the wrestling crowd to buy more to break. We encouraged them to buy two because breaking two would make them feel twice as good. We even had kids that would go around and help little old ladies who were to feeble, to break the records themselves. We loved it! A sale is a sale, and we could have cared less what they did with them. Unfortunately, that's why so few of them exist today.

Times have changed since those early, maverick days. The King has become a living legend, lauded internationally. He's recognized as a true hero; a hometown boy made good. Jerry is so many things other than a professional wrestler. He wears many crowns. He's an incredible artist, adept in any media. He's a ground breaking recording artist, movie star, WWE wrestler and Hall of Famer, wrestling superstar. The key word is Lawler is artist. He's a true artist who paints his life and careers with a broad stroke. This book covers those heydays from 1970 until 1996. These years chronicle Lawler's emergence as a world-class wrestler and national personality. His legend will continue to grow as long as his many facets are explored. This book gives you a ringside seat to over a quarter of a century of a Memphis anti hero. Enjoy!

James Blake
Barbarian Records

Quotes:

I contacted many people within the "Memphis Wrestling" family and let them know I was working on this book. I asked if they would be interested in giving me a quote, a story, etc. They all overwhelmingly wanted to. Not one hesitated. Below are their comments.

Shane Russell: Son Of Lance Russell

Jerry "THE KING" Lawler!!!! I can still hear my dad saying this on Monday nights at the Mid-South Coliseum. He introduced thousands of wrestlers through-out his career as the Voice of Memphis Wrestling but there was something about the way he announced Jerry Lawler's name that was different. When he bellowed Jerry's name, he would say it with a little more passion and conviction than anybody else, like he was personally proud that the "King" was coming to the ring. In fact, he was proud, almost like he was introducing his own son!!

Dad had known Jerry since he was 15 years old and had a little bit to do with getting Jerry in the wrestling business. Dad always said that Jerry had so much talent that he would have made it eventually, dad just happened to be in the right place at the right time to get the ball rolling. This was the start of an over 50 year relationship. Dad went on to WCW and Jerry went on to the WWF but they remained close friends.

When dad was selected to receive the Announcers Hall of Fame award at the annual Cauliflower Alley Club convention in 2016, he got to choose someone to introduce him at the dinner. I asked him had he thought about it and who would he like to ask. He looked at me like I was crazy!!! He said, in his great voice, "The King!!!!!" Dad was worried that with Jerry's busy schedule, he would already have a conflict. When Dad called Jerry about it, Jerry's response was, "I wouldn't miss it for anything, I'll be there!"

Lance Russell and Jerry Lawler, two names that are synonymous with Memphis Wrestling. Two friends that had a 50 year friendship in a business that was as cut-throat as any. In

2017, when dad passed away, Jerry cancelled everything to be at the funeral to pay his respects to the Lancer... his colleague and most importantly, his nearly lifelong friend!

Bill Dundee
Lawler was a great wrestler, I happened to be as was as well. That doesn't always bring about a good match. Jerry Jarrett put us in a feud together back in 1977, it was magic. I was booked as the underdog and Jerry was the mean, ol' King. It sold the territory out. From that point, whether it was against each another or as a team, the Memphis crowd always loved it. The truth is I knew my role. Jerry was the top guy and part owner of the territory, so that wasn't going to change. Being the #2 guy in Memphis was great and paid very well.

Jimmy Valiant
Oh man, Kingfish was always great to me. After those crazy Memphis wars with him in the late 1970s, they flipped me because the fans loved me so much. In the 1980s Kingfish would bring me in as his tag partner and the crowds couldn't get enough of it. Didn't matter if we were at the Union City High School Gym or the Mid-South Coliseum in Memphis, the fans bought the tickets. Jerry is like family, so if he calls me, I come to Memphis.

Ricky Morton: Rock n Roll Express
Lawler gets the credit for starting the Rock n Roll Express. It was all on him. Robert and I were at Ch 5 for the Saturday show in Memphis. Jerry walked into the dressing area and had me and Robert go with him. He told us what his plan was for the Rock n Roll Express. He brought a bag with him and pulled stack of current rock magazines and we all looked at the fashions. Jerry pulled out two pair of tights, one was purple and the other light tan color. I grabbed the purple ones and Robert was left with the light tan ones. I had only ever worn trunks, never the full tights, and didn't like them. When Robert tried his on, it looked like he was naked. Jerry reached into his bag again and brought out a bunch of things for our outfits, (bandanas, feathers, etc.) We went and got dressed and then looked at each other, with all the extras, and I told Robert there was no way I was going to the ring looking like that. Of course, you know we did. Lance Russell introduced us and the studio crowd went wild. It was hugely successful and the Rock n Roll Express were born. Jerry Lawler gave Ricky and I an opportunity by creating the Rock n Roll Express, and I am so glad he did because it made us superstars.

*Photo Courtesy of Jim Cornette
Ricky & Robert's 1st Day As
The Rock n' Roll Express

I have been a professional wrestler for 40 years. I have traveled all over the world and wrestled nearly everyone. I can tell you, that without a doubt, Jerry Lawler is the best wrestler I've ever been in the ring with. Thank you for everything Jerry!

Austin Idol: AustinIdolLive.com
So here we are, Jerry "The King" Lawler and the "Universal Heartthrob" Austin Idol, booked to wrestle each other at the Mid-South Coliseum for the Southern Heavyweight title. It was in the month of December when wrestling fans were enjoying their Christmas season but,

little did they know the Grinch was getting ready to ruin it for them! Gotta to tell you, I always liked playing the Grinch and if Fred Ward were alive today, I believe he would agree! I left the ring that night as the new Southern Heavyweight champion and really, the rest is history.

Despite Jerry and I having two colossal egos, we had a very special chemistry that made us like electricity in the ring. Year-in and year-out, we either feuded or were partners against some of the best in the wrestling industry and drew big time money in both scenarios. What we had in common the most was money, and we knew how to get it; although there were times I had to fight to get my fair share. The King and the Idol in a steel cage is a match that will never be forgotten! Looking back, it was a great run.

Jerry Lawler & Jimmy Hart

Jimmy Hart: Mouth Of The South

If it wasn't for Jerry Lawler, I would not be in the business I love, professional wrestling. Jerry Lawler was not only the top babyface in Memphis Wrestling, he was its top drawing heel. Long live the King!

Randy Hales: Power Pro Wrestling

I was very excited when Mark James ask me to write something for the Jerry Lawler Record Book. Then Mark gave me a headache when he asked me to do it in a paragraph. Jerry Lawler, the man who I am on record saying is the best professional wrestler who ever lived. Jerry Lawler, the man responsible for me ever being in the wrestling business. I am to do this in a paragraph. Jerry Lawler, the man who sold out the Memphis Mid-South Coliseum with Jack Brisco, Terry Funk, Harley Race, Dick the Bruiser, The Sheik, Rick Gibson, the Mongolian Stomper, Bill Dundee, Tommy Rich, Austin Idol, Bob Armstrong, Jackie Fargo and so many more. I have a paragraph. Jerry Lawler, who's career would fill up a library and I must write about it in a single paragraph. Jerry Lawler, who's career has spanned nearly fifty years, who dominated one city, Memphis, TN. like no other wrestler in history has dominated a city. I give up. I can't do this in one little paragraph... Read this book. Read all the results. Learn about all the wrestlers Jerry has been in the ring with. Read about all the World Champions he was in the ring with. Read about all the huge world-wide superstars he has been in the ring with. Read about the results of his matches with future Hall of Famers. Read the results of matches he had with people you have never heard of. Read about all the famous cities and countries he has wrestled in. Also, read about the small towns in Arkansas, Tennessee or Kentucky you have never heard of. Then, after you finish reading this book, you try to do what I can't do in one paragraph. You write a paragraph telling why Jerry Lawler is the best professional wrestler of all time.

Dave Millican: WWE Title Belt Maker & long-time friend of Jerry

It's not easy to be brief when trying to describe the influence that Jerry Lawler has had on my life. I probably have enough "King" stories to fill a book. In so many ways, I am who I am because of him. I make championship belts for a living. Without Jerry Lawler, I just don't think I would've ever cared enough to have paid any attention to a championship belt to have wanted to make my own. I've learned a lot about everything from public speaking to self promotion just by watching him for many years. I've also been fortunate to be able to call him my friend for about 30 years now. Jerry has a larger than life presence that is just part of him. No matter how long you've known him, it never fades. I didn't realize it until I got to know him, but it has nothing to do with fame. In fact, at times it is apparent to me that he's not even always aware of it. He would have that same charisma no matter what he had chosen as a profession. Fortunately for wrestling fans, he chose to entertain us. No one in my lifetime has ever done a better job of that than "The King".

Jerry Calhoun: Memphis Referee

I've known Jerry just about all my life. We went to the same high school (Treadwell) and married our high school sweethearts (sisters). I use to go with Jerry out of town on weekends when he wrestled, then he eventually got me into wrestling as a referee. We would play softball and football all the time. On Sunday nights we would go out to eat and then go to a movie with our second wives. I don't have enough positive words to say how much Jerry has meant to me as a friend and am so appreciative of all he has done for me. He has also had a major impact on so many people getting into wrestling and helping them along with their careers. I don't know of anyone that has the wrestling and communication skills he has, along with a mind for the wrestling business. We've done so much together and I will always cherish those wonderful memories. Thanks for making the world better (for the people you know), especially mine. You've made my life so much fun, thank you Jerry.

Dutch Mantell

Couple of things I'll always remember about Jerry was we shared the same birthday. And even odder was, we shared the same birth year. I used to travel with Jerry quite a bit and what I learned when he was booking, was to never over think an angle. Over-thinking took the original attractiveness of an angle and usually ruined it. Great talker, great performer and now with his WWE exposure is probably the most famous Memphian ever, even out distancing Jerry Lee Lewis and the Original King himself, Elvis Presley.

Jim Cornette

Jerry Lawler has had more than an incredible impact on Memphis Wrestling, he's had an incredible impact on my career as well--I told him one time I'd made more money with his material than he had! Unfortunately, that wasn't true, but I tried. The King is not only one of the great promo men of all time, and one of the all-time great ring psychologists, but his every match, whether in the hallowed Mid-South Coliseum before his most loyal subjects or anywhere else, was a clinic that ALL pro wrestling performers could learn from, for his body language, fire and intensity, and that immortal comeback. No one has had the career he's had, from the longevity, to the box office success, to the many facets in which he's excelled--wrestler, booker, announcer, personality. This book is a testament to that success.

Jerry, Jim Cornette & the King's Batmobille

LONG LIVE THE KING!

Jerry Jarrett: Memphis Wrestling Booker, Promoter & Owner
I've worked with thousands of wrestlers and promoted many of the top superstars in our industry. I can honestly say that Jerry Lawler stands head and shoulders about them all in creative ability, in-ring ability and verbal skills. Jerry and I were partners for many years in what has become known as the Memphis territory. Jerry's contributions both in the ring and in the business itself are invaluable to the extent that Memphis wrestling would not have the world-wide reputation it has today without him.

Dave Brown: Memphis Wrestling TV Show Co-Host
Jerry Lawler changed the Memphis Wresting landscape immeasurably in the early 1970s. As some of the big stars in the territory were past their prime, Lawler brought a fresh star to the promotion. He was a natural on camera, had a sense of humor that could either amuse or infuriate depending on whether he was a heel or a babyface at the time, and could cut a promo that was near perfect.

As the Jerry Lawler brand grew, the Memphis territory blossomed... aided of course by other fresh talent. By the 1980s when Memphis Wrestling was on top, Lawler was the steady constant in drawing money at the arena shows. His impact on the territory cannot be overstated.

I am proud to call him a friend for these many years.

Eddie Austin: Super-fan
During the summer of 1978, as an eight year old, I discovered Memphis Wrestling and Jerry Lawler. In 1979, as I watched Jerry's feud with Bill Dundee, I was hooked and there was no going back. Back then, I looked at Jerry as a real life superhero. Even now, forty years later, I still look at him through that 8 year old kid's eyes and still see a superhero. Thanks for the memories Jerry.

1970

Chapter 1

1970: West Memphis, AR?
w/Jerry Vickers lost via Count Out to the Executioners

Aug 17, 1970: Memphis, TN
lost to Mack York

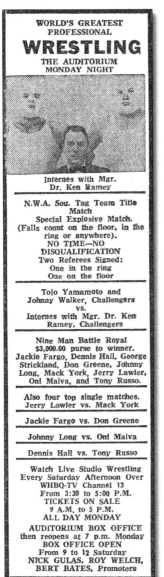

Aug 17, 1970: Jerry Lawler's First Monday Night In A Memphis Ring

Oct 6, 1970: Florence, AL
in Battle Royal

Jerry Lawler
218 lbs - Memphis, TN

Jerry Lawler: Rookie Year

1971

Chapter 2

Jan. 5, 1971: Memphis, TN
w/Gary Martin, lost to The Masked Outlaws

Jan 11, 1971: Memphis, TN
(sub for Eddie Marlin) & Gary Martin lost to the Outlaws

Jan 25, 1971: Memphis, TN
& Gary Martin vs. Tony & Chico Mendoza

Feb 9, 1971: Florence, AL
Jerry Lawler vs. The Green Shadow

Mar 18, 1971: Hopkinsville, KY
& Buddy Wayne Peale vs. Bobby Hart & Lorenzo Parente

Mar 25, 1971: Gadsden, AL
& Frankie Cain vs. The Samoans

April 8, 1971: Gadsden, AL
& Frankie Cain beat The Green Shadows

April 15, 1971: Gadsden, AL
in Battle Royal
- Winner gets Alabama Heavyweight Title

April 20, 1971: Florence, AL
beat Marcelle Varchon

May 15, 1971: Chattanooga, TN
beat Mack York
- Chattanooga debut

May 28, 1971: Anniston, AL
vs. Ricky Gibson
- 2 Out Of 3 Falls

June 4, 1971: Anniston, AL
vs. Johnny Long

June 11, 1971: Anniston, AL
vs. Sam Bass

June 25, 1971: Anniston, AL
& Bobby Whitlock vs. Roy Bass & Dick Taylor
- 2 Out Of 3 Falls

July 16, 1971: Anniston, AL
vs. Frank Hester
- 2 Out Of 3 Falls

July 17, 1971: Chattanooga, TN
beat Tony Mendoza

Aug 13, 1971: Anniston, AL
vs. Dick Taylor

Aug 19, 1971: Gadsden, AL
vs. Rick Sanchez

Aug 20, 1971: Anniston, AL
vs. Johnny Davila

Aug 26, 1971: Gadsden, AL
& Mr. X vs. Dick Taylor & Rick Sanchez

Aug 27, 1971: Anniston, AL
& Percy Bass vs. Jimmy Golden & Dick Taylor
- 2 Out Of 3 Falls

Sep 3, 1971: Gadsden, AL
& Steve Lawler vs. Jimmy Golden & Dick Taylor
- 2 Out Of 3 Falls
- Steve Lawler is Steve Kyle

Steve & Jerry Lawler

Oct 7, 1971: Gadsden, AL
vs. Jimmy Golden

Oct 8, 1971: Gadsden, AL
& Steve Lawler vs. Sam Bass & Ramon Perez

Oct 15, 1971: Gadsden, AL
& Steve Lawler vs. Jimmy Golden & Ramon Perez

Oct 22, 1971: Gadsden, AL
& Steve Lawler vs. Jimmy Golden & Ramon Perez

Oct 29, 1971: Gadsden, AL
& Steve Lawler vs. Percy Bass & Woodrow Bass

Nov 4, 1971: Anniston, AL
& Steve Lawler vs. Ramon Perez & Gary Martin

Nov 5, 1971: Gadsden, AL
& Steve Lawler vs. Woodrow Bass & Sam Bass

Nov 19, 1971: Gadsden, AL
& Steve Lawler vs. Ramon Perez & Woodrow Bass

Dec 2, 1971: Anniston, AL
w/Steve Lawler, Mr. X & Tony Russo vs. Ramon Perez, Gary Martin, Derek Windsor & Sammy Tucker

vs. Ramon Perez

Dec 9, 1971: Anniston, AL
lost to Gary Martin

Dec 16, 1971: Anniston, AL
won via DQ over Ramon Perez

A very young Jerry Lawler

1972

Chapter 3

Jan 13, 1972: Florence, AL
beat Joey Corea (unmasked Spoiler)

Jan 20, 1972: Anniston, AL
& Steve Lawler beat the Scufflin' Hillbillies(c)
- Tri-State Tag Title Match
- 2 Out Of 3 Falls

Jan 22, 1972: Gadsden, AL
& Steve Lawler lost to the Scufflin' Hillbillies
- Non-Title Match

Jan 27, 1972: Anniston, AL
& Steve Lawler(c) lost to the Scufflin' Hillbillies
- Tri-State Tag Title Match

Feb 3, 1972: Anniston, AL
w/Steve Lawler & Burrhead Jones vs. the
Scufflin' Hillbillies & Buddy Wayne

Feb 10, 1972: Florence, AL
beat Southern Jr. Champ Len Rossi
- Non Title Match
- Lawler won 2 out of 3 falls

Feb 16, 1972: Nashville, TN
& Sir Clements lost to Roy Lee Welch & Bearcat
Brown

Feb 22, 1972: Chattanooga, TN
& Green Shadow lost to Alex Medina & Roy Lee
Welch

Feb 24, 1972: Florence, AL
w/Sam Bass lost to Kevin Sullivan

Mar 2, 1972: Florence, AL
 w/Sam Bass drew vs Kevin Sullivan

Mar 3, 1972: Knoxville, TN
w/Sam Bass beat Mitsu Katayana

Mar 6, 1972: Birmingham, AL
& Jim White w/Sam Bass drew with Tom Drake
& Alex Medina

Mar 16, 1972: Florence, AL
& Jim White w/Sam Bass lost to Robert Fuller &
Kevin Sullivan

Mar 20, 1972: Birmingham, AL
w/Sam Bass beat Carlos Medina

Jerry Lawler & Sam Bass. Jerry probably
trying to explain to Bass that he doesn't
drink.

Mar 27, 1972: Birmingham, AL
w/Sam Bass drew with Dennis Hall

Mar 30, 1972: Florence, AL
& Jim White w/Sam Bass lost to Joey Rossi &
Eddie Marlin

Apr 5, 1972: Nashville, TN
w/Donna Christiantello & Diamond Lil vs. Cora
Combs, Darling Dagmar & Kevin Sullivan

Apr 8, 1972: Chattanooga, TN
& Pepe Lopez w/Sam Bass vs. Len Rossi & Tony
Charles
- Originally a Mid-America Tag Title Match but
Rossi & Charles dropped the belts earlier in the
day on Chattanooga TV.

Apr 10, 1972: Memphis, TN
& Jim White w/Sam Bass beat Jim Kent & Eddie
Marlin

Apr 12, 1972: Mobile, AL
& Masked Spoiler w/Sam Bass beat Ken Lucas &
Frank Dalton

Apr 13, 1972: Chattanooga, TN
& Jim White & Donna Christianello lost to Patty
Drake, Larry O'Day & Ron Miller

Apr 17, 1972: Memphis, TN
& Jim White w/Sam Bass beat Kevin Sullivan &
Eddie Marlin

Apr 18, 1972: Blytheville, AR
vs. Eric Von Brauner

Apr 19, 1972: Mobile, AL
w/Sam Bass lost to Mickey Doyle

April 20, 1972: Florence, AL
w/Sam Bass drew with Bearcat Brown
- Also in Battle Royal

Apr 25, 1972: Louisville, KY
& Jim White w/Sam Bass vs. Bearcat Brown &
Len Rossi

Apr 26: 1972: Mobile, AL
lost to Ken Lucas

Apr 27, 1972: Memphis, TN
w/Jim White, & Jim Kent lost to Tojo Yamamoto,
Oni Wiki Wiki & Tommy Gilbert

May 1, 1972: Memphis, TN
& Jim White w/Jim Kent beat Oki Wiki Wiki &
Tommy Gilbert

May 3, 1972: Evansville, IN
w/Jim White & Jim Kent beat via CO Tojo
Yamamoto, Oki Wiki Wiki & Roy Rowland

May 5, 1972: Tupelo, MS
& Jim White beat Alex Medina & Roy Rowland

May 8, 1972: Memphis, TN
& Jim White lost via DQ to Oki Wiki Wiki &
Tommy Gilbert

May 9, 1972: Louisville, KY
& Jim White w/Jim Kent vs. Dennis Hall &
Tommy Gilbert

May 12: Tupelo, MS
w/Jim White & Jim Kent beat Oki Wiki Wiki,
Tommy Gilbert & Tojo Yamamoto

May 15, 1972: Memphis, TN
& Jim White w/Jim Kent beat Larry O'Day & Ron
Miller

May 19, 1972: Tupelo, MS
w/Jim White & Jim Kent beat Tommy Gilbert,
Oki Wiki Wiki & Tojo Yamamoto

*Photo Courtesy of Dave Drason Burzynski
Jim White, Jimmy Kent (kneeling) & Jerry
Lawler.

May 22, 1972: Memphis, TN
& Jim White w/Jim Kent drew with Tojo
Yamamoto & Eddie Marlin

May 26, 1972: Tupelo, MS
w/Jim White & Jim Kent lost to Oki Wiki Wiki,
Tommy Gilbert & Tojo Yamamoto

May 29, 1972: Louisville, KY
& Jim White w/Jim Kent lost to the Gladiator &
Tojo Yamamoto

May 30, 1972: Blytheville, AR
 & Jim White w/Jim Kent vs. Alex Medina & Mike
Pappas

June 5, 1972: Memphis, TN
& Jim White w/Jim Kent drew with Norvell
Austin & Eddie Marlin

June 6, 1972: Blytheville, AR
& Jim White w/Jim Kent vs. Frank Martinez &
Jack Donovan

June 7, 1972: Bowling Green, KY
& Jim White w/Jim Kent vs. Sputnik Monroe &
Norvell Austin vs.

June 8, 1972: Florence, AL
& Jim White w/Jim Kent beat George Hultz &
Bearcat Brown

June, 12, 1972: Memphis, TN
w/Jim White & Jim Kent lost to Norvell Austin,
Eddie & Tommy Marlin

June 15, 1972: Florence, AL
& Jim White & Jim Kent lost to Bearcat Brown &
George Hultz
- Special referee: Joey Rossi
- Falls count anywhere

June 19, 1972: Birmingham, AL
w/Jim White & Jim Kent beat Oki Wiki Wiki,
Tommy Gilbert & Tojo Yamamoto
-Also in Battle Royal

June 22, 1972: Florence, AL
w/Jim White & Corsica lost via DQ to Joe George
Hultz, Bearcat Brown & Joey Rossi

June 26, 1972: Memphis, TN
w/Jim White, Jim Kent & Corsica Joe vs. Eddie
Marlin, Tojo Yamamoto, Oki Wiki Wiki & Frankie
Lane
- Also, won Battle Royal

June 29, 1972: Louisville, KY
& Jim White w/Jim Kent vs. Tojo Yamamoto &
the Gladiator

July 3, 1972: Birmingham, AL
w/Jim White & George Hultz beat Len Rossi,
Joey Rossi & Kevin Sullivan

July 10, 1972: Birmingham, AL
w/Jim White & George Hultz beat Len Rossi,
Joey Rossi & Kevin Sullivan

July 17, 1972: Birmingham, AL
w/Jim White & George Hultz beat Len Rossi,
Joey Rossi & Kevin Sullivan

July 19, 1972: Nashville, TN
& Jim White drew with Bearcat Brown & Tony
Charles

July 24, 1972: Birmingham, AL
& Jim White lost to Bearcat Brown & Kevin
Sullivan

July 29, 1972: Chattanooga, TN
& Jim White beat Robert Fuller & Kevin Sullivan

July 31, 1972: Birmingham, AL
& Jim White beat Bearcat Brown & Kevin
Sullivan

Aug 7, 1972: Birmingham, AL
w/Sam Bass & Jim White lost to Kevin Sullivan,
Bearcat Brown & Tommy Gilbert

Aug 14, 1972: Birmingham, AL
& Sam Bass lost to Bearcat Brown & Len Rossi

Aug 19, 1972: Chattanooga, TN
& Jim White w/Sam Bass beat Roy Lee Welch &
Frankie Lane

Aug 21, 1972: Birmingham, AL
& Jim White lost to Kevin Sullivan & Chief
Thunderfoot

Aug 23, 1972: Nashville, TN
& Jim White w/Sam Bass vs. Pepe Lopez & Chief
Thundercloud w/Onley Chewey

Aug 24, 1972: Florence, AL
& Jim White w/Sam Bass beat Bearcat Brown &
Kevin Sullivan
- No DQ

Aug 26, 1972: Chattanooga, TN
& Jim White w/Sam Bass beat Kevin Sullivan &
Frankie Lane

Aug 28, 1972: Birmingham, AL
w/Sam Bass & Jim White lost to Kevin Sullivan,
Chief Thundercloud & Bearcat Brown

Aug 30, 1972: Nashville, TN
& Jim White w/Sam Bass beat Leon Chandler &
Chief Thundercloud w/Little White Cloud

Aug 31, 1972: Florence, AL
& Jim White vs. Kevin Sullivan & Frankie Laine

Sept 4, 1972: Birmingham, AL
& Jim White drew with Kevin Sullivan & Chief Thundercloud

Sept 5, 1972: Blytheville, AR
& Jim White vs. Oni Wiki Wiki & Black Panther

Sept 7, 1972: Chattanooga, TN
& Jim White w/Sam Bass beat Tojo Yamamoto & Great Fuji w/Frankie Lane

Sept 11, 1972: Birmingham, AL
w/Diamond Lil, Jim White & Sam Bass lost to Little Darlin, Frankie Lane, Tom Drake & Chief Thundercloud

Sept 12, 1972: Blytheville, AR
& Jim White beat Roy Lee Welch & Chief Thundercloud

Sept 13, 1972: Nashville, TN
w/George Hultz & Jim White No Contest with Kevin Sullivan, Joey & Len Rossi w/Roy Lee Welch

Sept 16, 1972: Chattanooga, TN
w/Jim White & George Hultz beat Kevin Sullivan, Len & Joey Rossi

Sept 18, 1972: Birmingham, AL
& Jim White lost to Ox the Ripper & Dennis Hall

Sept 19, 1972: Blytheville, AR
& Jim White vs. Roy Lee Welch & Ken Lucas

Sept 20, 1972: Nashville, TN
w/Jim White & George Hultz beat Kevin Sullivan, Len & Joey Rossi
- No DQ

Sept 23, 1972: Chattanooga, TN
& Jim White & George Hultz lost to Kevin Sullivan, Joey & Len Rossi

September 25, 1972: Owensboro, KY
& Jim White w/Sam Bass vs. Chief Bold Eagle & Thundercloud w/drummer Little White Cloud

Sept 27, 1972: Nashville, TN
w/Jim White & George Hultz beat Kevin Sullivan, Joey Rossi & Len Rossi

Sept 28, 1972: Chattanooga, TN
w/Jim White & Sam Bass lost to Ken Lucas, Kevin Sullivan & Ox the Ripper

Oct 1, 1972: Louisville, KY
& Jim White beat Dennis Hall & Joey Rossi

Oct 2, 1972: Birmingham, AL
& Jim White beat Dennis Hall & Kevin Sullivan

Oct 4, 1972: Nashville, TN
& Jim White w/Sam Bass vs. Ken Lucas & Bearcat Brown w/Kevin Sullivan

Oct 9, 1972: Birmingham, AL
& Jim White beat Roy Lee Welch & Dennis Hall

Oct 10, 1972: Johnson City, TN
& Jim White vs. Frankie Lane & Hillbilly Vick

Oct 19, 1972: Birmingham, AL
& Jim White lost to Lorenzo Parente & Bobby Hart

Oct 23, 1972: Birmingham, AL
& Jim White drew with Dennis Hall & Bearcat Brown

Oct 24, 1972: Johnson City, TN
w/Jim White & Sam Bass vs. Kevin Sullivan, Frankie Lane & Vick the Hillbilly

Oct 26, 1972: Florence, AL
& Jim White lost to Joey Rossi & Frankie Lane

Oct 29, 1972: Chattanooga, TN
& Jim White drew with Tojo Yamamoto & Johnny Walker

Nov 2, 1972: Florence, AL
& Jim White beat Frankie Lane & Joey Rossi

Nov 4, 1972: Chattanooga, TN
& Jim White lost to Bearcat Brown & Dennis Hall

Nov 6, 1972: Birmingham, AL
& Jim White lost to Tojo Yamamoto & Bill Dromo

Nov 9, 1972: Chattanooga, TN
& Jim White w/Sam Bass lost to Dennis Hall & Bearcat Brown
- 2 out of 3 Falls

Nov 10, 1972: Knoxville, TN
& Jim White(c) beat Ken Lucas & Dennis Hall
- Mid-America Tag Title Match

Nov 10, 1972: Nashville, TN
& Jim White lost to Lorenzo Parente & Bobby
Hart
- Mid-America Tag Title Match

Nov 13, 1972: Memphis, TN
& Jim White drew with Eddie Marlin & Tommy
Gilbert

Nov 13, 1972: Knoxville, TN
& Jim White lost to Ken Lucas & Dennis Hall

Nov 18, 1972: Chattanooga, TN
& Jim White w/Sam Bass vs. Len Rossi & Tojo
Yamamoto

Nov 20, 1972: Memphis, TN
& Jim White lost to Ken Lucas & Dennis Hall
- Four Corner Elimination Match
- Also included Al & Don Greene plus Johnny
Walker & Frankie Lane

Nov 21, 1972: Louisville, KY
& Jim White w/Sam Bass vs. Len Rossi &
Bearcat Brown
& Jim White w/Sam Bass vs. Tojo Yamamoto &
Jerry Jarrett

Nov 24, 1972: Knoxville, TN
& Jim White beat Jack Donavon & Tommy
Gilbert

Nov 25, 1972: Chattanooga, TN
& Jim White w/Sam Bass beat Len Rossi &
Bearcat Brown

Nov 27, 1972: Memphis, TN
& Jim White beat Jackie Fargo & Tommy Gilbert

Nov 28, 1972: Louisville, KY
w/Jim White & Sam Bass lost to Bearcat Brown,
Len Rossi & Don Greene

Nov 29, 1972: Evansville, IN
w/Sam Bass & Jim White vs. Don Greene, Ken
Lucas & Dennis Hall

Dec 1, 1972: Knoxville, TN
Southern Tag Champs w/Jim White vs. the
Avengers

Dec 2, 1972: Chattanooga, TN
& Jim White w/Sam Bass lost to Ken Lucas &
Bearcat Brown

Dec 4, 1972: Memphis, TN
& Jim White w/Sam Bass lost via DQ to Johnny
Walker & Frankie Lane

Dec 5, 1972: Louisville, KY
w/Jim White & Sam Bass lost to Bearcat Brown,
Don Greene & Joey Rossi

Dec 7, 1972: Chattanooga, TN
& Jim White w/Sam Bass No Contest with
Dennis Hall & Ken Lucas

Dec 8, 1972: Knoxville, TN
& Jim White lost Southern Tag Titles to Bearcat
Brown & Tommy Gilbert

December 11, 1972: Memphis, TN
w/Sam Bass & Jim White vs. Johnny Walker,
Eddie Marlin & Tommy Gilbert
- Card canceled due to icy weather
- Len Rossi injured in car accident on this date

Dec 13, 1972: Nashville, TN
& Jim White lost via DQ to Bearcat Brown &
Joey Rossi

Dec 15, 1972: Knoxville, TN
& Jim White beat Dennis Hall & Dandy Jack
Donavon
- Also competed in Battle Royal

Dec 16, 1972: Chattanooga, TN
& Jim White w/Sam Bass lost to Dennis Hall &
Ken Lucas

Dec 17, 1972: Louisville, KY
& Jim White beat Tojo Yamamoto & Jerry Jarrett

Dec 18, 1972: Birmingham, AL
& Jim White beat Bearcat Brown & Frankie Lane

Dec 19, 1972: Memphis, TN
& Jim White drew with Dennis Hall & Ken Lucas

Dec 20, 1972: Nashville, TN
& Jim White w/Sam Bass vs. Tojo Yamamoto &
Jerry Jarrett

Dec 22, 1972: Knoxville, TN
& Jim White vs. Ron & Don Wright

Dec 23, 1972 Chattanooga, TN
& Jim White beat Dennis Hall & Ken Lucas

Dec 25, 1972: Birmingham, AL
& Jim White drew with Dennis Hall & Ken Lucas

Dec 26, 1972: Louisville, KY
w/Jim White & Sam Bass lost via DQ to Jackie
Fargo, Jerry Jarrett & Tojo Yamamoto

Dec 29, 1972: Knoxville, TN
& Jim White beat Buddy Atlas & Jack Donavon

Dec 30, 1972: Chattanooga, TN
w/George Hultz, Sam Bass, Jim White beat Don
Greene, Tojo Yamamoto, Dennis Hall & Ken
Lucas

1973

Chapter 4

Jan 2, 1973: Louisville, KY
w/Sam Bass & Jim White lost to Tojo
Yamamoto, Eddie Marlin (sub for Jackie Fargo)
& Jerry Jarrett
- Texas Tornado Death Match

Jan 3, 1973: Nashville, TN
& Jim White w/Sam Bass beat via CO Ken Lucas
& Dennis Hall
Sam Bass w/Jerry Lawler lost via DQ to Buddy
Atlas

Jan 6, 1973: Chattanooga, TN
& Jim White w/Sam Bass vs. Ken Lucas &
Dennis Hall
- Don Greene handcuffed to Sam Bass
- Loser of fall leaves town for 6 months

Jan 9, 1973: Louisville, KY
& Jim White w/Sam Bass lost to Tojo Yamamoto
& Jerry Jarrett

Jan 10, 1973: Nashville, TN
& Jim White w/Sam Bass beat Dennis Hall & Ken
Lucas
- Don Greene handcuffed to Sam Bass

Jan 11, 1973: Lexington, KY
& Jim White w/Sam Bass vs. Tojo Yamamoto &
Dennis Hall

Jan 13, 1973: Chattanooga, TN
& Jim White w/Sam Bass beat Dennis Hall &
Charlie Cook

Jan 15, 1973: Birmingham, AL
& Jim White w/Sam Bass No Contest with Al
Greene & Don Greene

Jan 16, 1973: Louisville, KY
& Jim White w/Sam Bass vs. Mid-America Tag
Champs Lorenzo Parente & Bobby Hart

Jan 17, 1973: Nashville, TN
& Jim White w/Sam Bass lost to Bearcat Brown
& Dennis Hall

Jan 19, 1973: Memphis, TN
& Jim White w/Sam Bass lost to Jackie Fargo &
Jerry Jarrett

Jan 23, 1973: Louisville, KY
& Jim White w/Sam Bass beat Eddie Marlin &
Tommy Gilbert

Jan 24, 1973: Evansville, IN
& Jim White w/Sam Bass vs. Jerry Jarrett & Tojo
Yamamoto

Jan 29, 1973: Memphis, TN
& Jim White w/Sam Bass lost to Southern tag
Champs Jerry Jarrett & Jackie Fargo
- Also Battle Royal

Jan 30, 1973: Louisville, KY
& Jim White w/Sam Bass drew with Bobby Hart
& Lorenzo Parente w/Don Duffy

Jan 31, 1973: Evansville, IN
& Jim White w/Sam Bass lost to Jerry Jarrett &
Jackie Fargo
- No DQ

Feb 5, 1973: Memphis, TN
& Jim White & Sam Bass lost to Bearcat Wright,
Burrhead Jones & Charlie Cook

Feb 6, 1973: Louisville, KY
& Jim White w/Sam Bass vs. Dennis Hall & Ben
Justice
- Also Battle Royal

Feb 7, 1973: Evansville, IN
& Jim White w/Sam Bass vs. Jackie Fargo & Tojo
Yamamoto

Feb 11, 1973: Chattanooga, TN
& Jim White w/Sam Bass drew with Eddie Marlin
& Tommy Gilbert
- Also Battle Royal

Feb 12, 1973: Memphis, TN
& Jim White, Sam Bass, Taro Marasaki & the
Great Fuji beat Bearcat Brown, Rufus R Jones,
Charlie Cook, Roy Welch & Bobby Lyons

Feb 14, 1973: Nashville, TN
& Jim White w/Sam Bass beat Jackie Fargo &
Jerry Jarrett

Feb 15, 1973: Florence, AL
& Jim White w/Sam Bass beat Bearcat Brown &
Roy Lee Welch

Feb 19, 1973: Memphis, TN
w/Jim White & Sam Bass beat Bearcat Brown,
Rufus R Jones & Charlie Cook
- 12th Round Texas Tornado Match

Sam Bass being interviewed by Dave Brown
while Jerry Lawler & Jim White look on.

Feb 20, 1973: Chattanooga, TN
w/Jim White & Sam Bass beat Bearcat Brown,
Burrhead Jones & Charlie Cook

Feb 21, 1973: Nashville, TN
w/Jim White & Sam Bass lost to Jackie Fargo,
Ben Justice & Jerry Jarrett

Feb 22, 1973: Florence, AL
& Jim White w/Sam Bass lost to Bearcat Brown
& Burrhead Jones (sub for Roy Lee Welch)

Feb 26, 1973: Chattanooga, TN
w/Sam Bass, Jim White, Taro Marasaki & the
Great Fuji beat Danny Dusek, Bearcat Brown,
Charlie Cook, Don Anderson & Tom Shaft

Feb 27, 1973: Louisville, KY
& Jim White w/Sam Bass vs. Tommy Gilbert &
Tommy Marlin

Feb 28, 1973: Evansville, IN
& Jim White w/Sam Bass vs. Don Anderson &
Joe Millich

Mar 1, 1973: Florence, AL
w/Jim White & Sam Bass beat Bearcat Brown,
Burrhead Jones & Lumberjack Dupree

Mar 5, 1973: Memphis, TN
& Jim White(c) w/Sam Bass beat Jackie Fargo &
Jerry Jarrett
- Southern Tag Title Match

Mar 6, 1973: Louisville, KY
w/Sam Bass & Jim White vs. Eddie Marlin,
Tommy Gilbert & Tommy Marlin

Mar 8, 1973: Florence, AL
& Jim White w/Sam Bass beat George Hultz &
Jack Donovan

Mar 12, 1973: Memphis, TN
& Jim White(c) w/Sam Bass No Contest w/Jerry
Jarrett & Jackie Fargo
- Southern Tag Title Match
- Titles held up

Mar 13, 1973: Louisville, KY
& Jim White w/Sam Bass vs. Eddie Marlin &
Tommy Gilbert(c)
- Mid-America Tag Title Match
- George Gulas Special Ref

Mar 18, 1973: Chattanooga, TN
& Jim White w/Sam Bass lost to Jackie Fargo &
Jerry Jarrett

Mar 19, 1973: Memphis, TN
& Jim White(c) w/Sam Bass lost to Jackie Fargo
& Jerry Jarrett
- Southern Tag Title Match
- Belts vs. Jarrett's hair

Mar 20, 1973: Blytheville, AR
& Jim White w/Sam Bass vs. Billy Wicks & Don
Anderson

Mar 26, 1973: Memphis, TN
& Jim White w/Sam Bass beat Jackie Fargo &
Jerry Jarrett(c) w/Tojo Yamamoto
- Southern Tag Titles vs Lawler's Hair
- No Time Limit - No DQ
- Jersey Joe Walcott Special Ref

Mar 27, 1973: Paducah, KY
& Jim White w/Bass vs. Bearcat Wright and
Charlie Cook

Mar 28, 1973: Nashville, TN
& Jim White w/Sam Bass beat Ron & Don
Wright(c)

Apr 2, 1973: Memphis, TN
& Jim White(c) w/Sam Bass No Contest with
Tojo Yamamoto & Roughhouse Fargo
- Southern Tag Title Match

Apr 4, 1973: Nashville, TN
& Jim White(c) w/Sam Bass beat Jackie Fargo &
Jerry Jarrett
- Southern Tag Title Match

Apr 6, 1973: Chattanooga, TN
vs. Mike Jackson

Apr 7, 1973: Chattanooga, TN
& Jim White w/Sam Bass drew with Bobby Hart
& Lorenzo Parente

Apr 9, 1973: Memphis, TN
& Jim White(c) w/Sam Bass lost to Tojo
Yamamoto & Roughhouse Fargo
- Southern Tag Title Match 2/3 Falls
- No DQ, Ring Enclosed In Bull Wire

Apr 11, 1973: Nashville, TN
& Jim White w/Sam Bass lost to Jackie Fargo &
Jerry Jarrett(c) w/Tojo Yamamoto
- Southern Tag Title Match
- Stunned ref gives belts accidently to White &
Lawler

Apr 16, 1973: Memphis, TN
& Jim White w/Sam Bass beat Tojo Yamamoto &
Roughhouse Fargo(c)
- Southern Tag Team Title Match
- Bass' & White's hair vs. titles

Apr 18, 1973: Nashville, TN
& Jim White(c) w/Sam Bass lost to Jerry Jarrett
& Jackie Fargo
- Southern Tag Title Match
- No Time Limit - No DQ - Titles vs Hair

Apr 23, 1973: Memphis, TN
& Jim White, Sam Bass & the Oriental Mystery
Man lost to Jerry Jarrett, Tojo Yamamoto, Jackie
& Roughhouse Fargo

Apr 24, 1973: Louisville, KY
& Jim White w/Sam Bass vs. Tojo Yamamoto &
Jerry Jarrett

Apr 25, 1973: Nashville, TN
Jim White, Sam Bass & Jerry Lawler lost to
Jackie Fargo, Tojo Yamamoto & Jerry Jarrett

Apr 30, 1973: Memphis, TN
lost to Jackie Fargo
- Also & Sam Bass & the Oriental Mystery Man
lost to Jackie & Roughhouse Fargo & Jerry
Jarrett

May 2, 1973: Nashville, TN
w/Jim White & Sam Bass lost to Jackie Fargo,
Tojo Yamamoto & Jerry Jarrett
- Hospital Elimination Match
- Also Jerry beat Jackie Fargo in singles match

May 7, 1973: Memphis, TN
& Jim White(c) w/Sam Bass won via DQ over
Jackie & Roughhouse Fargo
- Southern Tag Title Match

May 9, 1973: Nashville, TN
& Jim White w/Sam Bass beat Jackie Fargo &
Jerry Jarrett(c)
- Southern Tag Title Match
- Belts vs $300 to the fans

May 14, 1973: Memphis, TN
& Jim White(c) w/Sam Bass beat Jackie &
Roughhouse Fargo
- Southern Tag Title Match
- No DQ Match

May 15, 1973: Louisville, KY
w/Sam Bass & Jim White vs. Tojo
Yamamoto, Jackie Fargo & Jerry Jarrett
- Hospital elimination match
- Also vs. Tojo Yamamoto

May 16, 1973: Evansville, IN
& Jim White w/Sam Bass vs. Jerry Jarrett &
Jackie Fargo w/Tojo Yamamoto

May 21, 1973: Memphis, TN
& Jim White(c) w/Sam Bass beat Don Greene &
Charlie Cook
- Southern Tag Title Match

May 23, 1973: Evansville, IN
& Jim White w/Sam Bass vs. Jerry Jarrett &
Jackie Fargo w/Tojo Yamamoto

May 28, 1973: Memphis, TN
& the Great Fuji (sub Jim White) w/Sam Bass
lost to Eddie Marlin & Tommy Gilbert
- Lawler & White were Southern Tag Champs.
- White couldn't compete b/c of broken nose.

May 30, 1973: Evansville, IN
& Sam Bass w/Jim White vs. Jerry Jarrett &
Jackie Fargo w/Tojo Yamamoto

May 31, 1973: Louisville, KY
& Sam Bass w/Jim White vs. Johnny Eagle
Marlin & Tommy Marlin
- White has a broken nose

June 2, 1973: Chattanooga, TN
& Sam Bass w/Jim White drew with Jerry Jarrett
& Johnny Marlin

June 3, 1973: Louisville, KY
& Sam Bass w/Jim White vs. Eddie Marlin &
Tommy Gilbert

June 4, 1973: Memphis, TN
& Sam Bass w/Jim White beat Joey Rossi &
Jerry Jarrett w/Len Rossi & Lee Williams
- Lawler, White & Bass beat up Len afterwards
Jim White

June 7, 1973: Florence, AL
& Sam Bass w/Jim White beat Jackie Fargo &
Tojo Yamamoto

June 9, 1973: Chattanooga, TN
& Sam Bass w/Jim White beat Jerry Jarrett &
Devoy Brunson

June 11, 1973: Memphis, TN
& Sam Bass w/Jim White lost to Jerry Jarrett &
Joey Rossi w/Len Rossi & Lee Williams
- No DQ Match
- Lance Russell Special Ref

June 14, 1973: Florence, AL
& Sam Bass w/Jim White lost via DQ to Jackie
Fargo & Tojo Yamamoto

June 18, 1973: Memphis, TN
Southern Tag Tournament
Round 1
& Sam Bass w/Jim White beat Jackie &
Roughhouse Fargo

Round 2
& Sam Bass w/Jim White beat Don Greene &
Charles Cook

Round 3 - Finals
& Sam Bass w/Jim White beat Tojo Yamamoto &
Jerry Jarrett
- Win Tag Titles

Jim White, Sam Bass (kneeling) & Jerry
Lawler. Kent was the duo's first manager.

June 20, 1973: Nashville, TN
& Sam Bass w/Jim White drew with Jerry Jarrett
& Johnny Marlin

June 21, 1973: Florence, AL
& Sam Bass w/Jim White lost to Frankie Lane &
Billy Lane

June 23, 1973: Chattanooga, TN
& Jim White lost to Eddie Marlin & Tommy
Gilbert

& Jim White w/Sam Bass beat Jerry Jarrett &
Johnny Eagle Marlin
- Jim White cleared to wrestle.

June 25, 1973: Memphis, TN
& Jim White w/Sam Bass beat Joey Rossi &
Jerry Jarrett w/Len Rossi & Lee Williams
- Southern Tag Title Match

June 27, 1973: Nashville, TN
& Jim White & Sam Bass lost to Jerry Jarrett,
Eddie & Tommy Marlin

June 30, 1973: Chattanooga, TN
& Jim White(c) w/Sam Bass lost to Johnny
Marlin & Jerry Jarrett
- Southern Tag Title Match

July 2, 1973: Memphis, TN
& Jim White(c) w/Sam Bass beat Roughhouse
Fargo & Jerry Jarrett (Sub for Joey Rossi) w/Len
Rossi
- Southern Tag Title Match

July 4, 1973: Evansville, IN
& Jim White(c) w/ Sam Bass vs. Jerry Jarrett &
Tojo Yamamoto
- Southern Tag Title Match

July 5, 1973: Florence, AL
& Jim White(c) w/Sam Bass beat Jerry Jarrett &
Johnny Marlin
- Southern Tag Title Match

July 7, 1973: Chattanooga, TN
& Jim White w/Sam Bass beat Johnny Marlin &
Jerry Jarrett(c)
- Southern Tag Title Match
- Belts vs. Lawler's hair

July 9, 1973: Memphis, TN
& Jim White(c) w/Sam Bass lost to Roughhouse
Fargo & Jerry Jarrett
- Southern Tag Title Match

*Photo Courtesy of Mike Shields
Jim White & Jerry Lawler Checking On
Sam Bass After A Match

July 10, 1973: Blytheville, AR
& Jim White w/Sam Bass vs. Tojo Yamamoto &
Don Greene

July 11, 1973: Evansville, IN
& Jim White(c) w/ Sam Bass vs. Jerry Jarrett &
Tojo Yamamoto
- Southern Tag Title Match
- Sam Bass put in a straight jacket

July 12, 1973: Florence, AL
& Jim White w/Sam Bass beat Jerry Jarrett &
Johnny Marlin

July 14, 1973: Chattanooga, TN
& Jim White beat Jerry Jarrett & Johnny Marlin
 w/Tommy Marlin
- Southern Tag title Match

July 16, 1973: Memphis, TN
w/Sam Bass lost to Jerry Jarrett
- Bass' Hair vs. Jarrett's Hair Match

& Jim White w/Sam Bass lost to Roughhouse
Fargo & Jerry Jarrett(c)
- Southern Tag title Match

July 17, 1973: Blytheville, AR
& Jim White w/Sam Bass vs. Roy Lee Welch &
Charlie Cook

July 18, 1973: Nashville, TN
& Jim White w/Sam Bass lost via DQ to Billy &
Benny McGuire

July 19, 1973: Florence, AL
lost via DQ to Jerry Jarrett

w/Jim White & Sam Bass lost to Jerry Jarrett,
Tojo Yamamoto & Johnny Marlin

July 21, 1973: Chattanooga, TN
w/Sam Bass & Jim White lost to Jerry Jarrett,
Johnny Marlin & Tojo Yamamoto

w/Sam Bass beat Tommy Marlin

July 23, 1973: Memphis, TN
& Jim White & Sam Bass lost to Jerry Jarrett,
Tommy Gilbert & Eddie Marlin

July 24, 1973: Blytheville, AR
& Jim White w/Sam Bass vs. Jackie Fargo &
Roughhouse Fargo

July 25, 1973: Nashville, TN
& Jim White w/Sam Bass lost to Johnny Marlin &
Jerry Jarrett

July 28, 1973: Nashville, TN - TV Taping
w/Jim White and Sam Bass, take scissors to
Jerry Jarrett's hair. Jarrett is rescued by Eddie
Marlin & Tommy Gilbert

July 28, 1973: Chattanooga, TN
& Jim White beat Bearcat Brown & Charlie Cook

July 30, 1973: Birmingham, AL
& Jim White drew with Tommy Gilbert & Eddie Marlin

July 31, 1973: Memphis, TN
lost via DQ to Jerry Jarrett

Aug 1, 1973: Nashville, TN
w/Jim White & Sam Bass beat Tommy Gilbert, Eddie Marlin & Jerry Jarrett
- 2 out of 3 falls

Aug 4, 1973: Birmingham, AL TV
& Jim White(c) w/Sam Bass No Contest with Eddie Marlin & Tommy Gilbert
-Southern Tag Title Match

Aug 4, 1973: Chattanooga, TN
& Jim White(c) w/Sam Bass drew with Eddie Marlin & Tommy Gilbert
-Southern Tag Title Match

Aug 6, 1973: Birmingham, AL
& Jim White(c) w/Sam Bass beat Eddie Marlin & Tommy Gilbert
- Southern Tag Title Match
- 2 out of 3 falls

Aug 7, 1973: Memphis, TN
& Jim White(c) w/Sam Bass beat Tommy Gilbert & Eddie Marlin
- Southern Tag Title Match

Aug 8, 1973: Nashville, TN
w/Sam Bass lost to Jerry Jarrett
- Coal miners glove match:

& Jim White(c) w/Sam Bass beat Eddie Marlin & Tommy Gilbert
- Southern Tag Title Match

Aug 9, 1973: Chattanooga, TN
w/Sam Bass & Jim White lost to Eddie Marlin, Jerry Jarrett & Tommy Gilbert

Aug 13, 1973: Birmingham, AL
& Jim White(c) w/Sam Bass lost to Tommy Gilbert & Eddie Marlin w/Jim Garvin
- Southern Tag Title Match

Aug 15, 1973: Nashville, TN
& the Scorpion(c) lost to Eddie Marlin & Tommy Gilbert
- Southern Tag Title Match
- Special Ref: George Gulas
- Scorpion sub for Jim White
- Scorpion was a masked Don Duffy

* Jim White got in trouble with the promotion for dating one of the female wrestlers who happened to be black. When White refused to stop the relationship, he was fired by the promotion. This all came to a head between August 13 & 15, 1973. Don Duffy came out of retirement, and donned the mask to became Jerry Lawler's new partner, the Scorpion. The promotion also allowed the Scorpion to take over White's spot as tag champ with Jerry.

Aug 18, 1973: Chattanooga, TN
w/Sam Bass & the Scorpion lost to Jerry Jarrett, Tommy Gilbert & Eddie Marlin

Aug 20, 1973: Birmingham, AL
w/Sam Bass & Scorpion vs. Tommy Gilbert, Eddie Marlin & Jim Garvin

Aug 21, 1973: Memphis, TN
& the Scorpion(c) w/Sam Bass drew with Tommy Gilbert & Eddie Marlin
- Southern Tag Title Match

Aug 22, 1973: Evansville, IN
& the Scorpion w/Sam Bass vs. Tojo Yamamoto & Johnny Marlin

Aug 25, 1973: Chattanooga, TN
w/Sam Bass & the Scorpion lost to Eddie Marlin, Jerry Jarrett & Tommy Gilbert
- TexasTornado Death Match
- 7 Falls

Aug 29, 1973: Evansville, IN
w/the Scorpion & Sam Bass vs. Tojo Yamamoto, Jerry Jarrett & Johnny Marlin

Sep 4, 1973 Memphis, TN
& the Scorpion w/Sam Bass beat Benny & Billy McGuire

Sep 5, 1973: Evansville, IN
& the Scorpion w/Sam Bass vs. Roughhouse & Jackie Fargo

Sep 6, 1973: Florence, AL
& The Scorpion w/Sam Bass beat Tommy
Gilbert & Eddie Marlin(c)
- Southern Tag Title Match

Sep 9, 1973: Louisville, KY
& the Scorpion w/Sam Bass vs. Benny & Billy
McGuire

- Also, In A Battle Royal

Sep 10, 1973: Memphis, TN
w/the Scorpion w/Sam Bass vs. Jackie &
Roughhouse Fargo
- Doesn't look like this match took place

Sep 11, 1973: Birmingham, AL
& The Scorpion w/Sam Bass lost to Jackie &
Roughhouse Fargo & Jerry Jarrett
- Special referee George Gulas

Sep 12, 1973: Evansville, IN
& the Scorpion w/Sam Bass vs. Jerry Jarrett &
Johnny Marlin

Sep 13, 1973: Florence, AL
& the Scorpion w/Sam Bass lost to Tommy
Gilbert & Eddie Marlin(c)
- Mid-America Tag Title Match

Sep 17, 1973: Memphis, TN
<u>Southern Tag Team Tournament</u>
First Round
& the Scorpion w/Sam Bass beat Don Greene &
Larenzo Parente

Finals
w/the Scorpion lost to Tommy Gilbert & Eddie
Marlin

Sep 26, 1973: Nashville, TN
w/the Scorpion & Sam Bass lost to Jackie Fargo,
Roughhouse Fargo & Jerry Jarrett

Sep 30, 1973: Louisville, KY
& the Scorpion w/Sam Bass vs. Tojo Yamamoto
& Jerry Jarrett
- Texas Tornado Match - Falls Don't Count

Oct 1, 1973: Memphis, TN
& the Scorpion w/Sam Bass lost to Jackie Fargo
& Jerry Jarrett

Oct 3, 1973: Nashville, TN
& the Scorpion w/Sam Bass beat Jackie Fargo &
Jerry Jarrett w/Tojo Yamamoto

Oct 8, 1973: Memphis, TN
w/the Scorpion lost to Jerry Jarrett & Jackie
Fargo
- Texas Tornado Death Match

Oct 10, 1973: Nashville, TN
& The Scorpion w/Sam Bass lost to Jackie Fargo
& Tojo Yamamoto
- Texas Tornado Death Match

Oct 16, 1973: Memphis, TN
lost to Jerry Jarrett
- Piledriver Match

Oct 17, 1973: Nashville, TN
Jerry Lawler drew with Terry Lathan
- Also on card Scorpion unmasked (by Jackie
Fargo) to reveal Don Duffy

Oct 19, 1973: Adamsville, TN
& Don Duffy w/Sam Bass vs. Tojo Yamamoto &
Jerry Jarrett

Oct 22, 1973: Louisville, KY
& Don Duffy w/Sam Bass vs. Don Greene &
Bearcat Brown

Oct 24, 1973: Evansville, IN
& the Scorpion w/Sam Bass vs. Jerry Jarrett &
Tojo Yamamoto

Oct 29, 1973: Memphis, TN
& Al Greene(c) w/Sam Bass No Contest with
Eddie Marlin & Tommy Gilbert
- Southern Tag Title Match
- 2 out of 3 falls

Oct 31, 1973: Evansville, IN
& Sam Bass vs. Jackie Fargo & Tojo Yamamoto

Nov 1, 1973: Chattanooga, TN
& Sam Bass drew with Don Greene & Devoy
Brunson

Nov 5, 1973: Memphis, TN
& Al Greene(c) w/Sam Bass beat Eddie Marlin &
Tommy Gilbert w/Tojo Yamamoto
- Southern Tag Title Match
- No DQ

Nov 12, 1973: Memphis, TN
w/Sam Bass beat Tommy Gilbert

Nov 14, 1973: Evansville, IN
& the Scorpion w/Sam Bass vs. Johnny Marlin &
Jesse James

Nov 15, 1973: Florence, AL
& Al Greene w/Sam Bass lost to Lorenzo Parente
& Randy Curtis

Nov 19, 1973: Memphis, TN
lost to Tommy Gilbert
- Special Ref: George Gulas

Nov 26, 1973: Memphis, TN
w/Al Greene(c) w/Sam Bass lost to Tojo
Yamamoto & Jerry Jarrett
- Southern Tag Title Match

Nov 28, 1973: Evansville, IN
w/Don Duffy & Sam Bass lost to the Mighty
Yankees & George Harris

Dec 3, 1973: Memphis, TN
& Al Greene w/Sam Bass beat Benny & Billy
McGuire

Dec 10, 1973: Memphis, TN
w/Sam Bass beat Buddy Wayne Peale

Dec 18, 1973: Memphis, TN
& Al Greene w/Sam Bass vs. Tojo Yamamoto &
Jackie Fargo
- Also Won Battle Royal

Dec 19, 1973: Nashville, TN
& Al Greene w/Sam Bass beat Eddie Marlin &
Tommy Gilbert

Dec 22, 1973: Atlanta, GA - TV Taping
beat Bobby Starr

Dec 22, 1973: Chattanooga, TN
& Sam Bass drew with Johnny Marlin & Dennis
Hall

Dec 23, 1973: Memphis, TN
& Al Greene w/Sam Bass beat Buddy Wayne
Peale & Jerry Barber

Dec 26, 1973: Nashville, TN
w/Al Greene & Sam Bass drew with Eddie
Marlin, Dennis Hall & Tommy Gilbert

Dec 28, 1973: Atlanta, GA
beat Sputnik Monroe

Dec 29, 1973: Atlanta, GA - TV Taping
beat Jay French

Dec 29, 1973: Griffin, GA
vs. Tom Jones

Dec 30, 1973: Memphis, TN
& Al Greene w/Sam Bass lost to Jerry Jarrett &
Rufus R Jones

1974

Chapter 5

Jan 4, 1974: Atlanta, GA
& Bobby Shane lost to Bob Armstrong & Robert
Fuller

beat Bobby Cash

Jan 5, 1974: Atlanta, GA - TV Taping
beat Robert Fuller

Jan 5, 1974: Griffin, GA
lost to Lou Thesz

Jan 7, 1974: Savannah, GA
& Bobby Shane beat Robert Fuller & Bob
Armstrong

Jan 8, 1974: Macon, GA
beat Bobby Cash

Jan 10, 1974: Albany, GA
lost via DQ to Bobby Cash

Jan 11, 1974: Atlanta, GA
w/Gary Hart & Bobby Shane lost to Robert
Fuller, Bob Armstrong, & Buddy Fuller

Jan 12, 1974: Griffin, GA
vs. Bobby Cash

Jan 13, 1974: Atlanta, GA
vs. Ricky Gibson

Jan 15, 1974: Macon, GA
drew with Bobby Cash

Jan 16, 1974: Columbus, GA
drew with Roberto Soto

Jan 17, 1974: Albany, GA
vs. Roberto Soto

Jan 18, 1974: Atlanta, GA
& Bobby Duncum beat Roberto Soto & Bobby
Cash

w/Bobby Duncam lost to Robert Fuller & Bob
Armstrong
- was a draw, lost via coin toss

Jan 19, 1974: Griffin, GA
beat Roy Lee Welch

Jan 21, 1974: Macon, GA
beat Roy Lee Jones

Jan 22, 1974: Savannah: GA
beat Roberto Soto

Jan 23, 1974: Columbus, GA
vs Roberto Soto

Jan 24, 1974: Albany GA
& Bobby Duncum beat Tim Woods & Bobby Cash

Jan 25, 1974: Atlanta, GA
lost to Roberto Soto

Jan 28, 1974: Memphis, TN
w/Eddie Marlin w/Sam Bass lost to the Infernos
w/JC Dykes

- Jerry & Sam Bass turned babyface to help
Marlin

Jan 30, 1974: Columbus, GA
vs. Sputnik Monroe

Jan 31, 1974: Albany, GA
& Mr. Wrestling II lost via DQ to Tim Woods &
Robert Fuller

Feb 1, 1974: Atlanta, GA
beat Roberto Soto
- Loser Leaves Town Match

Feb 4, 1974: Memphis, TN
& Eddie Marlin w/Sam Bass lost to the
Infernos(c) w/JC Dykes
- Southern Tag Title Match

Feb 5, 1974: Macon, GA
beat Bobby Cash

Feb 6, 1974: Columbus, GA
vs. Roy Lee Welch

Feb 7, 1974: Albany, GA
& Mr. Wrestling II No Contest with Tim Woods &
Robert Fuller
- 2 Out Of 3 Falls Match

Feb 10, 1974: Atlanta, GA
& Tojo Yamamoto beat Eddie Marlin & Tommy Gilbert

Co-won a Battle Royal w/Robert Fuller

Feb 11, 1974: Memphis, TN
& Eddie Marlin w/Sam Bass lost to the Infernos(c) w/JC Dykes
- Southern Tag Title Match

Feb 12, 1974: Louisville, KY
& Eddie Marlin w/Sam Bass lost to Infernos(c) w/JC Dykes
- Southern Tag Title Match

Feb 13, 1974: Columbus, GA
& Bobby Duncum vs. Billy & Benny McGuire

Feb 15, 1974: Atlanta, GA
drew with Jackie Fargo

Feb 17, 1974: Louisville, KY
& Eddie Marlin w/Sam Bass lost to Infernos(c) w/JC Dykes
- Southern Tag Title Match
- 2 Refs

Feb 18, 1974: Memphis, TN
& Jackie Fargo w/Sam Bass lost to the Infernos(c) w/ JC Dykes
- Southern Tag Title Match

Feb 19, 1974: Savannah, GA
& Tojo Yamamoto beat Ricky Gibson & Roy Lee Welch

Feb 20, 1974: Columbus, GA
in Battle Royal

& Bobby Duncum vs. Robert Fuller & Roy Lee Welch

Feb 21, 1974: Albany, GA
& Bobby Duncum vs. Bobo Brazil & Bob Armstrong

Feb 22, 1974: Atlanta, GA
won via DQ over Robert Fuller
- Chain Match

Feb 26, 1974: Louisville, KY
& Eddie Marlin w/Sam Bass lost to Infernos(c) w/JC Dykes
- Southern Tag Title Match

Feb 27, 1974: Macon, GA
& Prince Lelani lost to Leon Ogle & Choo Choo Lynn

Feb 28, 1974: Albany, GA
& Art Nelson vs. Robert Fuller & Bobby Cash

Mar 1, 1974: Atlanta, GA
beat Robert Fuller

Mar 3, 1974: Macon, GA
w/Mr. Wrestling II Won a Tournament for the Macon Tag Team Titles

Mar 4, 1974: Memphis, TN
w/Sam Bass vs. Jackie Fargo

Mar 5, 1974: Louisville, KY
& Tojo Yamamoto w/Sam Bass drew with Infernos(c) w/JC Dykes
- Southern Tag Title Match

Mar 6, 1974: Columbus, GA
vs. Roy Lee Welch

Mar 8, 1974: Atlanta, GA
& Art Nelson beat Roy Lee Welch & Ricky Gibson

lost to Robert Fuller
- Lights Out Match

Mar 8, 1974: Atlanta, GA - TV Taping
vs. ?

Mar 9, 1974: Griffin, GA
lost to Robert Fuller

Mar 10, 1974: Savannah, GA
lost to Robert Fuller
- Lights Out Match

& Bill Costello lost to the Black Crusaders

Mar 10, 1974: Macon, GA - evening card
& Art Nelson beat the Black Crusaders

Mar 11, 1974: Memphis, TN
w/Sam Bass vs. Jackie Fargo w/Roughhouse Fargo

Mar 13, 1974: Columbus, GA
& Bill Costello vs. the Black Crusaders

Mar 14, 1974: Albany, GA
beat Black Crusader #2

Mar 15, 1974: Atlanta, GA
& Art Nelson drew with Rufus Jones & Tim Woods

& Art Nelson lost via DQ to Mr. Wrestling II & Robert Fuller

Mar 18, 1974: Memphis, TN
w/Sam Bass No Contest with Jackie Fargo
- Cage Match

Mar 19, 1974: Macon, GA
& Art Nelson drew with the Black Crusaders

Mar 20, 1974: Columbus, GA
vs. Sputnik Monroe

Also in 20-Man Battle Royal

Mar 21, 1974: Albany, GA
vs. Robert Fuller

Mar 22, 1974: Atlanta, GA
& Art Nelson lost to Mr. Wrestling II & Robert Fuller
- No DQ, Texas Tornado Death Match

Mar 23, 1974: Chattanooga, TN
& Jerry Jarrett beat Tojo Yamamoto & Ali Baba

Mar 25, 1974: Memphis, TN
w/Sam Bass beat Roughhouse Fargo

Mar 26, 1974: Macon, GA
& Mr. Wrestling II(c) lost to Bob Armstrong & Mr. Wrestling
- Macon Tag Title Match

Mar 28, 1974: Albany, GA
lost to Robert Fuller

Mar 29, 1974: Atlanta, GA
w/Art Nelson lost via DQ to Bob Armstrong & Robert Fuller(c)
- GA Tag Title Match

Mar 31, 1974: Louisville, KY
w/Sam Bass beat Roughhouse Fargo

Apr 1, 1974: Memphis, TN
& Lou Thesz w/Sam Bass beat Tommy Gilbert & Mike Jackson

w/Sam Bass beat Roughhouse Fargo
- Bullwire Match
- Also in Battle Royal

Apr 2, 1974: Macon, GA
won via DQ over Mr. Wrestling II

Apr 3, 1974: Columbus, GA
vs. Derrell Cochran

Apr 5, 1974: Atlanta, GA
& Art Nelson lost to Ron & Terry Garvin(c)
- No DQ
- GA Tag Title Match

Apr 6, 1974: Chattanooga, TN
w/Sam Bass beat Jerry Jarrett

Apr 8, 1974: Memphis, TN
& Lou Thesz w/Sam Bass beat Roughhouse Fargo & Tommy Gilbert
- Angle was done on this card where Lawler jumped Jackie Fargo to cover a legit injury. Fargo would be out 6-8 weeks.

Apr 9, 1974: Macon, GA
No Contest with Mr. Wrestling II

Apr 10, 1974: Columbus, GA
vs. Ricky Gibson

Apr 12, 1974: Atlanta, GA
& Art Nelson lost to Billy & Benny McGuire

Apr 13, 1974: Griffin, GA
& Art Nelson lost to Robert Fuller & Mr. Wrestling II

Apr 15, 1974: Memphis, TN
beat Tommy Gilbert(c)
- Southern Jr. Title Match
- 1st time Jerry won this title

Apr 16, 1974: Macon, GA
& Mr. Wrestling II lost to Bob Armstrong

Apr 17, 1974: Columbus, GA
vs. Tiger Conway Jr.

Apr 19, 1974: Atlanta, GA
w/Art Nelson, Bill Costello & Bobby Duncum beat Bob Armstrong, Ricky Gibson, Jerry Oates & Tiger Conway Jr.
- Also, In Battle Royal

Apr 22, 1974: Memphis, TN
(c)w/Sam Bass beat Tommy Gilbert w/Eddie Marlin
- Southern Jr Title Match

Apr 23, 1974: Macon, GA
lost to Jerry Brisco

Apr 24, 1974: Columbus, GA
vs. Mr. Wrestling II
- Chain Match

Apr 26, 1974: Atlanta, GA
& Art Nelson lost to Earl Maynard & Bob
Armstrong

Apr 28, 1974: Louisville, KY
w/Sam Bass beat Jerry Jarrett

Apr 29, 1974: Memphis, TN
lost to Tommy Gilbert
- Coal Miners Glove match
- Non-title match

May 1, 1974: Nashville, TN
(c) w/Sam Bass beat Roughhouse Fargo
-Southern Jr. Title Match

May 4, 1974: Chattanooga, TN
w/Sam Bass beat Steve Kovac(c)
- US Jr. Title Match

May 5, 1974: Louisville, KY
(c) w/Sam Bass beat Tommy Gilbert
-Southern Jr. Title Match

May 6, 1974: Memphis, TN
w/Sam Bass & Lou Thesz lost to Tommy Gilbert,
Eddie Marlin, & Ricky Gibson

May 8, 1974: Nashville, TN
w/Sam Bass beat Mike Jackson

May 12, 1974: Chattanooga, TN
(c) w/Sam Bass vs. Jerry Jarrett
- US Jr. Title Match

May 13, 1974: Memphis, TN
w/Sam Bass & Lou Thesz lost to Tommy Gilbert,
Eddie Marlin, & Jim Kent

May 15, 1974: Nashville, TN
(c) w/Sam Bass beat Tommy Gilbert
- Southern Jr. Title Match
- 2 out of 3 falls

May 20, 1974: Memphis, TN
(c) w/Sam Bass beat Ricky Gibson
- Southern Jr. Title Match

May 22, 1974: Nashville, TN
(c) w/Sam Bass beat Tommy Gilbert w/Eddie
Marlin
- Southern Jr. Title Match

May 23, 1974: Jackson, TN
w/Sam Bass vs Tony Ladue

May 25, 1974 Chattanooga, TN
(c) w/Sam Bass beat Ricky Gibson
- Southern Jr. Title Match

May 27, 1974: Memphis, TN
(c) w/Sam Bass DCO with Ricky Gibson
- Southern Jr. Title Match

May 29, 1974: Nashville, TN
& Sam Bass drew with Eddie Marlin & Tommy
Gilbert
- 60 min draw

June 1, 1974: Chattanooga, TN
(c) w/Sam Bass No Contest with Ricky Gibson
- Southern Jr. Title Match

June 2, 1974: Louisville, KY
(c) w/Sam Bass vs. Ricky Gibson
- Southern Jr. Title Match

June 3, 1974: Memphis, TN
(c) w/Sam Bass lost to Ricky Gibson
- Southern Jr. Title Match
- Special Ref - Jackie Fargo
- Fargo's first time back since Lawler "put him
out" two months earlier.

June 5, 1974: Nashville, TN
(c) w/Sam Bass beat Inferno #1 w/JC Dykes
- Southern Jr. Title Match
- Title vs Mask
- Inferno #1 revealed as Ronnie Bishop

June 6, 1974: Jackson, TN
w/Sam Bass vs Joey Rossi
- Indian Strap Match

June 8, 1974: Chattanooga, TN
(c) w/Sam Bass vs. Ricky Gibson
- Southern Jr. Title Match

June 9, 1974: Louisville, KY
(c) w/Sam Bass vs. Ricky Gibson w/Jackie Fargo
- Southern Jr. Title Match

June 10, 1974: Memphis, TN
w/Sam Bass beat Ricky Gibson(c) w/Jackie Fargo
- Southern Jr. Title Match
- Lawler's hair vs. Title

June 12:, 1974:Nashville, TN
w/Sam Bass beat Scufflin' Hillbilly (sub for Melvin Kimble)

June 13, 1974 @Florence, AL
(c) w/Sam Bass beat Ricky Gibson
- Southern Jr. Title Match

June 15, 1974: Chattanooga, TN
(c) w/Sam Bass lost to Ricky Gibson
- Southern Jr. Title Match
- Special Ref: Jackie Fargo

June 17, 1974: Memphis, TN
(c) w/Sam Bass No Contest with Jackie Fargo
- Southern Jr. Title Match

June 19, 1974: Nashville, TN
w/Sam Bass beat Frank Monte

June 20, 1974: Jackson, TN
& Al Greene w/Sam Bass vs Steve Kovac & Ricky Gibson

June 22, 1974 @Florence, AL
(c) w/Sam Bass vs. Ricky Gibson w/Jackie Fargo
- Southern Jr. Title Match

June 24, 1974: Memphis, TN
(c) w/Sam Bass lost to Jackie Fargo w/Ricky Gibson
- Southern Jr. Title Match
- No DQ

June 26, 1974: Nashville, TN
(c) w/Sam Bass beat Ricky Gibson
- Southern Jr. Title Match

* Some of the cities in the entire territory were isolated. While Lawler dropped the belt to Fargo in Memphis on 6/24, the card two days later in Nashville still listed Lawler as the Southern Jr. Champ. Without the internet to quickly transmit the title change info to fans in Nashville, the promotion was able to allow Lawler to drop the title to Fargo in different cities. Or as in this case, allowed a short payoff for the Memphis fans before Lawler took the belt back 7/8 Memphis card.

June 27, 1974: Jackson, TN
& Al Greene w/Sam Bass vs Steve Kovac & Ricky Gibson

June 29, 1974: Chattanooga, TN
& Mystery Man w/Sam Bass lost to Jackie Fargo & Ricky Gibson

July 1, 1974: Memphis, TN
w/Sam Bass defeated Jackie Fargo
- Steel Cage Match

July 3, 1974: Nashville, TN
(c) w/Sam Bass defeated Ricky Gibson
- Southern Jr. Title Match

July 4, 1974: Jackson, TN
& Don Kent w/Sam Bass vs Rufus R. Jones & Ricky Gibson

July 6, 1976: Chattanooga, TN
& Mystery Man vs. Jackie Fargo & Ricky Gibson
- Sam Bass locked in a cage

July 8, 1974: Memphis, TN
w/Sam Bass beat Jackie Fargo(c)
- Southern Jr. Title Match - No DQ

July 10, 1974: Nashville, TN
(c) w/Sam Bass vs. Jackie Fargo
- Southern Jr. Title Match

July 13, 1974: Chattanooga, TN
(c) w/Sam Bass beat Jackie Fargo w/Ricky Gibson
- Southern Jr. Title Match

July 15, 1974: Memphis, TN
(c) w/Sam Bass No Contest with the Sheik
- Southern Jr. Title Match

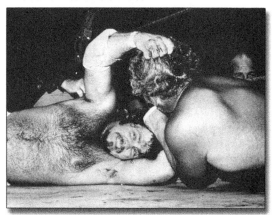
Jerry & The Sheik Being Dragged Apart

July 17, 1974: Nashville, TN
(c) w/Sam Bass No Contest with Jackie Fargo
w/Ricky Gibson
- Southern Jr. Title Match

July 18, 1974: Lexington, KY
(c) w/Sam Bass vs. Ricky Gibson w/Jerry Jarrett
- Southern Jr. Title Match

July 20, 1974: Chattanooga, TN
(c) w/Sam Bass lost to Jackie Fargo
- Southern Jr. Title Match
- Sam Bass locked in a cage

July 22, 1974: Memphis, TN
(c) w/Sam Bass beat Bobo Brazil
- Southern Jr. Title Match

July 27, 1974: Chattanooga, TN
w/Sam Bass defeated Jackie Fargo(c)
- Southern Jr. Title Match
- Title vs. Lawler's Hair
- Sam Bass locked in cage guarded by Rufus R. Jones

July 29, 1974: Memphis, TN
(c) w/Sam Bass lost via DQ to Mr. Wrestling II
- Southern Jr. Title Match
- Lawler tells everyone that Mr. Wrestling II is Johnny Walker (which is true).

*Photo Courtesy of Jim Blake
Jerry Lawler vs Bobo Brazil

*Photo Courtesy of Jim Blake
Jerry Lawler vs Mr. Wrestling II

July 23, 1974: Louisville, KY
(c) w/Sam Bass vs. Jackie Fargo
- Southern Jr. Title Match

July 24, 1974: Nashville, TN
w/Sam Bass lost to Jackie Fargo
- No DQ Cage Match
- Title not on the line

July 31, 1974: Nashville, TN
(c)w/Sam Bass defeated Jackie Fargo
- Steel Cage Match
- Non-title Match
- No DQ

Aug 5, 1974: Memphis, TN
(c) w/Sam Bass won via DQ over Bobo Brazil
- Southern Jr. Title Match

Aug 7, 1974: Nashville, TN
(c)w/Sam Bass lost to Jackie Fargo
- Southern Jr. Title Match
- No DQ
-Title & $300 vs $600

Aug 10 Chattanooga, TN
(c) w/Sam Bass beat Tojo Yamamoto
- Southern Jr. Title Match

Aug 12, 1974: Memphis, TN
(c) w/Sam Bass won via DQ over Dick the Bruiser
- Southern Jr. Title Match

Aug 22, 1974: Jackson, TN
(c) w/Sam Bass vs. Jackie Fargo
- Southern Jr. Title Match

Aug 27, 1974: Memphis, TN
(c) w/Sam Bass beat Rufus R. Jones
- Southern Jr. Title Match

Aug 29, 1974: Jackson, TN
(c) w/Sam Bass beat Jackie Fargo
- Southern Jr. Title Match

Aug 31, 1974: Chattanooga, TN
(c) w/Sam Bass beat Robert Fuller
- Southern Jr. Title Match

Sep 2, 1974: Memphis, TN
(c) w/Sam Bass lost via DQ to Robert Fuller
- Southern Heavyweight Title Match

*Photo Courtesy of Jim Blake
Jerry Lawler vs Dick the Bruiser

Aug 14, 1974: Nashville, TN
& Sam Bass lost to Ricky Gibson & Jackie Fargo

Aug 19, 1974: Memphis, TN
(c) w/Sam Bass beat Robert Fuller
- Southern Jr. Title Match

Aug 21, 1974: Memphis, TN
(c) w/Sam Bass beat Robert Fuller
- Southern Jr. Title Match

Jerry Lawler (wearing the Southern Title) with manager Sam Bass

* Jerry Jarrett decided to drop the "Junior" designation and make the title the Southern Heavyweight Title. The belt was over thirty-two years old by this point. Jarrett wanted to push Jerry Lawler as his top guy and he felt the "Jr." designation made it seem like the belt was for a smaller person. Not one who would go after the NWA World Heavyweight Title.

Sep 4, 1974: Evansville, IN
(c) w/Sam Bass beat Bearcat Brown

Sep 5, 1974: Jackson, TN
(c) w/Sam Bass beat Jackie Fargo
- Southern Heavyweight Title Match

Sep 7, 1974: Chattanooga, TN
(c) w/Sam Bass beat Robert Fuller
- Southern Heavyweight Title Match
- No DQ Match - No Ref

Sep 9, 1974: Memphis, TN
(c) w/Sam Bass beat Jerry Brisco
- Southern Heavyweight Title Match

Sep 10, 1974: Louisville, KY
(c) w/Sam Bass lost via DQ to Robert Fuller
w/Tojo Yamamoto
- Southern Heavyweight Title Match

Sep 11, 1974: Nashville, TN
& Sam Bass drew with Don Greene & Robert
Fuller

Sep 12, 1974: Jackson, TN
(c) w/Sam Bass beat Don Greene
- Southern Heavyweight Title Match

Sep 14, 1974: Chattanooga, TN
(c) w/Sam Bass beat Mr. Wrestling
- Southern Heavyweight Title Match

Sep 16, 1974: Memphis, TN
w/Sam Bass lost via DQ Jack Brisco(c)
- NWA World Heavyweight Title Match

* This World title shot for Jerry Lawler was also
a big deal for booker, Jerry Jarrett. Lawler was
the heir apparent to Jackie Fargo. For over a
year, Lawler had been the territory's top star.
He was consistently keeping the ticket sales
high, even having many sellouts of the Mid-
South Coliseum. The previous 6 months were a
setup for this match with Jack Brisco. Jarrett
called the program, "The Quest For The Gold".
Jarrett put the Southern belt on Lawler as the
first step. That was followed by feuds with
Jackie Fargo and Ricky Gibson. Then Jarrett
brought in highly established national stars like
The Sheik, Dick the Bruiser, Mr. Wrestling II,
Bobo Brazil, Rufus R, Jones, Jerry Brisco, etc.
With Lawler running through the NWA top ten
rankings it was a build up towards this match
with World champ, Jack Brisco. Though the
King came up short, it was an amazing Summer

in Memphis and the fans still talk about it, 44
years after the fact.

Sep 17, 1974: Louisville, KY
(c) w/Sam Bass beat Rufus R. Jones w/Tojo
Yamamoto
- Southern Title Match

Sep 18, 1974: Nashville, TN
(c) w/Sam Bass No Contest with Bobo Brazil
- Southern Heavyweight Title Match

Sep 19, 1974: Jackson, TN
(c) w/Sam Bass lost via DQ to Robert Fuller
- Southern Heavyweight Title Match

Sep 22, 1974: Louisville, KY
& Don Kent w/Sam Bass beat Jerry Jarrett &
Tojo Yamamoto

Sep 30, 1974: Memphis, TN
(c) w/Sam Bass beat Jerry Brisco
- Southern Title Match

Oct 1, 1974: Louisville, KY
& Don Kent w/Sam Bass lost to Jerry Jarrett &
Tojo Yamamoto
- Texas Tornado Death Match

Oct 2, 1974: Nashville, TN
(c) w/Sam Bass beat Rufus R. Jones
- Southern Title Match

*Photo Courtesy of Mike Shields
Jerry Lawler & Sam Bass Being Interviewed
By Len Rossi At A Nashville TV Taping.

Oct 3, 1974: Chattanooga, TN
(c) w/Sam Bass lost via DQ to Don Greene

- Southern Title Match

Oct 7, 1974: Memphis, TN
(c) w/Sam Bass won via DQ over Robert Fuller
- Southern Title Match

Oct 8, 1974: Louisville, KY
(c) w/Sam Bass beat Jerry Jarrett
- Southern Title Match

October 9, 1974: Nashville, TN
(c) w/Sam Bass No Contest with Robert Fuller
- Southern Title Match

Oct 10, 1974: Chattanooga, TN
(c) w/Sam Bass beat Harley Race
- Southern Title Match

Oct 14, 1974: Louisville, KY
w/Sam Bass lost via DQ to Jack Brisco(c)
- NWA World Heavyweight Title Match

Oct 15, 1974: Memphis, TN
(c) w/Sam Bass won via DQ over Robert Fuller
- Southern Title Match

Oct 17, 1974: Chattanooga, TN
(c) w/Sam Bass lost via DQ to Bobo Brazil
- Southern Title Match

Oct 22, 1974: Louisville, KY
(c) w/Sam Bass beat Robert Fuller
- Southern Title Match

Oct 23, 1974: Nashville, TN
(c) w/Sam Bass lost to Robert Fuller
- Southern Title Match
- Title vs Hair
- No DQ

Oct 24, 1974: Chattanooga, TN
w/Don Kent & Pepe Lopez beat Tojo Yamamoto,
Jerry Jarrett, & Don Greene

Oct 28, 1974: Memphis, TN
& Tojo Yamamoto beat Al Green & Phil
Hickerson w/Sam Bass
-Starts babyface run by Jerry Lawler

Oct 30, 1974: Nashville, TN
beat Robert Fuller(c)
- Southern Title Match
- Title vs Lawler's Hair
- No DQ

Nov 1, 1974: Louisville, KY
& Tojo Yamamoto beat Al Green & Phil
Hickerson w/Sam Bass

Nov 4, 1974: Memphis, TN
& Tojo Yamamoto won via DQ over Al Green &
Phil Hickerson w/Sam Bass

Nov 5, 1974: Louisville, KY
& Tojo Yamamoto lost to Al Green & Phil
Hickerson w/Sam Bass

Nov 6, 1974: Evansville, IN
& Tojo Yamamoto beat Al Green & Phil
Hickerson w/Sam Bass
- 2 out of 3 falls

Nov 7, 1974: Chattanooga, TN
w/Don Kent & Juan Sebastian beat Phil
Hickerson, Al Greene, & Dr. Death

Nov 11, 1974: Memphis, TN
& Tojo Yamamoto(c) beat Al Greene & Phil
Hickerson w/Sam Bass
- Southern Tag Title Match

Also - beat the Mummy

Nov 12, 1974: Louisville, KY
& Tojo Yamamoto lost to Al Green & Phil
Hickerson(c) w/Sam Bass
- Southern Tag Title Match

Nov 13, 1974: Evansville, IN
& Tojo Yamamoto vs. Al Green & Phil Hickerson
w/Sam Bass
- No DQ

Nov 14, 1974: Chattanooga, TN
w/Don Kent & Juan Sebastian lost to Dennis
Hall, George Gulas, & Jackie Fargo
- Winning team gets six-man tag titles & $3000

Nov 16, 1974: Florence, AL
(c) beat Silento Rodriguez

Nov 18, 1974: Memphis, TN
beat the Mummy
- Cage Match

Nov 19, 1974: Louisville, KY
& Tojo Yamamoto beat Al Green & Phil
Hickerson(c) w/Sam Bass
- Southern Tag Title Match
- Titles vs. Lawler's Hair
- No DQ

Nov 20, 1974: Evansville, IN
& Tojo Yamamoto beat Al Greene & Phil
Hickerson(c) w/Sam Bass
- Southern Tag Title Match
- Lawler's hair vs Titles

Nov 21, 1974: Chattanooga, TN
& Eddie Marlin lost via DQ to Count Drummer &
Duke Myers w/Sam Bass

Nov 25, 1974: Memphis, TN
w/Tojo Yamamoto beat the Mummy & Sam Bass

Nov 26, 1974: Louisville, KY
& Jerry Jarrett beat the Mummy & Sam Bass

Nov 28, 1974: Jackson, TN
& Tojo Yamamoto vs. Al Greene & Phil Hickerson
w/Sam Bass

Nov 30, 1974: Chattanooga, TN
& Eddie Marlin lost to Count Drummer & Duke
Myers

Dec 2, 1974: Memphis, TN
beat the Mummy w/Sam Bass
- Hair vs. Mask Match
-Mummy revealed as Ron Wright

December 4, 1974: Nashville, TN
& Tojo Yamamoto beat Al Greene & Phil
Hickerson w/Bass
Dec 5, 1974: Jackson, TN
& Eddie Marlin vs. Al Greene & Phil Hickerson
w/Sam Bass

Dec 7, 1974: Chattanooga, TN
w/Eddie Marlin & Tojo Yamamoto beat Duke
Myers, Count Drummer, & Sam Bass
- No DQ Match

Dec 8, 1974: Memphis, TN
& Ray Candy won via DQ over Al Greene & Phil
Hickerson(c) w/Sam Bass
- Southern Tag Title Match

December 11, 1974: Nashville, TN
& Tojo Yamamoto lost to Al Greene & Phil
Hickerson (c) w/Sam Bass
- Southern Tag Title Match

Dec 12, 1974: Jackson, TN
& Eddie Marlin vs. Phil Hickerson & John Gray
w/Sam Bass

Dec 13, 1974: Knoxville, TN
(c) vs. Ricky Gibson
- Southern Title Match

Dec 14, 1974: Chattanooga, TN
vs. Sam Bass
- Chain Match

Dec 15, 1974: Memphis, TN
beats Al Greene
- If Lawler wins, gets match with Sam Bass

beats Sam Bass

Dec 20, 1974: Knoxville, TN
vs. Nelson Royal

1975

Chapter 6

Jan 7, 1975: Louisville, KY
w/Jerry Bryant lost to Phil Hickerson & Doug Patton
- Southern Tag Title Tournament

Jan 8, 1975: Nashville, TN
drew with Don Kent(c) w/Sir Clements
Mid-America Title Match

Jan 13, 1975: Memphis, TN
beat Danny Hodge
lost to Steve Kovacs
- Round Robin 4-Man Tournament
- other participants: Ron Fuller & Danny Hodge
- Winner gets NWA World Title Shot

Jan 15, 1975: Nashville, TN
lost to Don Kent(c) w/Sir Clements
Mid-America Title Match

Jan 17, 1975: Knoxville, TN
beat Florentino Flores
won via DQ over Ron Wright
lost to Nelson Royal

Jan 19, 1975: Knoxville, TN
beat Jim Kent

Jan 20, 1975: Memphis, TN
& Dick the Bruiser lost via DQ to Ron Fuller & Danny Hodge

Jan 21, 1975: Louisville, KY
won via DQ over Pierre Bonet

Jan 22, 1975: Nashville, TN
vs. Mario Leone

Jan 23, 1976: Chattanooga, TN
w/Jerry Barber & George Gulas drew with Johnny Gray, Big Bad John & Lorenzo Parente
- 6-Man Title Match

* Exile For The King: It was about this time that Jerry Lawler made one of his first power plays with booker Jerry Jarrett. In simplest terms the King felt that the champion didn't travel to all the small cities. This meant he decided to start skipping some of the small towns on the Jarrett end of the territory. When Jerry Jarrett found out about it, he wasn't happy. His response was swift and harsh. He agreed with Jerry Lawler and took it a step further. He said, "Maybe the champ doesn't go to any of the cities in the territory..." Despite the huge success Jerry Lawler had helped the territory have during the Summer of 1974, Jerry Jarrett felt no wrestler was bigger than the promotion. This led Jarrett to have Lawler drop the Southern Title to Ron Fuller. After that, the King was shipped off to the Georgia territory for 6 months. The exile continued and saw Lawler sent to the Florida territory for 2 more months.

By late October 1975, Jerry Jarrett felt that Jerry Lawler had learned his lesson and was allowed to return to Memphis.

Jan 27, 1975: Memphis, TN
lost to Ron Fuller(c) w/Sam Bass
- Southern Title Match

Jan 28, 1975: Louisville, KY
won via DQ over Danny Hodge

Jan 29, 1975: Nashville, TN
w/Jerry Barber & George Gulas vs. John Gray, Big Bad John & Lorenzo Parente
- 6 Man Title Match

Jan 30, 1975: Chattanooga, TN
drew with Johnny Gray (sub for NWA Jr World Champ Ken Mantell)

Feb 3, 1975: Memphis, TN
lost to Jack Brisco(c)
- NWA World Heavyweight Title Match

Feb 4, 1975: Louisville, KY
lost to Ron Fuller(c) w/Sam Bass
- Southern Title Match
- Fan died of a heart attack during this match.

Feb 5, 1975: Evansville, IN
vs Ron Fuller(c)
- Southern Title Match

Feb 9, 1975: Chattanooga, TN
beat the Mummy
- Mummy unmasked as Melvin Kimble

Feb 14, 1975: Atlanta, GA
beat Steve Keirn

Feb 17, 1975: Augusta, GA
vs. Rocky Johnson(c)
- GA Heavyweight Title Match

Feb 21, 1975: Atlanta, GA
beat Ricky Gibson

Feb 24, 1975: Augusta, GA
vs. Ray Candy

Feb 25, 1975: Macon, GA
& Mongolian Stomper lost to Robert Fuller & Don
Muraco(c)
-Macon Tag Title Match

Feb 28, 1975: Atlanta, GA
beat Ray Candy

Mar 2, 1975: Macon, GA
beat Ricky Gibson

Mar 3, 1975: Augusta, GA
& Assassin II lost to Jerry Brisco & Rocky
Johnson(c)
- GA Tag Team Title Match

Mar 7, 1975: Atlanta, GA
& Assassin II lost to Jerry Brisco & Don Muraco

Mar 9, 1975: Macon, GA
& Don Greene beat Don Muraco & Robert
Fuller(c)
- Macon Tag Team Title Match

Mar 10, 1975: Augusta, GA
vs, Ray Candy

Mar 14, 1975: Atlanta, GA
drew with Don Muraco

Mar 21, 1975: Atlanta, GA
lost to Jerry Brisco

Mar 24, 1975: Augusta, GA
lost to Ray Candy

Mar 25, 1975: Macon, GA
& Don Greene(c) drew with Jerry Brisco & Don
Muraco
- Macon Tag Title Match

Mar 28, 1974: Atlanta, GA
w/Don Greene drew with Rocky Johnson & Jerry
Brisco

Mar 29, 1975 Griffin, GA
lost to Robert Fuller

Mar 31, 1975: Augusta, GA
vs. Ray Candy

Apr 1, 1975: Macon, GA
& Don Greene beat Rocky Johnson & Roberto
Soto

Apr 3, 1975: Rome, GA
& Don Greene vs. Jerry Brisco & Rocky
Johnson(c)
- GA Tag Title Match

Apr 8, 1975: Macon, GA
& Don Greene lost to Tommy Gilbert & Ricky
Gibson

Apr 10, 1975: Rome, GA
& Don Kent vs Jerry Brisco & Rocky Johnson

Apr 11, 1975: Atlanta, GA
drew with Rocky Johnson

Apr 13, 1975: Macon, GA
& Don Greene(c) drew with Tommy Gilbert &
Ricky Gibson
- Macon Tag Team Title Match

Apr 15, 1975: Atlanta, GA
& Assassin II lost to Bob Armstrong & Robert
Fuller

Apr 19, 1975: Griffin, GA
beat Robert Fuller

Apr 20, 1975: Savannah, GA
& Don Kent lost to Rocky Johnson & Jerry Brisco

Apr 21, 1975: Augusta, GA
vs. Rocky Johnson

Apr 25, 1975: Atlanta, GA
& Assassin II drew with Rocky Johnson & jerry
Brisco

Apr 26, 1975: Griffin, GA
& Don Greene lost to Bob Armstrong & Robert
Fuller

Apr 28, 1975: Augusta, GA
vs. Bob Armstrong

May 2, 1975: Atlanta, GA
drew with Jerry Brisco

May 4, 1975: Savannah, GA
& Assassin II lost to Bob Armstrong & Robert Fuller

May 8, 1975: Rome, GA
& Assassin II vs. Robert Fuller & Bob Armstrong
May 9, 1975: Atlanta, GA
lost to Dory Funk Jr.

May 16, 1975: Atlanta, GA
beat Tommy Gilbert

May 18, 1975: Savannah, GA
vs. Ricky Gibson

May 20, 1975: Macon, GA
& Don Greene lost to Andre the Giant

May 23, 1975: Atlanta, GA
drew with Jerry Brisco

May 27, 1975: Macon, GA
beat Bill Dromo

May 30, 1975: Atlanta, GA
w/Don Kent & Bob Orton Jr. lost to Bob Armstrong, Rocky Johnson & Robert Fuller

June 3, 1975: Macon, GA
vs. Mr. Wrestling II

June 6, 1975: Atlanta, GA
w/the Outlaws vs.Robert Fuller, Bob Armstrong & Mr. Wrestling

June 8, 1975: Savannah, GA
vs. Bob Armstrong

May 10, 1975: Macon, GA
& Abdullah the Butcher lost via DQ to Robert Fuller & Mr. Wrestling II

June 13, 1975: Atlanta, GA
beat Larry Zbyszko

June 17, 1975: Rome, GA
vs. Mr. Wrestling

June 20, 1975: Atlanta, GA
lost to Robert Fuller

June 24, 1975: Macon, GA
vs. Ricky Gibson

w/Bob Orton Jr, & Dudley Clements vs Ricky Gibson, Dennis Hall & Mike Stallings

June 26, 1975: Athens, GA
vs. Bob Armstrong

June 27, 1975: Atlanta, GA
drew with Bearcat Brown

June 30, 1975: Memphis, TN
DCO with Mongolian Stomper w/Bearcat Wright

July 7, 1975: Memphis, TN
lost to Mongolian Stomper w/Bearcat Wright
- No DQ

July 11, 1975: Atlanta, GA
beat Dennis Hall

July 14, 1975: Memphis, TN
won via DQ over Mongolian Stomper w/Bearcat Wright
- Southern Title Match

July 18, 1975: Atlanta, GA
lost to Bob Backland

July 21, 1978: Memphis, TN
w/Jackie Fargo DDQ with Mongolian Stomper(c) w/Bearcat Wright
- Southern Title Match

July 28, 1975: Memphis, TN
No Contest with Mongolian Stomper(c) w/Bearcat Wright
- Southern Title Match
- Special ref: Jackie Fargo

Aug 4, 1975 Memphis, TN
& Don Greene drew with Luke Graham & Bill Dundee

Aug 6, 1975: Nashville, TN
beat Sputnik Monroe

Aug 7, 1975: Jersey City, NJ
beat Larry Sharpe

Aug 11, 1975: Blytheville, AR
& Don Greene vs Bill Dundee & Luke Graham

Aug 12, 1975: Memphis, TN
w/Bob Armstrong, Robert Fuller, George Gulas & Don Greene beat Luke Graham, Bill Dundee, Frank Morell, Bill Costillo & Mr. Suzuki

Aug 14, 1975: Jackson, TN
& Roughhouse Fargo vs Cowboy Parker & Ken Dillinger

Aug 25, 1975: Orlando, FL
& Don Greene (Masked Superstars I & II) beat
Pepper Gomez & Mike Graham

Aug 26, 1975: Tampa, FL
& Don Greene (Masked Superstars I & II) beat
Ricky Gibson & Dennis Hall

Aug 27, 1975 Miami, FL
& Don Greene (Masked Superstars I & II) beat
Dennis Hall & Tony Charles

Aug 28, 1975: Porta Gorda, FL
& Don Greene (Masked Superstars I & II) beat
Mike Graham & Tony Charles

Aug 29, 1975: Fort Lauderdale, FL
& Don Greene (Masked Superstars I & II) vs.
Dennis Hall & Bobby Burns

Aug 30, 1975: Sarasota, FL
& Don Greene (Masked Superstars I & II) beat
Pepper Gomez & Dennis Hall

Sep 1, 1975: Orlando, FL
& Don Greene (Masked Superstars I & II) beat
Eddie Graham & Mike Graham

Sep 3, 1975: Miami, FL
& Don Greene (Masked Superstars I & II)beat
Tony Charles & Ricky Gibson

Sep 4, 1975: Jacksonville, FL
& Don Greene (Masked Superstars I & II) vs.
Tony Charles & Ricky Gibson

Sep 8, 1975: Orlando, FL
& Don Greene (Masked Superstars I & II)
beat Tony Charles & Mike George

Sep 9, 1975: Tampa, FL
& Don Greene (Masked Superstars I & II) beat
Mike Graham & Tony Charles

Sep 10, 1975: Miami, FL
& Don Greene (Masked Superstars I & II)
 beat Tony Charles & Ricky Gibson

Sep 11, 1975: Jacksonville, FL
& Don Greene (Masked Superstars I & II)
 vs. Mike George & Dennis Hall

Sep 12, 1975: Fort Lauderdale, FL
& Don Greene (Masked Superstars I & II) vs.
Cyclone Negro & Omar Negro

Sep 13, 1975: St. Petersburg, FL
& Don Greene (Masked Superstars I & II) lost
via DQ to Ricky Gibson & Jimmy Golden

Sep 16, 1975: Tampa, FL
& Don Greene (Masked Superstars I & II)
defeated Jimmy Golden & Ricky Gibson

Sep 17, 1975: Miami, FL
& Don Greene (Masked Superstars I & II) beat
Jimmy Golden & Ricky Gibson

Sep 19, 1975: Orlando, FL
& Don Greene (Masked Superstars I & II) lost to
Tony Charles & Tony Charles

Sep 20, 1975: Sarasota, FL
(as Masked Superstar II) in Battle Royal

Sep 22, 1975: West Palm Beach, FL
& Don Greene (Masked Superstars I & II) beat
Mike George & Omar Negro
-Also in Battle Royal

Sep 23, 1975: Tampa, FL
& Don Greene (Masked Superstars I & II) beat
Cyclone Negro & Omar Negro

Sep 24, 1975: Miami, FL
w/Don Greene lost to Florida Tag Champs
Cyclone & Omar Negro

Sep 25, 1975: Jacksonville, FL
& Don Greene (Masked Superstars I & II) vs
Mike George & Tony Charles
- Also in Battle Royal

Sep 26, 1975: Orlando, FL
& Don Greene (Masked Superstars I & II) lost to
Cyclone Negro & Omar Negro(c)
- FL Tag Title Match
- Also in Battle Royal

Sep 27, 1975: Lakeland, FL
Don Greene vs. Ricky Gibson & Jimmy Golden

Sep 29, 1975: West Palm Beach, FL
& Don Greene (Masked Superstars I & II) lost to
Mike George & Tony Charles

Sep 30, 1975: Tampa, FL
& Don Greene (Masked Superstars I & II) beat
Ricky Gibson & Jim Dillon

Oct 1, 1975: Miami, FL
& Don Greene (Masked Superstars I & II) beat
Omar & Cyclone Negro
- No DQ match

Oct 2, 1975: Jacksonville, FL
& Don Greene (Masked Superstars I & II) vs.
Omar & Cyclone Negro

Oct 3, 1975: Orlando, FL
& Don Greene (Masked Superstars I & II) won
via DQ over Jimmy Golden & Ricky Gibson

Oct 4, 1975: Sarasota, FL
& Don Greene (Masked Superstars I & II) beat
Jimmy Golden & Ricky Morton

Oct 6, 1975: West Palm Beach, FL
& Don Greene (Masked Superstars I & II) beat
Jimmy Golden & Ricky Gibson

Oct 7, 1975: Tampa, FL
& Don Greene (Masked Superstars I & II)beat
Jimmy Golden & Ricky Gibson

Oct 8, 1975: Miami, FL
& Don Greene (Masked Superstars I & II) beat
Eddie Graham & Mike Graham

Oct 10, 1975: Orlando, FL
& Don Greene (Masked Superstars I & II) &
Sam Bass lost to Cyclone Negro, Omar Negro &
Eddie Graham

Oct 13, 1975: West Palm Beach, FL
beat Tony Charles

Oct 14, 1975: Tampa, FL
beat Tony Charles

Oct 15, 1975: Miami, FL
lost to Mike George

Oct 16, 1975: Tallahassee, FL
vs. Mike George

Oct 17, 1975: Orlando, FL
drew with Ricky Gibson

Oct 20, 1975: West Palm Beach, FL
lost to Jimmy Golden

Oct 20, 1975: West Palm Beach, FL
w/Don Greene drew with Tony Charles & Billy
Robinson

Oct 21, 1975: Tampa, FL
lost to Mike Graham(c)
- US Jr Title Match

& Don Greene(Masked Superstars I & II) lost via
DQ to Billy Robinson & Tony Charles

Oct 22, 1975: Miami, FL
& Don Greene(Masked Superstars I & II) lost to
Jimmy Golden & Ricky Gibson

Oct 27, 1975: Memphis, TN
beat the Mongolian Stomper
- Loser Leaves town match

Oct 28, 1975: Blytheville, AR
vs. David Schultz

Oct, 29 1975: Nashville, TN
beat Golden Hawk

Oct 30, 1975: Chattanooga, TN
beat Mike Loren

Oct 31, 1975: Huntsville, AL
beat Bob Armstrong

Nov 1, 1975: Jonesboro, AR
w/Bill Dundee lost to the Infernos

Nov 3, 1975: Memphis, TN
won via DQ over the Sheik(c)
- US Title Match

Nov 4, 1975: Blytheville, AR
& Tommy Gilbert vs Rhode Island Red & Mr.
Suzuki

Nov 5, 1975: Nashville, TN
beat David Schultz

Nov 10, 1975: Memphis, TN
& Bob Armstrong lost to the Interns(c) w/Ken
Ramey
- Southern Tag Title Match

Nov 11, 1975: Blytheville, AR
& Tommy Gilbert vs Rhode Island Red & Mr.
Suzuki

Nov 17, 1975: Memphis, TN
beat Bob Armstrong

Nov 18, 1975: Blytheville, AR
w/Tommy Gilbert & Bobby Seals vs the Alaskan,
David Schultz & Ronnie Blaystein

Nov 19, 1975: Nashville, TN
& Jackie Fargo beat Phil Hickerson & Dennis
Condrey(c)
- US Tag Title Match

Nov 23, 1975: Chattanooga, TN
w/Jerry Jarrett & George Gulas lost to Phil
Hickerson, Dennis Condrey & Paul Maxwell

Nov 24, 1975: Memphis, TN
w/Sam Bass lost to Bob Armstrong(c)
- Southern Title Match

Nov 25, 1975: Louisville, KY
w/Sam Bass vs.Bob Armstrong

Nov 26, 1975: Nashville, TN
w/Sam Bass beat Bill Dundee

Dec 1, 1975: Memphis, TN
w/Sam Bass beat Tommy Giblert

Dec 1, 1975: Memphis, TN
w/Sam Bass No Contest with Bill Dundee

Dec 2, 1975: Louisville, KY
w/Sam Bass vs. Jerry jarrett

Dec 4, 1975: Bowling Green KY
w/Sam Bass vs Don Greene

*Photo Courtesy of Scott Teal Collection
Jerry Lawler vs Don Greene

Dec 8, 1975: Memphis, TN
w/Sam Bass lost to Bill Dundee
- No DQ Match

Dec 10, 1975: Nashville, TN
w/Sam Bass, Mitsu Arakawa, the Alaskan &
David Schultz vs Joey Rossi, Tommy Gilbert,
Don Anderson, Pez Whatley & Bearcat Brown

Dec 11, 1975: Bowling Green, KY
w/Sam Bass vs. Don Greene

Dec 15, 1975: Memphis, TN
<u>4- Man Southern Title Tournament</u>
Semi-finals
w/Sam Bass won via DQ over Dick the Bruiser

Finals
w/Sam Bass beat Ron Fuller
- Lawler wins Southern Title

Dec 16, 1975: Blytheville, AR
w/Sam Bass vs. Great Togo
- 2 out of 3 falls

Dec 17, 1975: Evansville, IN
w/Sam Bass beat Don Anderson

Dec 21, 1975: Memphis, TN
w/Sam Bass won via DQ over Ron Fuller
- Southern Title Match

& Sam Bass lost to Bob Armstrong & Bill Dundee

Dec 23, 1975: Evansville, IN
& David Schultz w/Sam Bass vs. Jerry Jarrett &
Tommy Rich

Dec 28, 1975: Memphis,TN
& Sam Bass lost to Bob Armstrong & Bill Dundee
- No DQ Match

Dec 23, 1975: Evansville, IN
& Sam Bass vs. Bill Dundee & Bob Armstrong

1976

Chapter 7

* You never knew who would show up. Adam West(TV's Batman), was in Memphis for the annual car show at the Cook Convention Center. In an effort to promote the car show, West, with his Batman cowl on, made a appearance on the Saturday morning Wrestling show. A brief verbal joust between Batman and the SuperKing took place. It's one of those little things that always seemed to happen on the live show. You never knew what to expect.

The King & Adam West At The Cook Convention Center In Memphis.

Jan 4, 1976: Memphis, TN
& Toru Tanaka lost to Jackie Fargo & Bill Dundee

Jan 6, 1976: Louisville, KY
& Sam Bass vs.Bob Armstrong & Bill Dundee

Jan 7, 1976: Evansville, IN
& Sam Bass lost via DQ to Bill Dundee & Jerry Jarrett

Jan 12, 1976: Memphis,TN
& Toru Tanaka won via DQ over Bill Dundee & Tojo Yamamoto

Jan 13, 1976: Louisville, KY
& Sam Bass No Contest with Jerry Jarrett & Bill Dundee
- Cage Match

Jan 14, 1976: Evansville, IN
& David Schultz w/Sam Bass vs. Bill Dundee & Jerry Jarrett

Jan 19, 1976: Memphis, TN
w/Sam Bass beat Ricky Gibson
- Southern Title Match
- Belt held up from previous Monday Night

Jan 20, 1976: Louisville, KY
& David Schultz w/Sam Bass No Contest with Bill Dundee & Jerry Jarrett

Jan 21, 1976: Evansville, IN
& David Schultz w/Sam Bass vs. Bill Dundee & Tojo Yamamoto

Jan 26, 1976: Memphis, TN
w/Sam Bass won via DQ over Ricky Gibson
- Southern Title Match
- Southern Title was held up previous week

Jan 27, 1976: Louisville, KY
& David Schultz w/Sam Bass No Contest with Bill Dundee & Tojo Yamamoto

Jan 28, 1976: Evansville, IN
(c) w/Sam Bass beat Ricky Gibson
- Southern Title Match

Jan 30, 1976: Blytheville, AR
w/Sam Bass vs. Bill Dundee

Feb 2, 1976: Memphis, TN
& David Schultz w/Sam Bass beat Tommy Rich & Bill Dundee

Feb 3, 1976: Louisville, KY
(c)w/Sam Bass beat Bill Dundee
- Southern Title Match

Feb 4, 1976: Evansville, IN
(c) w/Sam Bass beat Ricky Gibson
- Southern Title Match
- Title held up

Feb 6, 1976: Blytheville, AR
(c) w/Sam Bass vs. Bill Dundee
- No DQ Southern Title Match

Feb 8, 1976: Memphis, TN
(c) w/Sam Bass No Contest with Tommy Rich
- Southern Title Match

Feb 9, 1976: Birmingham, AL
vs. Masked Patriot

Feb 10, 1976: Louisville, KY
w/Sam Bass beat Bearcat Brown

w/Toru Tanaka, David Schultz & Sam Bass lost
to Tojo Yamamoto, Bill Dundee, Tommy Gilbert
& Bearcat Brown
- 8-man Tag Match

Feb 11, 1976: Evansville, IN
& David Schultz w/Sam Bass vs. Tommy Gilbert
& Bearcat Brown(c)
- Southern Tag Title Match

Feb 16, 1976: Memphis, TN
(c) w/Sam Bass lost via DQ to Tommy Rich
- Southern Title Match

*Photo Courtesy of Jim Cornette
Jerry Lawler Struggling With Tommy Rich.

Feb 17, 1976: Louisville, KY
(c) w/Sam Bass beat Rosey Jones (S.D. Jones)

Feb 22, 1976: Memphis, TN
(c) lost to Tommy Rich
- Southern Title Match
- No DQ - Sam Bass Banned From Ringside

Feb 24, 1976: Louisville, KY
w/Sam Bass lost to Tommy Rich

Mar 1, 1976: Louisville, KY
w/Sam Bass beat Tommy Rich
- No DQ - 2 out of 3 fall

Mar 2, 1976: Memphis, TN
vs. Dennis Hall

Mar 3, 1976: Nashville, TN
& David Schultz w/Sam Bass No Contest with
Bill Dundee & Tommy Rich

Mar 7, 1976: Memphis, TN
& Giant Frazier w/Sam Bass vs. Big Bad John &
Bill Dundee

w/Sam Bass lost via DQ to Ron Mikolajczyk
- Added match

March 9, 1976: Louisville, KY
w/Sam Bass lost to Tommy Rich(c)
- Southern Title Match
- No DQ - Bass Barred

Mar 10, 1976: Evansville, IN
(c)w/Sam Bass vs. Tommy Rich
- Southern Title Match

Mar 15, 1976: Memphis,TN
beat Tommy Gilbert
- Winner gets Southern Title Match

w/Sam Bass No Contest with Ron Mikolajczyk

Mar 16, 1976: Louisville, KY
& Sam Bass lost via Reversed Decision to
Tommy Rich (c) w/Big Bad John
- Southern Title Match

Mar 17, 1976: Evansville, IN
(c)w/Sam Bass vs. Tommy Rich
- Southern Title Match

Mar 20, 1976: Memphis, TN TV Show
w/Sam Bass beat Tommy Rich(c)
- Southern Title Match

Mar 22, 1976: Memphis,TN
& Plowboy Frazier w/Sam Bass lost via DQ to
Tommy Rich & Ron Mikolajczyk

Mar 23, 1976: Louisville, KY
& Plowboy Frazier w/Sam Bass beat Tommy
Rich & Big Bad John

Mar 24, 1976: Evansville, IN
(c) vs. Tommy Rich
- Southern Title Match

Mar 29, 1976: Memphis, TN
w/Sam Bass & Plowboy Frazier beat Tommy
Rich, Jerry Jarrett & Ron Mikolajczyk

March 30, 1976: Louisville, KY
& Plowboy Frazier w/Sam Bass over Tommy
Rich & Big Bad John w/Bill Dundee

Mar 31, 1976: Evansville, IN
& Plowboy Frazier w/Sam Bass vs. Tommy Rich
& Tojo Yamamoto

Apr 5, 1976: Memphis, TN
w/Sam Bass beat Ron Mikolajczyk
- 1st man to break rules loses

Apr 6, 1976: Louisville, KY
& Plowboy Frazier w/Sam Bass lost to
Tommy Rich & Ron Mickolajzcyk

Apr 7, 1976: Evansville, IN
w/Plowboy Frazier & Sam Bass lost to Tommy
Rich, Jerry Jarrett & Tojo Yamamoto

Apr 12, 1976: Memphis, TN
& Plowboy Frazier w/Sam Bass beat Ernie Ladd
& Ron Mikolajczyk in A Loser Leaves town match

April 13, 1976: Louisville, KY
w/Plowboy Frazier & Ernie Ladd No Contest with
Andre the Giant, Tommy Rich & Ron
Mickolajzcyk

Apr 14, 1976: Evansville, IN
(c)w/Sam Bass vs. Tommy Rich

Apr 19, 1976: Memphis, TN
& Plowboy Frazier(c) w/Sam Bass No Contest
w/Bill Dundee & Don Anderson
- Southern Tag Title Match

Apr 21, 1976: Evansville, IN
& Plowboy Frazier w/Sam Bass vs. Tommy Rich
& Ron Mickolajzcyk

April 23, 1976: Blytheville, AR
& Dr. X w/Sam Bass vs. Don Anderson & Bill
Dundee

Apr 26, 1976: Memphis, TN
& Plowboy Frazier w/Sam Bass lost via DQ to
Bill Dundee & Big Bad John
- Southern Tag Title Match

Photo Courtesy of Mike Shields
Jerry Lawler & Plowboy Frazier

Apr 27, 1976: Louisville, KY
& Plowboy Frazier(c) w/Sam Bass No Contest
with Bill Dundee & Don Anderson
- Southern Tag Title Match

Apr 28, 1976: Evansville, IN
w/Plowboy Frazier & Sam Bass lost to Tommy
Rich, Jerry Jarrett & Tojo Yamamoto
April 30, 1976: Blytheville, AR
& Dr. X w/Sam Bass vs. Don Anderson & Bill
Dundee

May 3, 1976: Memphis, TN
& Plowboy Frasier(c) w/Sam Bass lost to Bill
Dundee & Big Bad John
- Southern Tag Title Match

w/Sam Bass beat Don Anderson

May 4, 1976: Louisville, KY
& Plowboy Frazier w/Sam Bass lost via DQ to
Bill Dundee & Big Bad John(c)
- Southern Tag Title Match

May 5, 1976: Evansville, IN
& Plowboy Frazier(c) w/Sam Bass beat Bill
Dundee & Big Bad John
- Southern Tag Title Match

May 7, 1976: Blytheville, AR
w/Don Greene & The Scorpion vs. Don
Anderson, Bill Dundee & Tommy Rich

May 10, 1976: Memphis, TN
(c) w/Sam Bass won via DQ over Plowboy
Frazier

May 11, 1976: Louisville, KY
& Plowboy Frazier(c) w/Sam Bass DCOR with
Bill Dundee & Danny Miller

w/Sam Bass beat Don Anderson
- Lights Out Match

May 12, 1976: Evansville, IN
& Plowboy Frazier(c) w/Sam Bass won via DQ
over Bill Dundee & Don Anderson
- Southern Tag Title Match

May 17, 1976: Memphis, TN
w/Sam Bass lost to Plowboy Frazier w/Jarrett

May 18, 1976: Louisville, KY
w/Sam Bass over Plowboy Frazier

May 19, 1976: Nashville, TN
(c) w/Sam Bass beat Tommy Rich
- Southern Title Match

May 24, 1976: Memphis, TN
& Sam Bass lost to Jerry Jarrett & Plowboy
Frazier

May 26, 1976: Evansville, IN
w/Sam Bass won via DQ over Plowboy Frazier
May 28, 1976: Louisville, KY
w/Sam Bass lost to Plowboy Frazier w/Jerry
Jarrett

May 31, 1976: Memphis, TN
(c) w/Sam Bass beat Don Anderson
- Southern Title Match

& Sam Bass lost to Gentlemen Ben the
Wrestling Bear

June 1, 1976: Louisville, KY
& Sam Bass lost to Plowboy Frazier & Tommy
Rich
- Lawler's Crown On A 10' Pole

June 2, 1976: Evansville, IN
w/Sam Bass vs. Plowboy Frazier w/Tommy Rich
- No DQ

June 4, 1976: Blytheville, AR
& Sam Bass vs. Stan Frazier & Tommy Rich

June 7, 1976: Memphis, TN
(c) w/Sam Bass beat Don Anderson
- Southern Title Match
- 3 Refs

*Photo Courtesy of Jim Cornette
Jerry Lawler With The Southern Title.

June 9, 1976: Evansville, IN
w/Sam Bass vs. Plowboy Frazier w/Tommy Rich
- Cage Match
- Bass handcuffed to Rich

June 11, 1976: Blytheville, AR
(c) w/Sam Bass vs. Tommy Rich
- Southern Title Match

June 14, 1976: Memphis, TN
(c) w/Sam Bass beat Frankie Lane
- Southern Title Match

June 21, 1976: Memphis, TN
w/Sam Bass beat Rocky Johnson
- 15 Round Wrestling vs. Boxing Match

June 22, 1976: Louisville, KY
(c) w/Sam Bass beat Frankie Lane
- Southern Title Match

June 28, 1976: Memphis, TN
(c) w/Sam Bass beat Rocky Johnson
- Southern Title Match

June 29, 1976: Louisville, KY
(c) w/Sam Bass won via DQ over Jackie Fargo
- Southern Title Match

June 30, 1976: Evansville, IN
(c)w/Sam Bass vs. Frankie Lane
- Southern Title Match

July 4, 1976: Louisville, KY
w/Sam Bass lost to Rocky Johnson
- Boxing vs Wrestling Match
- Lawler wins by pin
- Johnson wins by KO
- 6th Rd KO for Johnson

July 6, 1976: Memphis, TN
w/Tommy Gilbert won via DQ over Jackie Fargo
& Don Anderson

(c) w/Sam Bass beat Gorgeous George Jr.
- Southern Title Match
- Tuesday Card because Elvis Presley Played
Mid-South Coliseum Monday Night

July 7, 1976: Evansville, IN
(c)w/Sam Bass No Contest Jackie Fargo
- Southern Title Match

July 11, 1976: Louisville, KY
(c) w/Sam Bass beat Gorgeous George Jr.
- Southern Title Match
- Decision was reversed and title held up

July 12, 1976: Memphis, TN
w/Sam Bass lost via 6th Rd KO from Rocky
Johnson
- Boxing vs. Wrestling Match
- Johnson did not wear gloves

July 14, 1976: Evansville, IN
w/Sam Bass beat Jackie Fargo
- Southern Title Match

July 18, 1976: Louisville, KY
w/Sam Bass lost to Gorgeous George Jr.
- Southern Title Match
- Title Change not acknowledged in Memphis

July 19, 1976: Memphis, TN
(c) w/Sam Bass beat by DQ Bobo Brazil

July 25, 1976: Louisville, KY
w/Sam Bass beat Gorgeous George Jr.(c)
- Southern Title Match
- Hair vs. Title

July 26, 1976: Memphis, TN
(c) w/Sam Bass beat Harley Race
- This was Sam Bass' last match.

The Deaths of Sam Bass, Frank Hester & Pepe Lopez
After the July 26, 1976 matches concluded in Memphis. The boys all piled into their cars and headed home. In those days, the booker, Jerry Jarrett required all of his wresters to live in the center of the territory, Nashville, TN. That night two journeymen wrestlers, Pepe Lopez and Frank Hester, who wore masks and wrestled as the Dominoes, caught a ride from Sam Bass, back to Nashville.

Sam Bass
Dec. 21, 1948 - July 27, 1976

In the early hours of Tuesday morning, July 27, 1976, a car traveling eastbound on I-40 crashed into the East Piney River Bridge, approximately 6 miles west of Dickson, TN. The impact knocked a 35 foot section of the bridge into the interstate. The east bound lanes were covered in concrete, metal and the wreckage of the car that had just made the mess. Bass had no time to react on this dark stretch of interstate. His car slammed it the debris

field. Just as quickly, a tractor trailer plowed through the first car, Bass' car and the remnants of bridge. The tractor trailer and Bass's car came to rest in the median, but immediately were engulfed in fire. Bass, Lopez and Hester were not able to get out of the car and all passed away.

When the fire was finally able to be put out, the bodies were burned beyond recognition. By this point many of the wrestling employees who had been in Memphis early Monday night had caught up the accident scene. One of the first ones there was Jerry Lawler. He had only been a few miles behind Bass' car. Pat Malone was there as well and he was the one who identified the bodies. Malone had witnessed Lopez & Hester get into Bass' car back at the Mid-South Coliseum in Memphis.

Jerry Jarrett had not made the trip to Memphis that week. In the early hours of July 27, 1976 he received a phone call from Jackie Fargo, who told him some of the boys had been killed in a wreck on the way home from Memphis. When Jarrett asked who it was, Jackie told him it was Sam Bass' car that burned up. Fargo picked up Jarrett and they raced out to the interstate near Dickson, TN. As they pulled up, Jerry Lawler saw them and came over. Jarrett had a little relief because he had worried that he had lost Lawler as well as Bass, because the two were known to travel together.

Wednesday night, the show would go on. It always goes on in wrestling. In Evansville, IN the fans turned out like they always did. In 1976, there was no internet, cable news, etc. Many of the Evansville fans learned about the car crash and the resulting deaths from an announcement given over the PA system at the Evansville Coliseum that night. As the announcer told the fans of the passing there was a silence. When it was announced that Sam Bass had perished as well, fans cheered. It's a testament to how hated Bass, as a heel manager, was. Jerry Jarrett says that Bass would have been ecstatic to know about that fan reaction. He had done his job perfectly. Sam Bass had the fans hating

him so much that they cheered when his death was announced. Now that is heat.

July 28, 1976: Evansville, IN
& Tommy Gilbert vs. Jackie Fargo & Frankie Lane

Aug 2, 1976: Memphis, TN
(c) beat Dory Funk Jr.
- Southern Title Match

August 3, 1976: Louisville, KY
(c) lost via DQ to Bill Dundee

Aug 9, 1976: Memphis, TN
(c) lost to Jack Brisco
- Southern Title Match

*Photo Courtesy of Jim Cornette
Jerry Lawler vs. Jack Brisco

Aug 11, 1976: Evansville, IN
 (c) vs. Jackie Fargo
- Southern Title Match

Aug 12, 1976: Bowling Green, KY
(c) vs. Charlie Cook
- Southern Title Match

Aug 15, 1976: Louisville, KY
(c) lost to Gorgeous George Jr.
- Southern Title Match

Aug 16, 1976: Memphis, TN Mid-South Coliseum, Monday
beat Jack Brisco(c)
- Southern Title Match

Aug 22, 1976: Memphis, TN Mid-South Coliseum, Monday
drew with Terry Funk(c)
- NWA World Title Match
- 60 minute draw

Aug 30, 1976: Memphis, TN
(c) won via DQ over Jackie Fargo
- Southern Title Match
w/Dennis Condrey & Phil Hickerson No Contest
w/Bill Dundee, Rocky Johnson & Tojo Yamamoto

Sep 1, 1976: Evansville, IN
w/Phil Hickerson, Dennis Condrey & Tommy Gilbert vs. Bill Dundee, Jackie Fargo, Tojo Yamamoto & Charlie Cook
- 8-Man Texas Tornado Death Match

Sep 5, 1976: Louisville, KY
w/Phil Hickerson & Dennis Condrey No Contest with Tojo Yamamoto, Bill Dundee & Plowboy Frazier

September 6, 1976: Memphis, TN
w/Dennis Condrey & Phil Hickerson went to A No Contest w/Tojo Yamamoto, Bill Dundee & Rocky Johnson

September 12, 1976: Louisville, KY w/Phil Hickerson & Dennis Condrey vs.Tojo Yamamoto, Bill Dundee & Plowboy Frazier

Sep 14, 1976: Memphis, TN
(c) lost to Tommy Rich
- Southern Title Match

- Jackie Fargo had a ringside ticket and during the match distracts Jerry to allow huge win by Tommy Rich.

Sep 15, 1976: Evansville, IN
w/Phil Hickerson & Dennis Condrey vs. Bill Dundee, Tojo Yamamoto & Plowboy Frazier

Sep 19, 1976: Louisville, KY
beat Plowboy Frazier
- Hair vs. Hair match

Sep 20, 1976: Memphis, TN
No Contest with Jackie Fargo

Sep 22, 1976: Evansville, IN
w/Phil Hickerson & Dennis Condrey vs. Bill Dundee, Tojo Yamamoto & Plowboy Frazier

Sep 26, 1976: Louisville, KY
beat Plowboy Frazier
- Lawler must bodyslam Frazier in 5:00 or head shaved

Sep 29, 1976: Evansville, IN
w/Phil Hickerson & Dennis Condrey vs. Bill Dundee, Tojo Yamamoto & Plowboy Frazier

Sep 30, 1976: Bowling Green, KY
& Tommy Gilbert vs Jackie Fargo & Plowboy Frazier

Oct 4, 1976: Memphis, TN
(c) lost to Jackie Fargo
- Southern Title Match
- Not acknowledged in other cities

Oct 6, 1976: Nashville, TN
(c) beat Bob Armstrong(c)
- Lawler's Southern Title vs. Armstrong's Mid-America Title

Oct 11, 1976: Memphis,
beat Dory Funk Jr.
- Texas Death Match

Jerry Lawler vs Dory Funk Jr.

Oct 13, 1976: Nashville, TN
(c) lost via DQ to Jackie Fargo
- Southern Title Match

Oct 18, 1976: Memphis, TN
lost via DQ to Terry Funk(c)
- NWA World Title Match
- Lawler won but ref reversed the decision

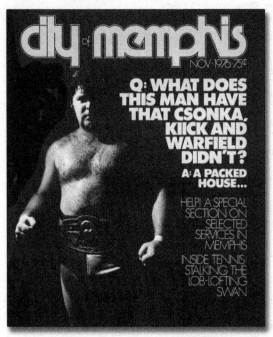

Jerry Lawler On A Local Magazine Cover

* When Lawler went to the dressing room with the World Title after the match with Terry Funk, he had a photo taken with the World Title. It was used on a local magazine cover.

Oct 19, 1976: Louisville, KY
(c) beat Tommy Rich
- Southern Title Match

*Photo Courtesy of Jim Cornette
Jerry Lawler Has Tommy Rich Under Control.

Oct 20, 1976: Nashville, TN
(c) beat Bill Dundee
- Southern Title Match

Oct 23, 1976: Chattanooga, TN
(c) beat Frankie Lane
- Southern Title Match

Oct 24, 1976: Evansville, IN
lost via DQ to Andre the Giant

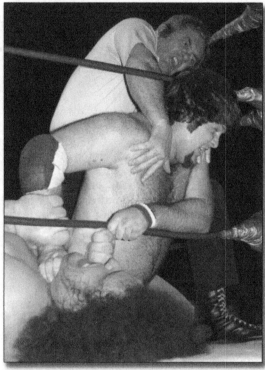

*Photo Courtesy of Jim Cornette
Jerry Lawler takes the battle to Andre the Giant

Oct 25, 1976: Memphis, TN
(c) beat Ron Fuller
- Southern Title Match

beat Mike Stark
- Special added non-title match

Oct 26, 1976: Louisville, KY
(c) lost to Tommy Rich
- Southern Title Match
- 3 refs

Oct 27, 1976: Nashville, TN
(c) beat Jackie Fargo
- Southern Title Match

Oct 28, 1976: Bowling Green, KY
& Gorgeous George Jr. vs. Tommy Rich & Don Anderson

Nov 1, 1976: Memphis, TN
(c) lost to Rocky Johnson
- Southern Title Match

Nov 2, 1976: Louisville, KY
beat Mike Stark

& Gorgeous George Jr. lost to Tommy Rich & Bill Dundee

Nov 3, 1976: Nashville, TN
was counted out against Jackie Fargo

Nov 8, 1976: Memphis, TN Mi
lost to Rocky Johnson(c)
- Southern Title Match

Nov 9, 1976: Louisville, KY
w/Gorgeous George Jr. vs. Bill Dundee & Tommy Rich
- Special Ref: Mike Stark

Nov 10, 1976: Evansville, IN
& Gorgeous George Jr. beat Bill Dundee & Don Anderson

beat Mike Stark

Nov 15, 1976: Memphis, TN
beat Jackie Fargo
- winner take all match

Nov 16, 1976: Louisville, KY
w/Gorgeous George Jr. & Tommy Gilbert lost to Bill Dundee, Plowboy Frazier & Tommy Rich

Nov 17, 1976: Evansville, IN
& Gorgeous George Jr. vs. Bill Dundee & Ricky Gibson
- Special ref: Plowboy Frazier

Nov 21, 1976: Louisville
went to a No Contest with Rocky Johnson(c)
- Southern Title Match

Nov 22, 1976: Memphis, TN
lost via DQ to Mike Stark

& Dutch Mantell lost via DQ to Danny Little Bear & Chief Thundercloud(c)
- Southern Tag Title Match

Nov 24, 1976: Evansville, IN
vs Rocky Johnson
- 15 Rounds, Boxer vs. Wrestlers, No Gloves

Nov 28, 1976: Louisville, KY
vs. Coyote Calhoun - WAKY DJ
vs. Rocky Johnson
- 15 Round Boxing Match
- Cancelled due to weather

Nov 29, 1976: Memphis, TN
& Gorgeous George Jr. No Contest with Rocky Johnson & Bill Dundee

Dec 1, 1976: Evansville, IN
(c) lost to Rocky Johnson
- Southern Title Match

Dec 6, 1976: Memphis, TN
Rocky Johnson(c) won via DQ over Mongolian Stomper w/Jerry Lawler
- Southern Title Match
- Lawler interferes

Dec 7, 1976: Louisville, KY
beat Coyote Calhoun - WAKY DJ
w/Gorgeous George Jr lost via reverse decision to Rocky Johnson w/Bill Dundee
- 15 Round Boxing Match

Dec 8, 1976: Evansville, IN
lost to Rocky Johnson(c)
- Southern Title Match
- Title vs. Crown

Dec 12, 1976: Memphis, TN
Rocky Johnson(c) w/Tommy Rich No Contest with Mongolian Stomper w/Jerry Lawler
- Southern Title Match

Dec 15, 1976: Evansville, IN
& Gorgeous George Jr. vs Rocky Johnson & Bill Dundee

Dec 16, 1976: Jackson, TN
& Russian Stomper vs. Rocky Johnson & Jackie Fargo

Dec 19, 1976: Memphis, TN
& Mongolian Stomper vs. Rocky Johnson & Jackie Fargo

Dec 21, 1976: Louisville, KY
David Schultz & Dutch Mantell w/Jerry Lawler
best Bill Dundee & Tommy Gilbert

Rocky Johnson(c) won via DQ over Mongolian
Stomper w/Jerry Lawler
- Southern Title Match

Dec 29, 1976: Evansville, IN
Mongolian Stomper w/Jerry Lawler lost via DQ
to Rocky Johnson(c)
- Southern Title Match

*Photo Courtesy of Jim Cornette
Gen. Lawler Managing The Mongolian
Stomper

*Photo Courtesy of Jim Cornette
Gen. Lawler laying the boots to Bill Dundee.

Dec 27, 1976: Memphis, TN
& Mongolian Stomper lost to Jackie Fargo &
Rocky Johnson
No DQ Match

Dec 28, 1976: Louisville, KY Louisville
Rocky Johnson(c) w/Bill Dundee No Contest with
Mongolian Stomper w/Jerry Lawler
- Southern Title Match

1977

Chapter 8

Jan 2, 1977: Knoxville, TN 3pm
lost via DQ to Rocky Johnson(c)
- Southern Title Match

Jan 2, 1977: Chattanooga, TN 7pm
lost via DQ to Rocky Johnson(c)
- Southern Title Match

Jan 3, 1977: Memphis, TN
lost via DQ to the Mongolian Stomper

Jan 4, 1977: Louisville, KY
w/Mongolian Stomper won by DQ over Bill
Dundee & Rocky Johnson

Jan 5, 1977: Evansville, IN
& Mongolian Stomper beat Rocky Johnson &
Tommy Gilbert

Jan 9, 1977: Memphis, TN Mid-South
w/Pvt. Diamond beat Mongolian Stomper
w/Rocky Johnson

Jan 11, 1977: Louisville, KY
& Mongolian Stomper lost to Bill Dundee &
Rocky Johnson
- No DQ Match

Jan 12, 1977: Evansville, IN
& Mongolian Stomper lost to Rocky Johnson &
Jackie Fargo
No DQ

Jan 17, 1977: Memphis, TN
won via DQ over the Mongolian Stomper
- Falls Count Anywhere Match

Jan 18, 1977: Louisville,
lost via reverse decision to Rocky Johnson(c)
- Southern Title Match

Jan 12, 1977: Evansville, IN
vs. Mongolian Stomper

Jan 22, 1977: Memphis, TN - TV results
Jerry Lawler with Dr. Frank's
- At TV Taping Dr. Frank was Jim Blake.

Jan 24, 1977: Memphis, TN
& Ernie Ladd beat Mongolian Stomper & Rocky
Johnson

Jan 25, 1977: Louisville, KY
w/Pvt. Diamond beat Rocky Johnson
- Lights Out Match
- Lawler win = gets crown back
- Johnson win = fan gets crown.

Jerry Lawler
The King of Wrestling

Jan 26, 1977: Evansville, IN
beat Rocky Johnson
- Non-Title Match
- Winner gets Lawler's Crown

Feb 7, 1977: Memphis, TN
No Contest with Bob Armstrong

Feb 8, 1977: Louisville, KY
& Gorgeous George Jr. w/Pvt. Diamond beat
Rocky Johnson & Bill Dundee(c)
-Southern Tag Title Match

Feb 9, 1977: Evansville, IN
& Gorgeous George Jr. beat Rocky Johnson &
Bill Dundee(c)
- Southern Tag Title Match

*Photo Courtesy of Jim Cornette
Jerry Lawler & Gorgeous George Jr., the
Southern Tag Champs.

Feb 14, 1977: Louisville, KY
& Gorgeous George Jr.(c) w/Pvt. Diamond beat
Billy & Benny McGuire
-Southern Tag Title Match
-Lawler also won Battle Royal

Feb 15, 1977: Memphis, TN
beat Bob Armstrong
- No DQ match

Feb 16, 1977: Evansville, IN
& Gorgeous George Jr.(c) beat Billy & Benny
McGuire
- Southern Tag Title Match

Feb 20, 1977: Memphis, TN
won via DQ over Bob Armstrong
- Steel Cage match

Feb 22, 1977: Louisville, KY
& George Wagner(c) beat Bill Dundee & Tommy
Rich
- Southern Tag Title Match

lost via reverse decision to Ricky Gibson
- To decide disputed Battle Royal victory from
Feb 14.

Feb 23, 1977: Evansville, IN
& George Wagner(c) lost to Bill Dundee &
Tommy Rich
- Southern Tag Title Match

*Photo Courtesy of Mike Shields
Jerry Lawler tees off on Bill Dundee.

Feb 28, 1977: Louisville, KY
beat Tommy Rich
- If Rocky Johnson wins the NWA World Title in
the main event, the winner of this match would
be the Southern Champion.

Mar 1, 1977: Memphis, TN
beat Tommy Rich
- If Rocky Johnson wins the NWA World Title in
the main event, the winner of this match would
be the Southern Champion.

Mar 2, 1977: Evansville, IN
beat Tommy Rich
- If Rocky Johnson wins the NWA World Title in
the main event, the winner of this match would
be the Southern Champion.

Mar 6, 1977: Memphis, TN
& Porkchop Cash beat George Wagner & Tommy
Rich

Mar 8, 1977: Louisville, KY
lost via DQ to George Wagner

Mar 9, 1977: Evansville, IN
w/Pvt. Diamond lost beat to Rocky Johnson(c)
- Southern Title Match

Mar 14, 1977: Memphis, TN
Southern Tag Title tournament:
First Round
& Jim White lost via DQ to George Wagner &
Tommy Rich

Mar 15, 1977: Louisville, KY
lost to George Wagner

Mar 16, 1977: Evansville, IN
w/Pvt. Diamond beat George Wagner

* Jerry Jarrett Splits From Nick Gulas. With the exception of Jackie Fargo and Tojo Yamamoto, all of the wrestlers already wrestling in Memphis sided and went with Jarrett. Jarrett gave Jerry Lawler 10% ownership of Memphis to stay with him.

Mar 20, 1977: Memphis, TN
No Contest with Bob Armstrong
- Stretcher Match: No Ref
-Debut card for Jerry Jarrett as Memphis
Territory Owner

Mar 22, 1977: Louisville, KY
lost to George Wagner
- Cage Match

Mar 23, 1977: Evansville, IN
lost to George Wagner
- Reverse decision
- Pvt Diamond handcuffed to Tommy Rich

Mar 27, 1977: Memphis, TN
beat Bob Armstrong

Mar 29, 1977: Louisville, KY
won via Count Out over George Wagner
- Indian Strap Match

Mar 23, 1977: Evansville, IN
lost to George Wagner
- Pvt Diamond barred from building

Apr 3, 1977: Memphis, TN
won by DQ over Rocky Johnson(c)
- Southern Title Match

Apr 5, 1977: Louisville, KY
lost by Count Out to Andre the Giant

*Photo Courtesy of Mike Shields
Jerry Lawler With A Headlock on Andre The Giant.

Apr 6, 1977: Evansville, IN
vs. George Wagner
- Indian Strap Match

Apr 11, 1977: Memphis, TN
beat Rocky Johnson
- Southern Title Match
- Southern Title was held up from earlier match

Apr 12, 1977: Louisville, KY
w/Rock Hunter lost via DQ to Rocky Johnson(c)
- Southern Title Match
- Belt held up after match

Apr 13, 1977: Evansville, IN
vs. George Wagner
- Submission Match

Apr 18, 1977: Memphis, TN
(c) lost via DQ to Rocky Johnson
- Southern Title Match
- Two refs

Apr 19, 1977: Louisville, KY
beat Rocky Johnson
- Southern Title Match
- No DQ
- Title Held Up After Apr 12 card

Apr 20, 1977: Evansville, IN
(c) beat Rocky Johnson
- Southern Title Match
- Title held up after match

Apr 24, 1977: Memphis, TN
(c) beat Jack Brisco
- Southern Title Match
- Famous photo taken that night.

*Photo Courtesy of Jim Blake
Jack Brisco vs. Jerry Lawler

Apr 26, 1977: Louisville, KY
(c) won via DQ over Rocky Johnson
- Southern Title Match
- Title can change on a DQ

Apr 27, 1977: Evansville, IN
beat Rocky Johnson
- Southern Title Match
- Title was held up after Apr 20th match

Apr 28, 1977: Knoxville, TN
(c) lost to Bob Armstrong
- Southern Title Match

May 1, 1977: Memphis, TN
- beat Bob Armstrong (c)
- Southern Title Match

*Photo Courtesy of Jim Cornette
Bob Armstrong Giving Jerry Lawler An
Atomic Drop

May 10, 1977: Louisville, KY
beat Bob Armstrong(c)
- Southern Title Match

May 11, 1977: Memphis, TN
(c) beat Robert Fuller
- Southern Title Match
- Special ref is George Wagner

May 12, 1977: Evansville, IN
w/Phil Hickerson & Dennis Condrey vs. Rocky
Johnson, Tommy Rich & George Wagner

May 17, 1977: Louisville, KY
w/Phil Hickerson & Dennis Condrey w/Mickey
Poole beat Rocky Jonson, Ricky & Robert Gibson
- Mickey Poole started managing Jerry Lawler

May 18, 1977: Memphis, TN
(c) w/Mickey Poole lost via DQ to Ron Fuller

May 19, 1977: Evansville, IN
won via Count Out over Bob Armstrong(c)
- Southern Title Match

May 20, 1977: Knoxville, TN
(c) beat Bob Armstrong
- Southern Title Match
- No DQ

May 23, 1977: Memphis, TN
(c) w/Poole beat Paul Orndorff
- Southern Title Match

May 24, 1977: Louisville, KY
(c) w/Poole lost via DQ to Paul Orndorff
- Southern Title Match

May 29, 1977: Memphis, TN
(c) w/Poole lost to Paul Orndorff
- Southern Title Match

*Photo Courtesy of Jim Cornette
The King In Trouble Against Paul Orndorff.

June 1, 1977: Evansville, IN
(c)w/Poole beat Paul Orndorff
- Southern Title Match

June 3, 1977: Blytheville, AR
w/Poole vs. Paul Orndorff(c)
- Southern Title Match
- 2 out of 3 falls

June 7, 1977: Louisville, KY
(c) w/Poole lost to Paul Orndorff
- Southern Title Match
- Belt Can Change On DQ:

June 8, 1977: Evansville, IN
(c) w/Poole lost via DQ to Paul Orndorff
- Southern Title Match

June 12, 1977: Memphis, TN
w/Poole won via DQ over- Dusty Rhodes

June 14, 1977: Louisville, KY
w/Poole lost to Paul Orndorff(c) w/Rocky
Johnson
- Southern Title Match

June 19, 1977: Memphis, TN
w/Poole No Contest with Dusty Rhodes

June 21, 1977: Louisville, KY
w/Poole beat Rocky Johnson
- Leather Strap On A 15' Pole Match

June 22, 1977: Evansville, IN
& Plowboy Frazier w/Poole beat Rocky Johnson
& Tommy Gilbert

June 24, 1977: Blytheville, AR
w/Poole vs. Paul Orndorff(c)
- Southern Title Match

June 27, 1977: Memphis, TN
w/Poole beat Rocky Johnson
- Leather Strap On A 15' Pole Match

June 28, 1977: Louisville, KY
w/Poole beat Rocky Johnson w/Paul Orndorff
- Loser Leaves Town Match

Bill Dundee over Leroy Brown w/Jerry Lawler
Brown must pin Dundee twice or lose Lawler's
$1000

June 29, 1977: Evansville, IN
w/Poole beat Rocky Johnson
- Leather Strap On A 15' Pole Match

July 1, 1977: Blytheville, AR
vs. Paul Orndorff(c)
- Southern Title Match
- Mickey Poole handcuffed to the ring post:

July 4, 1977: Memphis, TN
w/Poole lost to Bill Dundee
Lawler must pin Dundee twice or lose $4000

July 5, 1977: Louisville, KY
Leroy Brown w/Lawler lost to Bill Dundee.
- Cage Match
- Brown Must Win Twice In 15:00 Or Forfeit
Lawler's $1000

lost via reversed decision to Paul Orndorff(c)
- Southern Title Match
- Mickey Poole was handcuffed to a ring post

July 6, 1977: Evansville, IN
w/Poole lost via DQ to Paul Orndorff(c)
- Southern Title Match

July 11, 1977: Memphis, TN
w/Poole lost to Bill Dundee
- Cage Match
- Lawler's Cadillac vs. Dundee's $4,000
- Lawler must pin Dundee twice in 15 mins.

*Photo Courtesy of Jim Cornette
Jerry Lawler Cornering Bill Dundee In A Cage

July 12, 1977: Louisville, KY
w/Poole lost to Bill Dundee
- Lawler Must Pin Dundee Twice In 15 mins
- $2000 vs $2000 Winner Takes All

July 13, 1977: Evansville, IN
Leroy Brown w/Jerry Lawler lost to Bill Dundee
- Cage Match: $1,000 vs $1,000, winner take all
- Brown Must Pin Dundee twice in 15 mins.

lost to Paul Orndorff(c)
- Southern Title Match
- No DQ - Poole handcuffed to ring post

July 15, 1977: Blytheville, AR
w/Poole lost to Bill Dundee

July 18, 1977: Memphis, TN
w/Poole beat Paul Orndorff(c)
- Southern Title Match
- Winner gets NWA World Title Match vs H. Race

w/Poole went to a No Contest with Bill Dundee

July 19, 1977: Louisville, KY
w/Poole lost to Bill Dundee
- Cage Match
- Lawler Must Pin Dundee Twice In 15:00
- Dundee's $4000 vs Lawler's Cadillac

July 20, 1977: Evansville, IN
w/Poole lost to Bill Dundee
- $2,000 vs $2,000, winner takes all
- Lawler Must Pin Dundee Twice In 15:00

July 22, 1977: Blytheville, AR
(c)w/Poole vs. Bill Dundee
- Southern Title Match

July 25, 1977: Memphis, TN
(c)w/Poole lost to Bill Dundee
- Southern Title Match
- Title vs. Dundee's Cadillac

July 26, 1977: Louisville, KY
(c)w/Poole lost via DQ to Pat Barrett
- Southern Title Match

w/Poole lost via DQ to Bill Dundee
- Texas Bull Rope Match

July 27, 1977: Evansville, IN
w/Poole lost to Bill Dundee
- Dundee's $4,000 vs Lawler's Cadillac
- Lawler Must Pin Dundee Twice In 15:00

Aug 1, 1977: Memphis, TN
w/Poole beat Bill Dundee(c)
- Southern Title Match
- Dundee's Title & Cadillac vs Lawler's hair

Aug 2, 1977: Louisville, KY
(c) w/Poole lost to Bill Dundee
- Southern Title Match
- Title vs. Dundee's Cadillac

Aug 3, 1977: Evansville, IN
w/Poole No Contest with Bill Dundee
- Bull Rope Match

Aug 8, 1977: Memphis, TN
(c) w/Poole beat Paul Orndorff
- Southern Title Match

 (c) w/Poole lost to Bill Dundee
- Southern Title Match
- Cadillac vs Title
- Added match

Aug 9, 1977: Louisville, KY
beat Bill Dundee(c)
- Southern Title Match
- Cadillac & Title vs. Lawler's Hair
- Poole barred from ringside

Aug 10, 1977: Evansville, IN
(c)w/Poole lost to Bill Dundee
- Southern Title Match
- Dundee's Cadillac vs. Lawler's Title

Aug 15, 1977: Memphis, TN
(c) w/Poole beat Bill Dundee w/Paul Orndorff
- Southern Title Match
- Title & Poole's hair vs. Dundee's Cadillac

Aug 16, 1977: Louisville, KY
(c) w/Poole beat Mr. Wrestling
- Southern Title Match
- Mr. Wrestling was Dick Steinborn
w/Poole lost to Bill Dundee
- Cadillac Match

Aug 17, 1977: Evansville, IN
beat Bill Dundee(c)
- Southern Title Match
- Dundee's Cadillac & Title vs. Lawler's hair
- Mickey Poole banned from ringside

Aug 22, 1977: Memphis, TN
(c) w/Poole lost to Bill Dundee
- Southern Title Match
- Southern Title, Cadillac & Poole's Hair vs Dundee's Hair

Aug 23, 1977: Louisville, KY
w/Poole beats Bill Dundee(c)
- Winner gets the Cadillac

(c)w/Poole beat Mr. Wrestling
- Southern Title Match
- Mr. Wrestling was a sub for Paul Orndorff

Aug 24, 1977: Evansville, IN
(c)w/Poole lost to Bill Dundee
- Southern Title Match
- Dundee's Cadillac vs. Lawler's Title

Aug 29, 1977: Memphis, TN
w/Poole beat Bill Dundee(c)
- Southern Title Match
- Texas Tornado Death Match
- Dundee's Title & Cadillac vs. Lawler's hair

Aug 30, 1977: Louisville, KY Louisville Gardens, Tuesday
w/Poole beat Mr. Wrestling
Loser Leaves Louisville Match

(c) w/Poole lost to Bill Dundee
- Southern Title Match
- Lawler's Title & Cadillac vs. Dundee's hair

Aug 31, 1977: Evansville, IN
(c) No Contest with Bill Dundee
- Southern Title Match
- Poole in a cage
- Title vs Dundee's Cadillac

Sep 2, 1977: Blytheville, AR
w/Poole beat Norvell Austin
- 2 Out Of 3 Falls

Sep 5, 1977: Memphis, TN
(c) beat Bill Dundee
- Southern Title Match
- Hair vs. Hair
- Poole locked in cage at ringside
- Dundee's head was shaved.

Sep 7, 1977: Evansville, IN
(c) w/Poole beat Mr. Wrestling w/Bill Dundee
- Southern Title Match
- Loser Leaves Town

Sep 11, 1977: Louisville, KY
w/Poole lost to Mr. Wrestling

Sep 13, 1977: Memphis, TN
(c) beat Bill Dundee
- Southern Title Match
- No DQ
- Lawler's Hair vs. Dundee's Wife's Hair
- Lawler retires after the win

Sep 14, 1977: Evansville, IN
(c) beat Bill Dundee
- Southern Title Match
- Loser Leaves Town
- Lawler retires after match

Sep 16, 1977: Knoxville, TN
beat Ron Fuller(c)
- Southeastern Title Match

Oct 3, 1977: Memphis, TN
During the last intermission, (before the Main Event), Jerry Lawler and his band played a mini-concert for the wrestling fans. Handsome Jimmy Valiant came out and busted a guitar over the King's head, busting him open.

* Retirement Angle: How do you top the amazing Summer feud between Lawler & Dundee? That's what Jerry Jarrett was tasked with. His booking and Jerry Lawler's talent had turned the King into the area's biggest heel, ever. No one had ever generated as much heat as Jerry Lawler had during 1977. The only option Jarrett had left was to turn the King into the greatest hero the territory had ever seen. Step one was the retirement angle after winning the feud with Bill Dundee. Jerry Lawler wanted to go on the road full time with his band. It was perfect with the local death of Elvis Presley still on the mind of the Memphis fans. The next step took place on the Oct 3 card, the new bad guy in Memphis, Jimmy Valiant, had attacked and left the King bloodied during his concert for the fans. Valiant had gone through several contenders for the Southern Heavyweight Title. On the Oct 8 Saturday morning TV Taping, Valiant explained to the Memphis fans that Oct 10 would be his last night in Memphis. After that he would take the Southern Title back to New York City with him and they would NEVER see it again. At the end the taping, Eddie Marlin made a call to Jerry Lawler and asked if he would come back out of retirement to face Valiant because he was the last hope of the promotion. Jerry agreed to face Valiant, and the fans were behind the King. Just like that.

Oct 10, 1977: Memphis, TN
beats Jimmy Valiant(c)
- Southern Title Match
- Lawler ends retirement

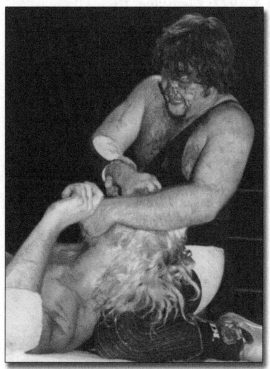

*Photo Courtesy of Jim Cornette
Jerry Lawler and Jimmy Valiant, Bloody One Another.

Oct 17, 1977: Memphis, TN
(c) beats Jimmy Valiant
- Southern Title Match
- NY State Ref
- Ref ended up being Johnny Valiant

& Norvell Austin lost to Phil Hickerson & Dennis Condrey

Oct 18, 1977: Louisville, KY
beats Jimmy Valiant(c)
- Southern Title Match
- 1st Lawler match here since retirement

Oct 21, 1977: Blytheville, AR
& Norvell Austin No Contest with Phil Hickerson & Dennis Condrey

Oct 24, 1977:Memphis, TN
w/Bill Dundee beat Jimmy & Johnny Valiant

Oct 25, 1977: Louisville, KY
(c) wins via DQ over Jimmy Valiant
- Southern Title Match
- NY State Ref
- Ref ended up being Johnny Valiant

& Norvell Austin No Contest with Dennis
Condrey & Phil Hickerson

*Photo Courtesy of Jim Cornette
Norvell Austin & Jerry Lawler

Oct 26, 1977: Evansville, IN
beat Jimmy Valiant
- Southern Title Match
- 1st Lawler match here since retirement

Oct 28, 1977: Blytheville, AR
& Norvell Austin No Contest With Phil Hickerson
& Dennis Condrey
- 2 Out Of 3 Falls

Oct 30, 1977: Memphis, TN
& Bill Dundee No Contest with Phil Hickerson &
Dennis Condrey w/Al Costello
- Hospital Elimination Match

Nov 1, 1977: Louisville, KY
& Norvell Austin lost to Phil Hickerson & Dennis
Condrey w/Al Costello

& Bill Dundee beat Jimmy & Johnny Valiant
- Added Match

Nov 2, 1977: Evansville, IN
(c) won via DQ over Jimmy Valiant
- Southern Title Match

& Norvell Austin lost to Phil Hickerson & Dennis
Condrey w/Al Costello

Nov 4, 1977: Blytheville, AR
w/Norvell Austin & Big Red vs. Phil Hickerson,
Dennis Condrey & Al Costello
-2 Out Of 3 Falls

Nov 7, 1977: Memphis, TN
w/Bill Dundee & Norvell Austin beat Jim Valiant,
Phil Hickerson & Dennis Condrey

Nov 8, 1977: Louisville, KY
& Bill Dundee beat Phil Hickerson & Dennis
Condrey
- Hospital Elimination Match

*Photo Courtesy of Jim Cornette
Former Enemies, Now Partners: Bill Dundee
& Jerry Lawler

Nov 9, 1977: Evansville, IN
w/Bill Dundee beat Jimmy & Johnny Valiant

& Norvell Austin lost to Phil Hickerson & Dennis
Condrey

Nov 14, 1977: Memphis, TN
beat Jimmy Valiant
- Dog Fight match

Nov 15, 1977: Louisville, KY
w/Bill Dundee & Norvell Austin beat Jimmy
Valiant, Dennis Condrey & Phil Hickerson

Nov 16, 1977: Evansville, IN
& Bill Dundee No Contest with Phil Hickerson &
Dennis Condrey w/Al Costello
- Hospital Elimination Match

Nov 20, 1977: Owensboro, KY
w/Bill Dundee & Norvell Austin over Phil
Hickerson, Dennis Condrey & Al Costello

(c) over Phil Hickerson w/Al Costello
- Southern Title Match

Nov 21, 1977: Memphis, TN
(c) beat Mr. Wrestling
- Southern Title Match

Nov 22, 1977: Louisville, KY
beat Jimmy Valiant
- Dog Fight Match
- No Referee in ring
- Win by KO-ing opponent for a 20 Count

Concert by Jimmy Hart & the Gentry's along
with Jerry Lawler, MC'ed by Lance Russell

Nov 23, 1977: Evansville, IN
w/Bill Dundee & Norvell Austin vs. Phil
Hickerson, Dennis Condrey & Jimmy Valiant

Concert by Jimmy Hart & the Gentry's along
with Jerry Lawler.

Nov 25, 1977: Blytheville, AR
& Big Red vs the Samoans(c)
- Southern Tag Tournament

Nov 28, 1977: Memphis, TN
(c) lost to Jimmy Valiant
- Stretcher Match
- Lawler's Title vs. Valiant's $20,000

Nov 29, 1977: Louisville, KY
& Big Red w/Robert Gibson beat the
Samoans(c)
- Southern Tag Title Match

Nov 23, 1977: Evansville, IN
& Bill Dundee won via DQ over the Samoans(c)
- Southern Title Match

Dec 5, 1977: Memphis, TN
beat Jimmy Valiant(c)
- Stretcher Match
- Southern Title On The Line
- Barbed Wire Around The Ring
- Valiant's Title vs. Lawler's $20,000

Dec 6, 1977: Louisville, KY
(c) lost to Jimmy Valiant
- Stretcher Match
- Southern Title On The Line
- Lawler's Title vs. Valiant's $20,000

beat Mike Stark
- Grudge Match

Dec 7, 1977: Evansville, IN
& Big Red won via DQ over the Samoans(c)
- Southern Title Match

Dec 11, 1977: Memphis, TN
60 min. draw with Harley Race
- NWA World Title Match

Dec 13, 1977: Louisville, KY
beat Jimmy Valiant(c)
- Stretcher Match
- Southern Title On The Line
- Valiant's Title vs. Lawler's $20,000

Dec 14, 1977: Evansville, IN
beat Jimmy Valiant
- Dog Fight Match
- No Referee in ring
- Win by KO-ing opponent for a 20 Count

Dec 18, 1977: Memphis, TN
lost via stoppage to Harley Race(c)
- NWA World Title Match
- No DQ Match
- 90 Minute Time Limit
- Last defense of NWA World Title in Memphis
till 1982
- Jimmy Valiant jumped into the ring and busted
a liter, glass coke bottle over the head of
Lawler. Then Jimmy picked up pieces of the
glass stabbed Jerry in the left shoulder with it.
Lawler could not continue and the ref had no
choice but to stop the match.

Dec 20, 1977: Louisville, KY
Competed in a Battle Royal

Bill Dundee & Big Red w/Lawler won by DQ over
Phil Hickerson & Dennis Condrey(c) w/Al
Costello
- Southern Tag Title Match

Dec 21, 1977: Evansville, IN
beat Jimmy Valiant(c)
- Stretcher Match
- Southern Title On The Line
- Valiant's Title vs. Lawler's $20,000

Dec 26, 1977: Memphis, TN
Lawler at ringside getting fans to sign a petition
to have Jimmy Valiant reinstated so the King
can get his revenge, in the ring.

Dec 27, 1977: Louisville, KY
Lawler at ringside getting fans to sign a petition
to have Jimmy Valiant reinstated so the King
can get his revenge, in the ring.

Dec 28, 1977: Evansville, IN
Lawler at ringside getting fans to sign a petition
to have Jimmy Valiant reinstated so the King
can get his revenge, in the ring.

1978

Chapter 9

Jan 2, 1978: Memphis, TN
lost to Jimmy Valiant

Jan 3, 1978: Louisville, KY
vs. Jimmy Valiant

Jan 4, 1978: Evansville, IN
lost via DQ (ref reversal) to Jimmy Valiant
- Southern Title Match

Jan 6, 1978: Blytheville, AR
& Big Red beat Sonny King & Frankie Lane

Jan 9, 1978: Memphis, TN
w/flag holder Bill Dundee lost to Jimmy Valiant
w/flag holder Frankie Lane
- Loser Waves The Flag Match
- Lane KO'ed Dundee and waved Lawler's flag.

Jan 11, 1978: Evansville, IN
w/flag holder Bill Dundee lost to Jimmy Valiant
w/flag holder Frankie Lane
- Loser Waves The Flag Match
- Lane KO'ed Dundee and waved Lawler's flag.

Jan 13, 1978: Blytheville, AR
beat Sonny King
- 15 Rounds of Boxing

Jan 16, 1978: Memphis, TN
bear Jimmy Valiant
- Submission Match

Jan 18, 1978: Evansville, IN
vs. Jimmy Valiant
- Submission Match
- Cancelled Due To Weather

Jan 20, 1978: Blytheville, AR
beat Sonny King
- 15 Rounds of Boxing

Jan 23, 1978: Memphis, TN
No Contest with Jimmy Valiant
- Southern Title Match
- Hair vs. Hair
- No hair cut and fans got mad. Destroyed chairs, lit some on fire, police and fire dept. called. Jarrett paid a lot of money to the Mid-South Coliseum to pay for damage.

Jan 25, 1978: Evansville, IN
vs. Black Jack Lane
- Submission Match
- Cancelled Due To Weather 2nd week in a row

Jan 30, 1978: Memphis, TN
(c) beat Mr. Wrestling(c)
- Southern Title vs North American Title
- Mr. Wrestling was still Dick Steinborn

*Photo Courtesy of Jim Cornette
Jerry Lawler vs. Mr. Wrestling (Dick Steinborn)

Jan 31, 1978: Louisville, KY
beat Frankie Lane
- Submission match

Feb 1, 1978: Evansville, IN
beat Jimmy Valiant
- Submission Match

Feb 3, 1978: Blytheville, AR
(c) beat Sonny King
- Southern Title Match

Feb 5, 1978: Memphis , TN
(c) beat Jimmy Valiant
- Southern Title Match

Feb 7, 1978: Louisville, KY
(c) beat Jimmy Valiant
- Southern Title Match

Feb 8, 1978: Evansville, IN
lost to Jimmy Valiant
- Lumberjack Match

Feb 11, 1978: Madisonville, KY
(c) beat Sonny King
- Southern Title Match

- In a Battle Royal

Feb 13, 1978: Memphis, TN
(c) beat Jimmy Valiant
- Southern Title Match

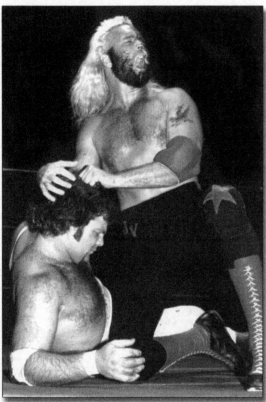

*Photo Courtesy of Jim Cornette
Jerry Lawler vs. Jimmy Valiant: The War
Continues!

Feb 15, 1978: Evansville, IN
(c) beat Mr. Wrestling(c)
- Southern Title vs North American Title
- Mr. Wrestling was still Dick Steinborn

Feb 17, 1978: Blytheville, AR
(c) beat Sonny King
- Southern Title Match

Feb 19, 1978: Memphis, TN
(c) beat Jimmy Valiant
- Southern title vs. $5000

Feb 28, 1978: Memphis, TN
(c) beat Jimmy Valiant
- Southern Title Match

Bill Dundee w/Lawler No Contest with Norvell
Austin w/Sonny King

Mar 1, 1978: Evansville, IN
(c) beat Jimmy Valiant
- Southern Title Match

Mar 5, 1978: Memphis, TN
(c) beat Jim Valiant
- Southern Title Match
- Title vs. 1978 Corvette

Mar 8, 1978: Evansville, IN
(c) beat Jimmy Valiant
- Southern Title Match
- Title vs. Valiant's $5,000

Mar 11, 1978: Jonesboro, AR
(c) beat Sonny King
- Southern Title Match

Mar 13, 1978: Memphis, TN
(c) won by DQ over Joe Leduc
- Southern Title Match

& Bill Dundee (c) beat Sonny King & Norvell
Austin
- Southern Tag Title Match

Mar 15, 1978: Evansville, IN
(c) beat Sonny King
- Southern Title Match

Mar 17, 1978: Blytheville, AR
(c) beat Jim Starr
- Southern Title Match

Mar 20, 1978: Memphis, TN
(c) w/Steve Kyle won by DQ over Joe Leduc
w/Sonny King

Mar 22, 1978: Evansville, IN
& Bill Dundee beat Sonny King & Joe Leduc
- Leduc's Evansville Debut
- Jimmy Valiant & Sonny King were originally
supposed to team but Leduc & King beat him
up.

Mar 24, 1978: Blytheville, AR
(c) beat Sonny King
- Southern Title Match

Mar 27, 1978: Memphis, TN
(c) beat Jimmy Valiant
- Southern Title Match
- Winner must win by a 5-count

Mar 29, 1978: Evansville, IN
lost to Joe Leduc w/Sonny King

Mar 31, 1978: Blytheville, AR
& Steve Kyle beat Sonny King & Norvell Austin

Apr 1, 1978: Jonesboro, AR
lost to Ron Slinker
- Karate vs. wrestling

April 2, 1978: Knoxville, TN
(c) lost by DQ to Robert Fuller
- Southern Title Match

Apr 3, 1978: Memphis, TN
lost to Ron Slinker
- Karate vs. wrestling

Apr 5, 1978: Evansville, IN
w/Steve Kyle beat Joe Leduc w/Sonny King
- Kyle was seated with Sonny King

Apr 8, 1978: Chattanooga, TN - TV results
& Bill Dundee(c) beat Norvell Austin & Blackjack Frankie Lane
- Southern Tag Title Match

Apr 10, 1978: Memphis, TN
(c)beat Ron Slinker
- Southern Title Match

Apr 12, 1978: Evansville, IN
beat Ron Slinker
- 15 round karate vs. wrestling

Apr 14, 1978: Blytheville, AR
(c) won by DQ over Joe Leduc w/Sonny King
- Southern Title Match

Apr 17, 1978: Memphis, TN
lost to John Louie w/Sonny King

Apr 19, 1978: Evansville, IN
beat Jimmy Valiant(c)
- Southern Title Match

Apr 22, 1978: Chattanooga, TN - TV Results
& Bill Dundee (c) beat Mr. Seki & Danny Davis
- Southern Tag Title Match

Apr 24, 1978: Memphis, TN
beat John Louie
- Texas Tornado Death Match - Hair on the line.

Apr 26, 1978: Evansville, IN
& Bill Dundee(c) lost to Joe Leduc & John Louie
- Southern Tag Title Match

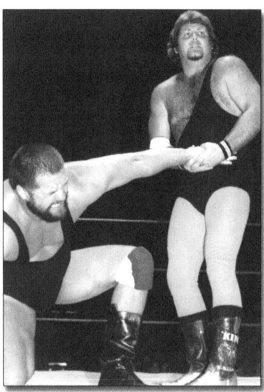

*Photo Courtesy of Jim Cornette
Jerry Lawler With An Armbar on John Louie.

Apr 29, 1978: Chattanooga, TN - TV results
w/Plowboy Frazier & Bill Dundee beat Mr. Seki, The Red Shadow & The Darth Vader

May 1, 1978: Memphis, TN
w/Bill Dundee & Jimmy Valiant No Contest with Joe Leduc, John Louie & Sonny King

May 2, 1978: Louisville, KY
w/Bill Dundee & Jimmy Valiant beat Joe Leduc, Sonny King & John Louie

May 6, 1978: Chattanooga, TN TV results
& Bill Dundee drew with Norvell Austin & Ron Slinker

May 6, 1978: Jackson, TN TV results
beat Ron Slinker

May 8, 1978: Memphis, TN
w/Jimmy Valiant & Bill Dundee beat Joe Leduc,
John Louie & Sonny King
No DQ, no stopping the match

May 11, 1978: Lexington, KY
(c) beat Gorgeous George Jr.
- Southern Title Match

May 13, 1978: Chattanooga, TN TV results
& Bill Dundee(c) won by DQ over Norvell Austin
& Mr. Seki

May 13, 1978: Jackson, TN TV results
& Plowboy Frazier lost to Joe Leduc & John Louie

May 15, 1978: Memphis, TN
& Bill Dundee & Jimmy Valiant lost to Joe Leduc,
John Louie & Sonny King

May 16, 1978: Louisville, KY
(c) vs. Sonny King
- Southern Title Match
- Dog fight, no referee:

Competed in 22-Man Battle Royal

May 19, 1978: Blytheville, AR
(c) beat Gorgeous George Jr.
- Southern Title Match

May 20, 1978: Chattanooga, TN TV results
lost to John Louie
- Non-Title Match

May 22, 1978: Memphis, TN
& Jimmy Valiant No Contest with Joe Leduc &
John Louie w/Sonny King(c)
- Southern Tag Title Match
- Titles Held Up

May 23, 1978: Louisville, KY
& Jimmy Valiant vs. Joe Leduc & John Louie(c)
- Southern Tag Title Match

May 24, 1978: Evansville, IN
& Bill Dundee won via DQ over Joe Leduc & John
Louie(c)

May 26, 1978: Blytheville, AR
& Porkchop Cash lost to Frankie Lane & Mike
Boyer

May 27, 1978: Chattanooga, TN TV results
beat The Marvel

May 29, 1978: Memphis, TN
& Jimmy Valiant beat Joe Leduc & John Louie to
win Southern Tag Team Titles

June 2, 1978: Blytheville, AR
(c) beat John Louie
- Southern Title Match

June 5, 1978: Memphis, TN
2-Ring, 20-Man Battle Royal
Winner: Jerry Lawler

w/Jimmy Valiant lost via DQ to Joe Leduc(c)
w/Sonny King
- Southern Title Match

*Photo Courtesy of Jim Cornette
Joe Leduc Dropping The Leg Down On
Jerry Lawler

June 6, 1978: Louisville, KY
won via DQ over Joe Leduc w/Sonny King

June 7, 1978: Evansville, IN
w/Bill Dundee & Jimmy Valiant won via DQ over
Joe Leduc, John Louie & Sonny King

June 8, 1978: Lexington, KY
& Jimmy Valiant won via DQ over Joe Leduc,
John Louie(c)
- Southern Tag Title Match

June 9, 1978: Blytheville, AR
beat John Louie
- No DQ

June 10, 1978: Chattanooga, TN TV results
(c) by DQ over John Louie
- Southern Title Match

June 12, 1978: Memphis, TN
beat Joe Leduc(c)
- Southern Title Match
- No DQ
- After match. Leduc throws Lawler over the top rope onto the ringside table and legit damages his thigh muscle. Jerry has to sit out 3 weeks til the July 3rd show.

June 25, 1978: The Jerry Jarrett promotion publically changed their allegiance to the AWA. Previously it had been a member of the NWA. This was done for the fans only, Memphis remained a paying member of the NWA. Jerry Jarrett only made the switch to be able to bring in the AWA World champion whenever he wanted, (the AWA didn't have events on Mondays.)

July 3, 1978: Memphis, TN
(c) lost via DQ to Joe Leduc w./Sonny King
- Southern Title Match
- Got revenge and sent Leduc to the hospital (it was a work).

July 5, 1978: Evansville, IN
(c) beat Joe Leduc w/Sonny King
- Southern title Match

July 6, 1978: Lexington, KY
(c) beat Joe Leduc
- Southern Title Match

July 9, 1978: Louisville, KY
(c) beat John Louie
- Southern title match

July 9, 1978: Owensboro, KY
(c) beat Joe Leduc
- Southern title match

July 10, 1978: Memphis, TN
(c) beat Sonny King
- Southern Title Match
- Loser Leaves Town
- Sonny King was gone from Memphis after this match.

July 11, 1978: Chattanooga, TN
(c) beat Joe Leduc
- Southern Title Match

July 12, 1978: Evansville, IN
beat Sonny King
- Loser Leaves Match

July 14, 1978: Knoxville, TN
vs. Jimmy Golden
Round One: Car Tournament

July 16, 1978: Louisville, KY
(c) beat Joe Leduc
- Southern Title Match

*Photo Courtesy of Jim Cornette
Joe Leduc Gives Jerry Lawler A Huge Backdrop.

July 17, 1978: Memphis, TN Mid-South Coliseum, Monday
(c) beat Joe Leduc
- Southern Title Match - No DQ

July 18, 1978: Chattanooga, TN
(c) beat Joe Leduc
- Southern Title Match - No DQ

July 19, 1978: Evansville, IN
(c) won via DQ over Joe Leduc
- Southern Title Match

July 24, 1978: Memphis, TN
(c) beat Dennis Condrey
- Southern Title Match

July 25, 1975: Chattanooga, TN
(c) beat via DQ Joe Leduc
- Southern Title Match

July 26, 1978: Evansville, IN
(c) beat Joe Leduc
- Southern Title Match
- No ref in the ring

July 30, 1978: Louisville, KY
(c) beat Joe Leduc
- Southern Title Match

July 31, 1978: Memphis, TN
(c) beat Joe Leduc

Aug 2, 1978: Evansville, IN
(c) beat Joe Leduc
- Southern Title Match
- Lumberjack Match

Aug 4, 1978: Blytheville, AR
(c) beat John Louie
- Southern Title Match

Aug 5, 1978: Jonesboro, AR
(c) beat Frankie Lane
- Southern Title Match

Aug 7, 1978: Memphis, TN
(c) lost to Joe Leduc
- Southern Title Match
- Set up for this match had Leduc cutting his
arm with his ax on Memphis TV Aug 5, 1978. He
called it "A Blood Oath".

Aug 10, 1978: Lexington, KY
(c) lost to Joe Leduc
- Southern Title Match
- 2 refs in ring

Aug 11, 1978: Blytheville, AR
lost to Joe Leduc(c)
- Southern Title Match

Aug 12, 1978: Jonesboro, AR
beat John Louie

Aug 14, 1978: Memphis, TN
beat Joe Leduc(c)
- Southern Title Match
- Winner To Face AWA World Champ on July 21.

Aug 18, 1978: Blytheville, AR
(c) beat Joe Leduc
- Southern Title Match

Aug 19, 1978: Jonesboro, AR
(c) beat Joe Leduc
- Southern Title Match

Aug 20, 1978: Chattanooga, TN
& Bill Dundee No Contest with Jimmy & Johnny
Valiant

Aug 21, 1978: Memphis, TN
won by DQ over Nick Bockwinkel (c) w/Bobby
Heenan
- AWA World Title Match
- Heenan interferes
- 1st AWA World Title Match in Memphis

*Photo Courtesy of Jim Cornette
Jerry Lawler With A Headlock on Nick
Bockwinkel.

Aug 22, 1978: Owensboro, KY
(c) beat Joe Leduc
- Southern Title Match

Aug 24, 1978: Huntingdon, TN, Thursday
& Bill Dundee won by DQ over Joe Leduc & John Louie(c)
- Southern Tag Title Match

Aug 25, 1978: Blytheville, AR
& Wayne Farris lost to Joe Leduc & John Louie(c)
- Southern Tag Title Match

Aug 27, 1978: Louisville, KY
& Bill Dundee beat Jimmy & Johnny Valiant

Aug 28, 1978: Memphis, TN
(c) lost to Joe Leduc
- Southern Title Match

*Photo Courtesy of Jim Cornette
The King Pulling Out A Chain

Aug 29, 1978: Chattanooga, TN
won via DQ over Joe Leduc(c)
- Southern Title Match

Sep 1, 1978: Blytheville, AR
beat Frankie Lane
- Boxing Match

Sep 3, 1978: Louisville, KY
lost to Joe Leduc(c)
- Southern Title Match
- Title vs. Leduc Leaving Town

Sep 4, 1978: Memphis, TN
by DQ over Joe Leduc(c)
- Southern Title Match

- 50-Man $10,000 Battle Royal
- Winner: Jerry

Sep 5, 1978: Chattanooga, TN
won via DQ over Joe Leduc
- Southern Title Match

Sep 7, 1978: Lexington, KY
(c) beat Joe Leduc
- Southern Title Match
- Inside a cage

Sep 9, 1978: Jonesboro, AR
& the Mongolian Stomper lost via DQ to Joe Leduc & John Louie(c)
- Southern Tag Title Match

Sep 10, 1978: Louisville, KY
& the Mongolian Stomper lost via DQ to Joe Leduc & John Louie(c)
- Southern Tag Title Match

Sep 12, 1978: Memphis, TN
& the Mongolian Stomper lost via DQ to Joe Leduc & John Louie(c)
- Southern Tag Title Match

Sep 13, 1978: Evansville, IN
(c) lost via DQ to Joe Leduc
- Southern Title Match

Sep 18, 1978: Memphis, TN
& the Mongolian Stomper beat Joe Leduc & John Louie(c)
- Southern Tag Title Match
- Cage Match
- No DQ

Sep 19, 1978: Owensboro, KY
(c) lost to Joe Leduc
- Southern title match

Sep 20, 1978: Evansville, IN
(c) lost to Joe Leduc
- Southern Title Match
- Inside a cage

Sep 21, 1978: Lexington, KY
& Mongolian Stomper beat Joe Leduc & John Louie(c)
- Southern Tag Title Match
- No DQ

Sep 23, 1978: Jonesboro, AR
w/Tommy Gilbert beat Joe Leduc with John Louie
-Texas Tornado Death Match

Oct 2, 1978: Memphis, TN
won by DQ over the Mongolian Stomper

* Advertised as AWA World Tag Champs Jim Brunzell & Greg Gagne vs. Lawler & Stomper. On Sat TV show, Stomper turned on Lawler.

*Photo Courtesy of Jim Cornette
The King vs. The Stomper!

Oct 4, 1978: Evansville, IN
beat Joe Leduc(c)
- Southern Title Match
- Dogfight Match

Oct 5, 1978: Lexington, KY
& Mongolian Stomper beat Joe Leduc & John Louie(c)
- Southern Tag Title Match

Oct 6, 1978: Blytheville, AR
(c) vs. Joe Leduc
- Southern Title Match

Oct 8, 1978: Louisville, KY
(c) beat Joe Leduc
- Southern Title Match
- Texas Death Match

Oct 9, 1978: Memphis, TN
Southern tag title tournament - Round one:
& Wayne Farris lost to Nelson Royal & Don Fargo

beat the Mongolian Stomper
- No DQ Lights Out Match

Oct 11, 1978: Evansville, IN
(c) beat Joe Leduc
- Southern Title Match: Loser gets 10 lashes

Oct 18, 1978: Evansville, IN
& Bill Dundee beat Joe Leduc & Nelson Royal

Oct 16, 1978: Memphis, TN
(c) beat Nelson Royal
- Southern Title Match

*Photo Courtesy of Jim Cornette
Nelson Royal With A Front Facelock On The King.

Oct 18, 1978: Evansville, IN
& Bill Dundee beat Nelson Royal & Joe Leduc

Oct 20, 1978: Tupelo, MS
& Robert Gibson lost to the Bounty Hunters(c)
w/Chuck Malone

- Southern Tag Title Match
- Bounty Hunters were Jerry & David Novak
- Won the tag titles in Memphis, on Oct 9, 1978.

Oct 22, 1978: Louisville, KY
(c) won by DQ over Joe Leduc
- Southern Title Match

Oct 23, 1978: Memphis, TN
beat Nelson Royal
- Texas Death Match

Oct 29, 1978: Louisville, KY
& Jackie Welch lost to the Bounty Hunters(c)
w/Chuck Malone
- Southern Tag Title Match

Oct 30, 1978: Memphis, TN
& Bill Dundee beat Joe Leduc & Don Fargo

Nov 1, 1978: Evansville, IN
& Bill Dundee won via DQ over Joe Leduc & Don
Fargo w/Al Greene

Nov 6, 1978: Memphis, TN
& Bill Dundee beat The Bounty Hunters(c)
w/Chuck Malone

Nov 7, 1978: Frankfort, KY
& Jackie Welch won via DQ over Bill Dromo &
Joe Leduc

Nov 8, 1978: Evansville, IN
& Bill Dundee w/Robert Gibson won via DQ over
Joe Leduc & Don Fargo w/Al Greene

Nov 9, 1979: Lexington, KY
beat Nelson Royal
- Texas Tornado Death Match

Nov 12, 1978: Louisville, KY
& Bill Dundee beat Don Fargo & Joe Leduc

Nov 13, 1978: Memphis, TN
& Bill Dundee(c) beat the Bounty Hunters
w/Chuck Malone
- Southern Tag Title Match
- Titles vs. Malone's Hair
- Malone Had Head Shaved

Nov 17, 1978: Blytheville, AR
beat Jimmy Valiant

Nov 18, 1978: Jonesboro, AR
& Bill Dundee(c) beat the Bounty Hunters
w/Chuck Malone
- Southern Tag Title Match

Photo Courtesy of Jim Cornette
Jerry Lawler & Bill Dundee
Southern Tag Champs

Nov 19, 1978: Louisville, KY
& Bill Dundee(c) No Contest with Jimmy Valiant
& Wayne Farris
- Southern Tag Title Match

Nov 20, 1978: Memphis, TN
& Bill Dundee(c) No Contest with Jimmy Valiant
& Wayne Farris
- Southern Tag Title Match

Nov 22, 1978: Evansville, IN
& Bill Dundee(c) beat the Bounty Hunters
w/Chuck Malone
- Southern Tag Title Match

Nov 24, 1978: Blytheville, AR
& Koko Ware lost to Don Fargo & Jimmy Valiant

Nov 25, 1978: Jonesboro, AR
w/Bill Dundee & Koko Ware beat the Bounty
Hunters & Chuck Malone

Nov 26, 1978: Louisville, KY
& Bill Dundee(c) beat Jimmy Valiant & Wayne
Farris
- Southern Tag Title Match
- No DQ

Nov 27, 1978: Memphis, TN
& Bill Dundee(c) beat Jimmy Valiant & Wayne
Farris
- Southern Tag Title Match
- No DQ, No Stopping For Blood

Nov 29, 1978: Evansville, IN
& Bill Dundee(c) No Contest with Jimmy Valiant
& Wayne Farris
- Southern Tag Title Match

Dec 1, 1978: Blytheville, AR
won via DQ over Wayne Farris

w/Jackie Welch, Bearcat Brown & Koko Ware
lost to Don Fargo, Al Greene, Jimmy Valiant &
Wayne Farris

Dec 2, 1978: Jonesboro, AR
beat Bounty Hunter Jerry Novak

w/ Bill Dundee & Koko Ware beat the Bounty
Hunters & Chuck Malone

Dec 4, 1978: Memphis, TN
beat Tommy Gilbert(c)
- Southern Title Match
- Gilbert had won belt from Don Fargo.

Dec 6, 1978: Evansville, IN
& Bill Dundee(c) beat Jimmy Valiant & Wayne
Farris
- Southern Tag Title Match

Dec 7, 1978: Lexington, KY
& Bill Dundee(c) beat Jimmy Valiant & Wayne
Farris
- Southern Tag Title Match

Dec 9, 1978: Madisonville, KY
& Bill Dundee(c) beat the Bounty Hunters
w/Chuck Malone
- Southern Tag Title Match

Dec 11, 1978: Memphis, TN
(c) drew with Bill Dundee
- Southern Title Match
- 60 min draw

Dec 13, 1978: Evansville, IN
& Bill Dundee beat Wayne Farris & Jimmy
Valiant
- Hospital elimination match

Dec 16, 1978: Jonesboro, AR
& Koko Ware No Contest with Dennis Condrey &
Phil Hickerson

Dec 18, 1978: Memphis, TN
& Bill Dundee(c) lost to Phil Hickerson & Dennis
Condrey
- Southern Tag Title Match

*Photo Courtesy of Jim Cornette
Phil Hickerson Eating A Jerry Lawler Fist.

Dec 19, 1978: Louisville, KY
(c) beat Jimmy Valiant
- Southern Title Match

Dec 20, 1978: Evansville, IN
& Bill Dundee(c) beat Jimmy Valiant & Wayne
Farris
- Southern Tag Title Match

Dec 25, 1978: Memphis, TN
(c) lost to Austin Idol
- Southern Title Match

Dec 26, 1978: Louisville, KY
& Bill Dundee(c) lost to Phil Hickerson & Dennis
Condrey
- Southern Tag Title Match

Dec 27, 1978: Evansville, IN
(c) lost via DQ to Jimmy Valiant
- Southern Title Match

Dec 30, 1978: Jonesboro, AR
& Bill Dundee lost to Phil Hickerson & Dennis
Condrey(c)
- Non-Title Match
- Two straight falls

1979

Chapter 10

Jan 1, 1979: Memphis, TN
vs. Austin Idol(c)
- Southern Title Match
- Card Cancelled Because Of Snow

Jan 2, 1979: Louisville, KY
lost to Austin Idol(c)
- Southern Title Match

Jan 3, 1979: Evansville, IN
& Bill Dundee(c) lost to Phil Hickerson & Dennis Condrey
- Southern Tag Title Match

Jan 5, 1979: Tupelo, MS
& Pez Whatley lost to Phil Hickerson & Dennis Condrey(c)
- Southern Tag Title Match

Jan 8, 1979: Memphis, TN
No Contest with Austin Idol (c)
- Southern Title Match
- Ref injury caused match stoppage

Jan 10, 1979: Evansville, IN
& Pez Whatley lost to Phil Hickerson & Dennis Condrey(c)

* Lawler passes blood before matches but wrestles despite ring doctor's warnings not to. He drives to Nashville after the matches where he passes out at the airport and is hospitalized. It is reported later that the problem was a traumatic reaction to a kick in the stomach from Austin Idol on the Jan 8 Memphis card

Jan 15, 1979: Memphis, TN
Ron Fuller (sub for injured Jerry Lawler) beats Austin Idol(c)
- Southern Title Match

Jan 21, 1979: Memphis, TN
beat Austin Idol

*Photo Courtesy of Jim Cornette
Austin Idol Traps Jerry Lawler In A Bearhug.

Jan 23, 1979: Louisville, KY
& Robert Gibson vs. Phil Hickerson & Dennis Condrey(c)
- Southern Tag title Match

Jan 24, 1979: Evansville, IN
& Robert Gibson vs. Phil Hickerson & Dennis Condrey(c)
- Southern Tag title Match

Jan 26, 1979: Tupelo, MS
beat Phil Hickerson

Jan 28, 1979: Louisville, KY
vs. Austin Idol

Jan 29, 1979: Memphis, TN
& Jackie Fargo beat Mil Mascaras & Austin Idol
- Stretcher Match
- Fargo's first time in Memphis since Jarrett-Gulas split in 1977.

Jan 31, 1979: Evansville, IN
& Tommy Gilbert won by DQ over David Schultz
& Wayne Farris

Feb 2, 1979: Tupelo, MS
& Koko Ware won by DQ over David Schultz &
Wayne Farris

Feb 3, 1979: Jonesboro, AR
w/Koko Ware & Tommy Gilbert beat Austin Idol,
Chris Colt & Don Fargo

Feb 5, 1979: Memphis, TN
& Jackie Fargo beat Austin Idol & Tojo
Yamamoto

Feb 6, 1979: Louisville, KY
beat Austin Idol
- I Quit match
- Loser Leaves town

Feb 7, 1979: Evansville, IN
beat Austin Idol

Feb 8, 1979: Lexington, KY
won via DQ over Austin Idol(c)
- Southern Title Match

Feb 9, 1979: Tupelo, MS
& Bill Dundee No Contest with Don Carson &
Dennis Condrey

Feb 10, 1979: Memphis, TN - TV Taping
won by DQ over Austin Idol
-Don Carson and Dennis Condrey interfere

Feb 12, 1979: Memphis, TN
w/Jackie & Roughhouse Fargo lost to Austin
Idol, Dennis Condrey & Don Carson

Feb 13, 1979: Louisville, KY
beat Don Carson
- Lawler won in under a minute.

**Feb 16, 1979: Tupelo, MS Sports Arena,
Friday**
w/Bill Dundee, Jimmy Golden, Roger Howell &
Buzz Sawyer No Contest with Don Carson, Chris
Colt, Dennis Condrey & the Assassins

beat Don Carson

Feb 18, 1979: Memphis, TN
beat Austin Idol
- Canadian Lumberjack match

Feb 20, 1979: Louisville, KY
lost by forfeit to Don Carson
- Lawler was not able to make it to town by bell
time.

Feb 21, 1979: Evansville, IN
& Robert Fuller won by DQ over Don Carson &
Dennis Condrey(c)
- Southern Tag Title Match

Feb 26, 1979: Memphis, TN
won via DQ over Toru Tanaka(c)
- Southern Title Match
- Austin Idol interfered and threw in in Lawler's
eyes.

Mar 24, 1979: Louisville, KY - TV Taping
Jerry Barber lost via DQ against Austin Idol
- Jerry Lawler attacks Idol

Mar 25, 1979: Chattanooga, TN
& the Mexican Angel won via DQ over Terry
Gordy & Michael Hayes

Mar 27, 1979: Louisville, KY
Bill Dundee by DQ over Austin Idol
- Jerry Lawler attacks Idol after the match

Mar 28, 1979: Evansville, IN
& Bill Dundee lost via DQ to Professor Toru
Tanaka & Austin Idol

Mar 31, 1979: Memphis, TN - TV Taping
& Robert Fuller beat Hans Schroder & Black
Inferno

Apr 2, 1979: Memphis, TN
& Robert Fuller beat Austin Idol & Toru Tanaka
Texas Tornado Death Match

Apr 3, 1979: Louisville, KY
beat Masked Idol
- Idol had previously lost a Loser Leaves Town
match to Lawler and that was the reason for the
mask.

Apr 4, 1979: Evansville, IN
beat Austin Idol

Apr 5, 1979: Lexington, KY
lost via DQ to Austin Idol

2-Ring 16-Man Battle Royal.
Ring 1 Winners:
Prof Toru Tanaka & Mongolian Stomper.

Ring 2 winners:
Jerry Lawler & Bill Dundee

Final:
Lawler & Dundee beat Tanaka & Stomper
-Stomper refuses to tag in to Tanaka

Apr 6, 1979: Tupelo, MS
vs. Mongolian Stomper

Apr 7, 1979: Jonesboro, AR
won by DQ over Mongolian Stomper(c)
- Southern Title Match

Apr 8, 1979: Chattanooga, TN
& Bill Dundee drew with Terry Gordy & Michael Hayes

Apr 9, 1979: Memphis, TN
& Toru Tanaka lost to Austin Idol & Mongolian Stomper
- No DQ Match

Apr 10, 1979: Louisville, KY
beat the Masked Idol
- Steel Cage match

Apr 11, 1979: Evansville, IN Coliseum, Wednesday
beat Austin Idol
- Steel Cage Match

Apr 12, 1979: Croydon, IN
won by DQ over the Mongolian Stomper(c)
- Southern Title Match

Apr 13, 1979: Tupelo, MS
& Prof. Tanaka vs. the Mongolian Stomper & Gorgeous George Jr.

Apr 14, 1979: Memphis, TN - TV Taping
lost via Count Out to Jimmy Golden
Lawler left match to chase Austin Idol

Apr 14, 1979: Jackson, TN
& Prof. Tanaka vs Austin Idol & Mongolian Stomper

Apr 16, 1979: Memphis, TN
by DQ over Austin Idol
- Steel Cage Match

Apr 17, 1979: Louisville, KY
beat the Masked Idol
- Steel Cage Match
- Lawler's Hair vs Idol Mask

- Prof Tanaka Guards Cage Door
- Was unmasked as Austin Idol and exiled from Louisville.

Apr 18, 1979: Evansville, IN
beat the Austin Idol
- Steel Cage Match
- Loser Leaves Town
- Prof Tanaka Guards Cage Door

Apr 23, 1979: Memphis, TN
beat the Austin Idol
- Steel Cage Match
- Lawler's Hair vs Idol Leaves Town
- Prof Tanaka Guards Cage Door

*Photo Courtesy of Jim Cornette
Jerry Lawler Controls Austin Idol In A Cage.

Apr 6, 1979: Tupelo, MS
w/Bill Dundee & Robert Fuller vs The Assassins & Mongolian Stomper

Apr 30, 1979: Memphis, TN
beats Jimmy Golden
- Winner gets a Southern Title Shot

May 1, 1979: Louisville, KY
No Contest with Jimmy Golden
- Winner gets a Southern Title Shot

May 2, 1979: Evansville, IN
beats Jimmy Golden
- Winner gets a Southern Title Shot

May 3, 1979: Lexington, KY
beat the Austin Idol
- Steel Cage Match
- Lawler's Hair vs Idol Leaves Town
- Prof Tanaka Guards Cage Door

May 4, 1979: Humboldt, TN
won via DQ over the Mongolian Stomper(c)
- Southern Title Match

May 5, 1979: Jonesboro, AR
won via DQ over Jimmy Golden

May 7, 1979: Memphis, TN
lost to the Mongolian Stomper(c)
- Southern Title Match

May 8, 1979: Louisville, KY
beat Jimmy Golden
- No DQ
- Winner Gets Southern Title Match

May 12, 1979: Jonesboro, AR
beat Jimmy Golden
- No DQ

May 14, 1979: Memphis, TN
beat Jimmy Golden
- No DQ
- Loser Leaves Town Match

the Mongolian Stomper(c) lost via DQ against mystery opponent Terry "Hulk" Boulder who was presented by Jerry Lawler. This was Hulk Hogan's debut in Memphis

May 15, 1979: Louisville, KY
won via DQ over Mongolian Stomper(c)
- Southern Title Match

May 17, 1979: Owensboro, KY
& Bill Dundee won via DQ over the Assassins w/Gorgeous George, Jr.

May 18, 1979: Tupelo, MS
beat Jimmy Golden

May 19, 1979: Jonesboro, AR
won via DQ over Mongolian Stomper(c)
- Southern Title Match

May 21, 1979: Memphis, TN
& Terry Boulder beat Mongolian Stomper & Gorgeous George Jr.
- Cage Match

May 22, 1979: Louisville, KY
& Terry Boulder won via Count Out over Mongolian Stomper & Gorgeous George Jr.

May 23, 1979: Evansville, IN
won by DQ over Mongolian Stomper w/GG Jr.
- Southern Title Match

May 24, 1979: Booneville, MS
beat Gorgeous George Jr.

May 25, 1979: Brownsville, TN
beat Prof Toru Tanaka

May 26, 1979: Jonesboro, AR
beat Gorgeous George Jr.

May 28, 1979: Memphis, TN
Van Tournament
1st Round
lost to Mongolian Stomper w/Joe Leduc

May 29, 1979: Louisville, KY
& Thunderbolt Patterson beat Mongolian Stomper & Gorgeous George Jr.
- No DQ
- Steel Cage match
- Patterson was a sub for Hulk.

w/Robert Fuller & Bill Dundee No Contest with Professor Toru Tanaka, Mr. Fuji & Gorgeous George, Jr.

May 30, 1979: Evansville, IN
w/Bill Dundee & Robert Fuller beat Mongolian Stomper, Prof Tanaka & Gorgeous George Jr.
- No DQ

June 1, 1979 Tupelo, MS
won via DQ over Mongolian Stomper(c)
- Southern Title Match

June 4, 1979: Memphis, TN
& Bill Dundee beat Toru Tanaka & Mr. Fuji(c)
- Southern Tag Title Match
- Dundee was a sub for Thunderbolt Patterson.

June 5, 1979: Louisville, KY
beat Mongolian Stomper w/Gorgeous George, Jr.

was a sub for Thunderbolt Patterson w/Robert Fuller & Bill Dundee No Contest with Toru Tanaka, Mr. Fuji & Gorgeous George, Jr.

June 6, 1979: Evansville, IN Coliseum, Wednesday
w/Bill Dundee, Robert Fuller No Contest with Mongolian Stomper, Professor Toru Tanaka, Mr. Fuji w/Gorgeous George, Jr.
- Texas tornado tag match

June 8, 1979: Tupelo, MS Sports Arena, Friday
& Bill Dundee(c) beat Larry Latham & Wayne Farris (Blond Bomber)
- Southern Tag Title Match

June 9, 1979: Memphis, TN - TV Taping
& Bill Dundee(c) over Danny Davis & Sputnik Monroe, Jr.
- Non-Title Match

June 9, 1979: Jackson, TN
& Bill Dundee(c) beat Larry Latham & Wayne Farris
- Southern Tag Title Match

June 11, 1979: Memphis, TN
& Bill Dundee beat Prof. Toru Tanaka & Mr Fuji
- Southern Tag Title Match

June 12 Louisville, KY
w/Bill Dundee, Robert Fuller & Plowboy Frazier beat Toru Tanaka, Mr. Fuji, Mongolian Stomper & Gorgeous George Jr.
- Loser leave town
- Texas Death & Tornado Rules

June 13, 1979: Evansville, IN
w/Bill Dundee, Plowboy Frazier & Robert Fuller beat Toru Tanaka, Mr. Fuji, Mongolian Stomper & Gorgeous George Jr.
- Loser leave town
- Texas Death & Tornado Rules
- Steel Cage Match

June 14, 1979: Lexington, KY
1979 Lincoln Tournament
Round 1: won via DQ over Mongolian Stomper

Round 2: beat Gorgeous George Jr.

Round 3: beat Larry Latham

Finals: beat Wayne Farris

June 15, 1975: Tupelo, MS
& Bill Dundee(c) lost to Larry Latham & Wayne Farris
- Southern Tag Title Match
- Aftermath of the match was the "Tupelo Concession Stand Brawl"

June 16, 1979: Jonesboro, AR
& Tommy Gilbert lost to Larry Latham & Wayne Farris(c)
- Southern Tag Title Match

June 18, 1979: Memphis, TN
& Bill Dundee lost to Larry Latham & Wayne Farris(c)
- Southern Tag Title Match

June 19, 1979: Louisville, KY
& Bill Dundee beat Hans Schroder & the Gestapo
- Gestapo was Rick Oliver

June 20, 1979: Evansville, IN
& Bill Dundee beat Hans Schroder & the Gestapo

June 23, 1979: Jonesboro, AR
beat Larry Latham

w/Eddie & Tommy Gilbert lost to Larry Latham, Wayne Farris & Danny Davis

June 25, 1979: Memphis, TN
& Bill Dundee lost to Larry Latham & Wayne Farris(c)
- Southern Tag Title Match

June 26, 1979: Louisville, KY
& Bill Dundee No Contest with Larry Latham & Wayne Farris(c)
- Southern Tag Title Match

June 27, 1979: Evansville, IN
& Bill Dundee won via DQ over Larry Latham & Wayne Farris(c)
- Southern Tag Title Match

June 28, 1979: Forrest City, AR
& Bill Dundee won via DQ over Larry Latham & Wayne Farris(c)
- Southern Tag Title Match

June 29, 1979: Tupelo, MS
w/Bill Dundee & Jerry Jarrett won via DQ over Larry Latham, Wayne Farris & Danny Davis

June 30, 1979: Jonesboro, AR
& Johnny Starr lost to Wayne Farris & Larry Latham(c)
- Southern Tag Title Match

July 2, 1979: Memphis, TN
w/Steve Regal & Jackie Fargo lost to Larry Latham, Wayne Farris & Danny Davis

July 3, 1979 Louisville, KY
& Bill Dundee lost to Larry Latham & Wayne Farris(c) w/Danny Davis
- Southern Tag Title Match

July 4, 1979 Evansville, IN
& Bill Dundee lost to Larry Latham & Wayne Farris(c) w/Danny Davis
- No DQ match

July 5, 1979: Lexington, KY
& Bill Dundee lost to Wayne Farris & Larry Latham(c) w/Danny Davis
- Southern Tag Title Match

July 7, 1979: Central City, KY
& Bill Dundee lost to Wayne Farris & Larry Latham(c) w/Danny Davis
- Southern Tag Title Match

July 9, 1979: Memphis, TN
w/Jackie Fargo & bill Dundee beat Wayne Farris, Larry Latham & Danny Davis

July 10, 1979: Louisville, KY
w/Bill Dundee & Jerry Jarrett lost to Wayne Farris, Larry Latham & Danny Davis

July 11, 1979: Evansville, IN
w/Bill Dundee & Jerry Jarrett No Contest with Wayne Farris, Larry Latham & Danny Davis

July 12, 1979: Gore Springs, MS
& Randy Tyler win via DQ over Wayne Farris & Larry Latham(c) w/Danny Davis
- Southern Tag Title Match

July 14, 1979: Memphis, TN - TV Taping
& Bill Dundee drew with Michael Hayes & Terry Gordy - Fabulous Freebirds
- 1 Fall to each team when time expired.

July 14, 1979: Blytheville, AR
w/Bill Dundee & Jerry Jarrett won by DQ over Wayne Farris, Larry Latham & Danny Davis

July 16, 1979: Memphis, TN
& Bill Dundee lost by DQ to Wayne Farris & Larry Latham

*Photo Courtesy of Jim Cornette
Jerry Lawler Coming Off The Second Second Turnbuckle, With A Fist To Larry Latham's Jaw.

July 17, 1979: Louisville, KY
w/Bill Dundee & Jerry Jarrett beat Larry Latham, Wayne Farris & Pete Austin

July 18, 1979: Evansville, IN
w/Jerry Jarrett & Bill Dundee beat Wayne Farris, Larry Latham & Pete Austin

July 20, 1979: Osceola, AR
& Bill Dundee won via DQ over Larry Latham & Wayne Farris w/Danny Davis
- Southern Tag Title Match

July 21, 1979: Memphis, TN - TV Taping
& Bill Dundee beat the Gestapo & Hans Schroder

July 21-24, 1979
WFIA convention in Memphis, TN at the Holiday Inn Rivermont
Wrestler of the year: Bill Dundee
Tag team of the year: Bill Dundee & Jerry Lawler
- Promotion used this award and Lawler not getting Wrestler of the Year to initiate the King's heel turn.

July 21, 1979: Jackson, TN
w/Eddie & Terry Boulder beat Ron Bass, Pete Austin & Danny Davis
- Terry Boulder was Hulk Hogan
- Eddie Boulder was Brutus Beefcake

July 23, 1979: Memphis, TN
& Bill Dundee beat the Freebirds: Terry Gordy & Michael Hayes

July 24, 1979: Louisville, KY
w/Jackie Fargo & Bill Dundee beat Danny Davis, Wayne Farris & Larry Latham

July 25, 1979: Evansville, IN
& Bill Dundee won by DQ over Larry Latham & Wayne Farris(c) w/Danny Davis
- Southern Tag Title Match

July 26, 1979: Booneville, MS
w/Jerry Jarrett & Bill Dundee beat Wayne Farris, Larry Latham & Danny Davis

Wins 2-ring tag team Battle Royal w/Bill Dundee
- they defeat Farris & Latham in the finals.

July 27, 1979: Adamsville, TN
& Bill Dundee won by DQ over Larry Latham & Wayne Farris(c) w/Danny Davis
- Southern Tag Title Match

July 28, 1979: Memphis, TN - TV Taping
over Bub Smith

July 28, 1979: Jonesboro, AR
Jerry Lawler & Steve Regal beat Hans Schroeder & the Gestapo

Jerry Lawler, Bill Dundee & Jerry Jarrett beat Wayne Farris, Larry Latham & Danny Davis
- Southern Title Match

July 30, 1979: Memphis, TN
& Randy Tyler lost to the Fabulous Freebirds: Terry Gordy & Michael Hayes

July 31, 1979: Louisville, KY
& Bill Dundee drew with Freebirds: Terry Gordy & Michael Hayes

Aug 1, 1979: Evansville, IN
& Bill Dundee No Contest with Terry Gordy & Michael Hayes

Aug 2, 1978: Lexington, KY
w/Jerry Jarrett & Bill Dundee beat Wayne Farris, Larry Latham & Danny Davis

Aug 3, 1979: Tupelo, MS
& Bill Dundee lost to Michael Hayes & Terry Gordy

Aug 4, 1979: Memphis, TN - TV Taping
Interview with Jerry Lawler & Bill Dundee. They show Memphis tape from July 30, 1979: Nick Bockwinkel (AWA World Champ) beats Bill Dundee. During interview Lawler gets angry when it's revealed Dundee will get a rematch vs. Bockwinkel on Aug 20, 1979.

Aug 4, 1979: Madisonville, KY
w/Jerry Jarrett & Bill Dundee beat Larry Latham, Wayne Farris & Sgt. Danny Davis

Aug 8, 1979: Nashville, TN
& Bill Dundee lost via DQ Wayne Farris & Larry Latham(c) w/Danny Davis

Aug 9, 1979: Woodland, MS
w/Jerry Jarrett & Bill Dundee beat Wayne Farris, Larry Latham & Danny Davis

Aug 11, 1979: Memphis, TN - TV Taping
Interview: Bill Dundee says he is giving up his AWA title shot to Jerry Lawler. Lawler comes out and says he will wrestle Dundee for the shot.

Aug 15, 1979: Nashville, TN
w/Bill Dundee & Ken Lucas beat David Schultz, Latham & Farris

Aug 17, 1979: Blytheville, AR
& Steve Regal lost to Michael Hayes & Terry Gordy

Aug 18, 1979: Memphis, TN TV Taping
Interview with Jerry Lawler
beats Dallas Montgomery
-Lawler bloodies Montgomery until Tommy Gilbert, Steve Regal and Bill Dundee make the save
- Jerry Lawler is in full heel mode now.

Aug 18, 1979: Jonesboro, AR
& Eddie Gilbert lost to Pete Austin & Sonny King

Aug 20, 1979: Memphis, TN
beats Bill Dundee
- Winner faces Nick Bockwinkel for AWA World Title.

*Photo Courtesy of Jim Cornette
Jerry Lawler Gives Bill Dundee A Piledriver.

Aug 22, 1979: Nashville, TN
& Ken Lucas beat Larry Latham & Wayne Farris w/Sgt Davis

Aug 25, 1979: Memphis, TN TV Taping
Replay Memphis tape, Aug 20, 1979: Bill Dundee loss to Jerry Lawler
Dave Brown interviews Jerry Lawler
beats Koko Ware
- fist drop & pin

Aug 25, 1979: Jonesboro, AR
No Contest with Tommy Gilbert

Aug 27, 1979: Memphis, TN
drew with Nick Bockwinkel(c)
- AWA World Title Match
- 60 min draw

Aug 28, 1979: Louisville, KY
beat Bill Dundee(c)
- Southern Title Match

Aug 29, 1979: Bolivar, TN
No Contest with Tommy Gilbert

Aug 31, 1979: Blytheville, AR
beat Steve Regal

Sep 1, 1979: Memphis, TN TV Taping
Memphis tape from Aug 27: Nick Bockwinkel (AWA champ) 60 min draw with Jerry Lawler
Lance Russell interviews Jerry Lawler
beat Jerry Bryant

Sep 1, 1979: Jonesboro, AR
w/Wayne Farris & Larry Latham beat Eddie Marlin, Tommy & Eddie Gilbert

Sep 3, 1979: Memphis, TN
lost to Superstar Bill Dundee(c)
- Non-Title Match

Sep 4, 1979: Louisville, KY
No Contest with Bill Dundee

Sep 5, 1979: Evansville, IN
No Contest with Bill Dundee

Sep 6, 1979: Lexington, KY
No Contest with Bill Dundee

Sep 7, 1979: Tupelo, MS
No Contest with Bill Dundee

Sep 8, 1979: Memphis, TN - TV Taping
Recap of Memphis tape, Sep 3: Bill Dundee vs. Jerry Lawler. Lance interviews Jerry Lawler, Jimmy Hart.
w/Jimmy Hart No Contest with Ricky Morton w/Sonny King.
- Hart slaps Morton in match
- Jimmy Hart is now Jerry Lawler's manager.

Sep 8, 1979: Jackson, TN, Saturday
w/Jimmy Hart No Contest with Bill Dundee

Sep 10, 1979: Louisville, KY
w/Jimmy Hart lost to Bill Dundee w/Sonny King
- No DQ match

Sep 11, 1979: Memphis, TN
w/Jimmy Hart lost via DQ to Sonny King

Sep 12, 1979: Evansville, IN
w/Jimmy Hart lost to Bill Dundee
- No DQ match

Sep 13, 1979: Savannah, TN
& Ron Bass w/Hart beat Bill Dundee & Roger Howell

Sep 14, 1979: Tupelo, MS
w/ Hart lost to Bill Dundee

Sep 15, 1979: Memphis, TN - TV Taping
Interview with Jerry Lawler & Jimmy Hart
w/Hart lost via DQ to Steve Regal
- Lawler caught using chain

*Photo Courtesy of Jim Cornette
Lance Russell Interviews Jerry Lawler, With Jimmy Hart In The Background.

Sep 17, 1979: Memphis, TN
w/Hart lost via DQ to Sonny King
- Pole Match
- Strap on top of pole

Sep 18, 1979: Louisville, KY
w/Hart lost via DQ to Sonny King

Sep 19, 1979: Evansville, IN
w/Hart lost via DQ to Sonny King

Sep 22, 1979: Jonesboro, AR
& Ron Bass w/Hart lost to Bill Dundee & Eddie Marlin

Sep 23, 1979: Owensboro, KY
vs Randy Savage

* This was not a scheduled match, and there was no chance of it actually happening. Randy Savage was attempting to gain ground for his ICW outlaw promotion. Savage was openly challenging Jerry Lawler and other members of Jerry Jarrett's promotion to just show up for the card. Just show up and they can have $5,000. There was no way Jarrett would allow any of his guys to show up at a ICW event. This behavior by Savage helped him build a reputation as a bit of a lunatic.

Sep 24, 1979: Memphis, TN
w/Hart beat Bill Dundee(c)
- Southern Title Match
- Title vs Lawler's $5,000
- Card @ Cook Convention Center

Sep 25, 1979: Louisville, KY
w/Hart lost via DQ to Sonny King
- Pole Match
- Strap on top of pole

Sep 29, 1979: Jonesboro, AR
w/Ron Bass & Jimmy Hart drew with Bill Dundee, Eddie & Tommy Marlin
Oct 1, 1979: Memphis, TN Mid-South Coliseum, Monday
(c) w/Hart lost Southern Title to Bill Dundee
- Southern Title Match
- No DQ
- Title & $5,000 vs Dundee's hair

Oct 2, 1979: Louisville KY
w/Hart lost via DQ Bill Dundee
- Southern Title Match
- Title vs Lawler's $5,000

Oct 3, 1979: Evansville, IN
w/Hart lost via DQ Bill Dundee
- Southern Title Match
- Title vs Lawler's $5,000

Oct 4, 1979: Booneville, MS
w/Hart lost via DQ Bill Dundee

Oct 5, 1979: Tupelo, MS
w/Hart & Wayne Farris No Contest with Bill
Dundee & Hector Guerrero w/Eddie Marlin

Oct 6, 1979: Jonesboro AR
w/Hart lost via DQ to Hector Guerrero

Oct 7, 1979: Lexington KY
w/Hart lost via DQ to Bill Dundee

Oct 8, 1979: Memphis TN
& Plowboy Frasier w/Hart lost via DQ to Jimmy
Valiant & Bill Dundee
- Dundee interfered

Oct 9, 1979: Louisville KY
& Ron Bass w/Hart lost to Bill Dundee & Jimmy
Valiant

w/Wayne Farris & Larry Latham beat Ricky
Morton, Eddie & Tommy Marlin

Oct 10, 1979: Evansville, IN
w/Wayne Farris, Larry Latham & Danny Davis
w/Hart beat Eddie & Tommy Marlin, Sonny King
& Rick Morton

w/Ron Bass & Jimmy Hart lost via DQ to Bill
Dundee, Jimmy Valiant & Hector Guerrero

Oct 11, 1979: Booneville, MS
w/Hart beat Hector Guerrero

Oct 15, 1979: Memphis TN
w/Hart beat Bill Dundee(c)
- Southern title match,
- Winner gets CWA World Title Match

w/Hart lost to Bill Dundee
- Blindfold match

Oct 16, 1979: Louisville, KY
& Plowboy Frazier w/Hart lost to Bill Dundee &
Hector Guerrero

Oct 17, 1979: Evansville, IN
& Plowboy Frazier w/Hart lost to Bill Dundee &
Hector Guerrero

Oct 19, 1979: Tupelo, MS
& Jimmy Hart vs. Eddie Marlin & Tommy Marlin

Oct 22, 1979: Memphis, TN
(c) w/Hart beat Bill Dundee
- Southern Title Match
- Hart in a cage at ringside

Oct 23, 1979: Louisville, KY
(c) w/Hart beat Bill Dundee
- Southern Title Match
- Winner gets CWA World Title Match

lost to Tommy Marlin
- Blindfold Match

Oct 24, 1979: Evansville, IN
 (c) w/Hart beat Bill Dundee
- Southern Title Match
- Winner gets CWA World Title Match

*Photo Courtesy of Jim Cornette
Jerry Lawler Uses A Rope To Hang Bill
Dundee.

Oct 25, 1979: Clarkton, MO
w/Hart lost via DQ to Plowboy Frazier

Oct 26, 1979: Tupelo, MS
(c) w/Hart beat Bill Dundee
- Southern Title Match

Oct 29, 1979: Memphis, TN
& Jimmy Hart beat Bill Dundee & Cowboy Lang

Oct 30, 1979: Louisville, KY
(c) w/Hart beat Bill Dundee
- Southern Title Match
- Hart in a cage at ringside

Oct 31, 1979: Evansville, IN
(c) w/Hart beat Bill Dundee
- Southern Title Match
- Hart in a cage at ringside

Nov 2, 1979: Tupelo, MS
(c) w/Hart beat Bill Dundee
- Southern Title Match

Nov 3, 1979: Memphis, TN - TV Taping
w/Hart beat Koko Ware

Nov 3, 1979: Jonesboro, AR American Legion Arena, Saturday
w/Larry Latham & Wayne Farris w/Jimmy Hart won by DQ over Bill Dundee, Steve Kyle & Koko Ware

Nov 5, 1979: Memphis, TN
(c) w/Hart beat Paul Orndorff
- Southern Title Match

Nov 6, 1979:Louisville, KY
& Jimmy Hart beat Bill Dundee & Cowboy Lang

Nov 7, 1979: Evansville, IN
& Jimmy Hart beat Bill Dundee & Cowboy Lang

Nov 8, 1978: Lexington, KY
w/Jimmy Hart beat Superstar Billy Graham(c)
- CWA World Title Match

*Photo Courtesy of Jim Cornette
Jerry Lawler Battling Billy Graham For the CWA World Title.

Nov 9, 1979: Tupelo, MS
& Jimmy Hart beat Bill Dundee & Cowboy Lang

Nov 12, 1979: Memphis, TN
(c) w/Hart beat Billy Graham
- CWA World Title Match

*Photo Courtesy of Jim Cornette
Jerry Lawler: CWA World Champ

Nov 13, 1979: Louisville, KY
(c) w/Hart beat Steve Regal
- Southern Title Match

Nov 14, 1979: Evansville, IN
(c) w/Hart beat Steve Regal
- Southern Title Match

Nov 17, 1979: Jonesboro, AR
(c) w/Hart won by DQ over Sonny King
- Southern Title Match

Nov 19, 1979: Memphis, TN
(c) w/Hart lost via DQ to Superstar Billy Graham
- CWA World Title Match

Nov 21, 1979: Nashville, TN
(c) w/Hart beat Superstar Billy Graham
- CWA World Title Match

Nov 22, 1979: Jackson, TN
(c) w/Hart lost via DQ to Jackie Fargo
- Southern Title Match

Nov 23, 1979: Tupelo, MS
(c) w/Hart lost via DQ to Sonny King
- Southern Title Match

Nov 24, 1979: Jonesboro, AR
& Steve Kyle w/Hart lost to Sonny King & Rick Morton

Nov 25, 1979: Louisville, KY
(c) w/Hart beat Bobo Brazil
- CWA World Title Match

Nov 26, 1979: Memphis, TN
(c) w/Hart beat Dick the Bruiser
- CWA World Title match

Nov 28, 1979: Evansville, IN
(c)w/Hart lost via DQ to Dick the Bruiser
- CWA World Title Match

Dec 1, 1979: Jonesboro AR
& Jimmy Hart lost via DQ to Jerry Jarrett & Big Red

Dec 2, 1979: Memphis, TN
(c) w/Hart won by DQ over Austin Idol

Dec 4, 1979: Louisville, KY
w/Hart lost to Ken Lucas
- Non-Title Match

Dec 5, 1979: Evansville, IN
w/Hart beat Jackie Fargo(c)
- Southern Title Match

Dec 6, 1979: Lexington, KY
(c) w/Jimmy Hart beat Jackie Fargo
- CWA World Title

Dec 8, 1979: Memphis, TN TV Taping
w/Hart beat Koko Ware

Dec 8, 1979: Chattanooga, TN
& Ken Lucas lost to Wayne Farris & Larry Latham

Dec 10, 1979: Memphis, TN Mid-South Coliseum, Monday
(CWA Champ) w/Hart lost via DQ to Nick Bockwinkel (AWA champ
- CWA World Title vs AWA World Title

Dec 11, 1979: Louisville, KY
w/Hart won by DQ over Ken Lucas

Dec 12, 1979: Nashville, TN
(c) w/Hart lost via DQ to Jackie Fargo
- CWA World Title Match

Dec 15, 1979: Chattanooga, TN
(c) beat via DQ Tony Atlas
- CWA World Title Match

Dec 16, 1979: Memphis, TN
w/Hart lost to Ken Lucas

*Photo Courtesy of Jim Cornette
Jerry Lawler vs. Ken Lucas

Dec 18, 1979: Louisville, KY
w/Hart beat Ken Lucas
- Ref position outside ring

Dec 23, 1979: Louisville, KY, Sunday
& Jimmy Hart lost to Ken Lucas & Jerry Jarrett

Dec 23, 1979 Prime Time Sunday with Tom Snyder
NBC TV show features a segment on wrestling focusing on the Jerry Jarrett promotion. Segment features Jerry Lawler, Jimmy Hart, Bill Dundee, Tommy Gilbert, Ron Bass, Lance Russell, Hector Guerrero, Michael Hayes, Paul Morton, Jerry Calhoun, Sonny King, Guy Coffey

Dec 25, 1979: Memphis, TN
w/Hart beat Ken Lucas

w/Hart beat Steve Regal

Dec 27, 1979: Springfield, KY Washington County High School, Thursday
w/Tojo Yamamoto & Sonny King w/Hart beat Big Red, Steve Regal & Rick Morton

w/Hart beat Steve Regal-14:48

Dec 28, 1979: Tupelo, MS
w/Hart vs. Paul Ellering

Dec 30, 1979: Louisville, KY
(c) w/Hart beat Jerry Jarrettt
- CWA World Title Match

16-Man Battle Royal
Finals
w/Hart lost to Ricky Morton

1980

Chapter 11

Jan 1, 1980: Memphis, TN
& Jimmy Hart beat Ken Lucas & Steve Regal

*Photo Courtesy of Jim Cornette
Jerry Lawler & Jimmy Hart

Jan 2, 1980: Evansville, IN
& Jimmy Hart beat Jerry Jarrett & Ken Lucas

Jan 3, 1980: Lexington, KY
& Jimmy Hart lost to Jerry Jarrett & Ken Lucas

Jan 5, 1980: Jonesboro, AR
(c) w/Hart beat Paul Ellering
- CWA World Title Match

Jan 7, 1980: Memphis, TN
w/Jimmy Valiant & Jimmy Hart beat Big Red, Steve Regal & Ricky Morton

Jan 8, 1980: Louisville, KY
& Jimmy Valiant w/Hart beat Ricky Morton & Steve Regal

Jan 9, 1980: Evansville, IN
w/Jimmy Valiant & Jimmy Hart beat Paul Ellering, Ken Lucas & Steve Regal

Jan 11, 1980: Tupelo, MS
& Jimmy Hart vs Jerry Jarret & Bill Dundee

Jan 12, 1980: Memphis, TN - TV results
& Jimmy Valiant w/Hart lost via DQ to Ricky & Robert Gibson

Jan 12, 1980: Jonesboro, AR
(c) w/Hart lost via DQ to Jerry Jarrett
- CWA World Title Match

Jan 14, 1980: Memphis, TN
w/Jimmy Valiant & Jimmy Hart beat Steve Regal. Rick Morton & Big Red

Jan 15, 1980: Louisville, KY
w/Jimmy Valiant & Jimmy Hart lost via DQ to Jerry Jarrett, Bill Dundee & Ken Lucas

Jan 16, 1980: Evansville, IN
w/Jimmy Valiant & Jimmy Hart vs. Ken Lucas, Bill Dundee & Jerry Jarrett

Jan 19, 1980: Memphis, TN - TV results
w/Hart beat Ricky Morton

Jan 19, 1980: Jonesboro, AR
& Jimmy Hart lost to Jerry Jarrett & Bill Dundee

Jan 21, 1980: Memphis, TN
(c) w/Hart lost via DQ to Bill Dundee
- CWA World Title Match

Jan 22, 1980: Louisville, KY
w/Jimmy Valiant & Jimmy Hart lost to Jerry Jarrett, Ken Lucas & Bill Dundee
- No DQ match

Jan 23, 1980: Evansville, IN
w/Jimmy Valiant & Jimmy Hart beat Ken Lucas, Bill Dundee & Jerry Jarrett
No DQ Match

Jan 19, 1980: Memphis, TN - TV results
& Jimmy Valiant w/Hart defeated Larry Hardin and Ricky Morton

Jan 26, 1980: Jonesboro, AR
(c) w/Hart drew with Jerry Jarrett
- CWA World Title Match

w/Sonny King & Jimmy Hart lost to Jerry Jarrett, Bill Dundee and Ricky Morton

Jan 28, 1980: Memphis, TN
& Jimmy Valiant w/Hart lost via DQ to Bill Dundee & Jackie Fargo

Jan 29, 1980: Louisville, KY
(c) w/Hart beat Bill Dundee
- CWA World Title Match

Photo Courtesy of Jim Cornette
Bill Dundee Uppercuts Jerry Lawler

* Jerry Lawler Breaks Leg: In a not so friendly game of tag football, Jerry Lawler broke his leg and would end up being out almost all of 1980. This caused the territory to struggle and several people had to stand up and carry the promotion on their shoulder, including Bill Dundee, Tommy Rich & Jimmy Valiant. Perhaps none so much as rookie manager Jimmy Hart.

Jimmy had just started to manage Jerry Lawler. With Lawler out, it allowed Hart to flourish and make a name for himself. It also gave the promotion the ultimate villain for Lawler to battle upon his return.

June 2, 1980: Memphis, TN
An appearance at ringside by Jerry Lawler

Photo Courtesy of Jim Cornette
Jerry Lawler Returns To Monday Night.

June 9, 1980: Memphis, TN
An appearance at ringside by Jerry Lawler

July 14, 1980: Memphis, TN - TV results
Eddie Marlin signs Jerry Lawler to a new contract

June 16, 1980: Memphis, TN
An appearance at ringside by Jerry Lawler

June 18, 1980: Evansville, IN
An appearance at ringside by Jerry Lawler

Aug 16, 1980: Memphis, TN - TV Results
Show was hosted by Lance Russell, Dave Brown & Jerry Lawler

Winner gets a Southern title shot: Tommy Rich beat Bill Dundee - Rich gives Dundee a low blow turning heel. Afterwards, Lance Russell & Jerry Lawler interview Tommy Rich - Rich shoves Lawler

Aug 30, 1980: Memphis, TN - TV results
Lance interviews Jerry Lawler
-out comes Jimmy Hart & Karl Krupp
-Hart slaps Lawler

Sep 1, 1980: Memphis, TN
beat Jimmy Hart

Sep 8, 1980: Louisville, KY
beat Jimmy Hart

Sep 9, 1980: Memphis, TN Mid-South Coliseum, Tuesday
beat Killer Karl Krupp
- Cast Match - Both men wearing cast on 1 leg.

Jimmy Valiant (c) w/Jerry Lawler beat Tommy Rich w/Jimmy Hart
- Southern Title Match

Sep 10, 1980: Evansville, IN
beat Jimmy Hart

Sep 12, 1980: Tupelo, MS
beat Jimmy Hart

Sep 13, 1980: Jonesboro, AR
Bill Dundee w/Jerry Lawler beat Gypsy Joe w/Hart

Sep 16, 1980: Louisville, KY
beat Killer Karl Krupp
- Cast Match - Both men wearing cast on 1 leg.

* Jerry was supposed to follow up the Sep 16 card and fight Krupp again on the Sep 17 card in Evansville, IN but it didn't happen. Jerry reinjured his leg in this match which set the healing back 3 months. He would not be able to return to the ring fully until the end of December. Jerry Lawler would be out of action nearly eleven months during 1980.

Oct 8, 1980: Evansville, IN
Tommy Rich w/Jimmy Hart beat Jimmy Valiant
- Jimmy Hart handcuffed to Jerry Lawler

Oct 29, 1980: Nashville, TN
Tojo Yamamoto & Bill Dundee w/Jerry Lawler beat Tommy Rich & Bobby Eaton w/Jimmy Hart

Oct 30, 1980: Campbellsburg, IN
beat Jimmy Hart

Nov 1, 1980: Jonesboro, AR
& Bill Dundee beat Tommy Rich & Jimmy Hart

Nov 6, 1980: Lexington, KY
beat Jimmy Hart

Nov 11, 1980: Lexington, KY
beat Jimmy Hart

Dec 3, 1980: Nashville, TN
& Ricky Morton vs. Bobby Eaton & Jimmy Hart

Bobby Eation Gets Blasted by Jerry Lawler

Dec 6, 1980: Jonesboro, AR
& Carl Fergie lost via DQ to Bobby Eaton & The Angel w/Jimmy Hart
- Jimmy Hart's Hair At Stake

Dec 11, 1980: Lexington, KY
& Carl Fergie beat Bobby Eaton & Jimmy Hart

Dec 12, 1980: Tupelo, MS
& Carl Fergie beat Bobby Eaton & Jimmy Hart

Dec 19, 1980: Tupelo, MS
& Bill Dundee lost to tThe Angel & Bobby Eaton
w/Hart

Dec 26, 1980: Tupelo, MS
beat Bobby Eaton & Jimmy Hart

Dec 29, 1980: Memphis, TN
beat the Dream Machine w/Hart
- If Lawler wins he gets 5 mins vs. Hart:

Jerry Lawler beat Jimmy Hart
- 5 Minute Match

*Photo Courtesy of Jim Cornette
Jerry Lawler Finally Returns For Good!

1981

Chapter 12

* With Jerry Lawler finally back in the ring, the territory was on fire. Jerry Lawler was running through a rogue's gauntlet on a weekly basis as Jimmy Hart was bringing in some of the best talent Memphis had seen in years. It was an amazing time to be a Jerry Lawler & Memphis Wrestling fan.

Jan 1, 1981: Nashville, TN
beat Dream Machine w/Hart
- If Lawler wins, he gets 5 mins vs. Hart:

Jerry Lawler No Contest with Jimmy Hart

*Photo Courtesy of Jim Cornette
Jerry Lawler vs. Dream Machine

Jan 2, 1981: Evansville, IN
beat the Dream Machine w/Hart

beat Jimmy Hart

Jan 3, 1981: Nashville, TN
& Bill Dundee beat The Angel, Dream Machine & Jimmy Hart
Handicap Match

Jan 5, 1981: Memphis, TN
beat Paul Ellering w/Hart
- If Lawler wins he faces Hart and partner Hart chooses.

beat Jimmy Valiant & Jimmy Hart
- Handicap Match

Jan 6, 1981: Louisville, KY
beat Dream Machine w/Hart
- If Lawler wins, he gets 5 mins vs. Hart:

beat Jimmy Hart

Jan 7, 1981: Evansville, IN
& Ricky Morton beat the Dream Machine, the Angel & Jimmy Hart

Jan 8, 1981: Lexington, KY
beat Dream Machine w/Hart
- If Lawler wins, he gets 5 mins vs. Hart:

beat Jimmy Hart
Jan 10, 1981: Nashville, TN
& Ken Lucas beat The Angel & Dream Machine w/Hart
- Pole Match with Strap on top

Jan 12, 1981: Memphis, TN
beat Austin Idol w/Hart
- Hart's gold record (Keep On Dancing) at stake.

Jan 13, 1981 Louisville, KY
beat Paul Ellering w/Hart
- If Lawler wins he faces Hart and partner Hart chooses.

beat Jimmy Valiant & Jimmy Hart
- Handicap Match

Jan 14, 1981: Evansville, IN
beat Paul Ellering w/Hart
- If Lawler wins he faces Hart and partner Hart chooses.

beat Jimmy Valiant & Jimmy Hart
- Handicap Match

Jan 17, 1981: Jonesboro, AR
vs. the Angel w/Jimmy Hart

Jan 18, 1981: Memphis, TN
lost via DQ to Joe Leduc w/Hart
- If Lawler wins, gets to give 10 belt lashes to Hart. If Leduc wins, Hart gives Lawler 10 lashes.
- Sunday, 3pm Card

Jan 20, 1981: Louisville, KY
beat Austin Idol w/Hart

Jan 21, 1981: Evansville, IN
beat Austin Idol w/Hart

Jan 24, 1981, Jonesboro, AR
w/Tommy & Eddie Gilbert vs. the Dream Machine, the Angel & Skull Murphy w/Hart

Jan 26, 1981: Memphis, TN
beat Ron Bass w/Hart
- Bass was a sub for Joe Leduc

Jan 27, 1981: Louisville, KY
beat the Dream Machine w/Hart
- Dream was a sub for Leduc

Jan 28, 1981: Evansville, IN
beat the Dream Machine w/Hart
- Dream was a sub for Leduc

* Joe Leduc must have had an injury. He had been booked against Lawler for the entire week.

Jan 29, 1981: Nashville, TN
beat Bill Irwin w/Hart

Feb 2, 1981: Memphis, TN
beat Austin Idol
- Jimmy Hart was banned from ringside

Feb 3, 1981: Louisville, KY
beat Austin Idol
- Jimmy Hart was banned from ringside

Feb 4, 1981: Evansville, IN
beat Austin Idol
- Jimmy Hart was banned from ringside

Feb 5, 1981: Winslow, IN
beat the Dream Machine w/Hart

Feb 7, 1981: Jonesboro, AR
won via DQ over Jimmy Valiant(c) w/Hart
- Southern Title Match

Feb 8, 1981: Jackson, TN
beat the Dream Machine w/Hart

Feb 9, 1981: Memphis, TN
won via DQ over Hulk Hogan w/Hart

*Photo Courtesy of Jim Cornette
Jerry Lawler & Referee Jerry Calhoun

Feb 10, 1981 Louisville, KY
beat the Dream Machine w/Hart
- if Dream loses, Hart gets 10 lashes.
- Originally listed as Southern Title Match with Lawler vs Valiant.

Feb 11, 1981: Evansville, IN
vs. Jimmy Valiant(c) w/Hart
- Southern Title Match

Feb 12, 1981: Lexington, KY
beat the Dream Machine w/Hart
- if Dream loses, Hart gets 10 lashes.
- Dream was a sub for Leduc

Feb 13, 1981: Murray, KY, Friday
beat Dream Machine w/Hart

Feb 14, 1981: Nashville, TN
beat Austin Idol w/Hart

Feb 15, 1981: Memphis, TN
beat Jimmy Valiant(c) w/Hart
- Southern Title Match
- Sunday card

beat Austin Idol

Feb 17, 1981: Louisville, KY
beat Austin Idol

Feb 18, 1981: Evansville, IN
won via DQ over Austin Idol w/Hart

Feb 23, 1981: Louisville, KY
beat Jimmy Valiant(c) w/Hart
- Southern Title Match

won by DQ over Austin Idol w/Hart
- Dutch Mantell interferes for Idol

Feb 24, 1981: Memphis, TN
& Jackie Fargo won via DQ over Austin Idol &
Dutch Mantell w/Hart
- Tuesday Card

Feb 25, 1981: Evansville, IN
beat Jimmy Valiant(c) w/Hart
- Southern Title Match

won by DQ over Austin Idol w/Hart

Mar 1, 1981: Memphis, TN
w/Jackie & Roughhouse Fargo beat Jimmy Hart,
Austin Idol & Dutch Mantell
- Sunday Card

Mar 3, 1981: Louisville, KY
& Plowboy Frazier won via DQ over Austin Idol &
Dutch Mantell w/Hart

Mar 4, 1981: Evansville, IN
& Plowboy Frazier beat Austin Idol & Dutch
Mantell w/Hart

Mar 5, 1981: Nashville, TN
& Plowboy Frazier beat Austin Idol & Dutch
Mantell w/Hart

Mar 7, 1981: Nashville, TN
(c) beat Jimmy Valiant w/Hart
- Southern Title Match
- Loser Leaves town match

Mar 8, 1981: Jackson, TN
(c) beat Jimmy Valiant w/Hart
- Southern Title Match

Mar 9, 1981: Memphis, TN
(c) beat Jimmy Valiant w/Hart
- Southern Title Match

Mar 10, 1981: Louisville, KY
(c) beat Jimmy Valiant
- Southern Title Match
- Loser leaves town match

Mar 11, 1981: Evansville, IN
(c) beat Jimmy Valiant w/Hart
- Southern Title Match
- Loser leaves town match

Mar 12, 1981: Lexington, KY
(c) beat Jimmy Valiant w/Hart
- Southern Title Match
- Loser leaves town match

Mar 16, 1981: Memphis, TN
(c) beat Jack Brisco w/Hart
- Southern Title Match
- Brisco was the heel

Mar 17, 1981: Louisville, KY
won via DQ over Jimmy Hart
- Lawler had one hand tied behind his back.

**Mar 18, 1981: Evansville, IN Coliseum,
Wednesday**
won via DQ over Jimmy Hart
- Lawler had one hand tied behind his back.

Mar 21, 1981: Nashville, TN
w/Bill Dundee & Dream Machine beat Tojo
Yamamoto, Wayne Farris & Jimmy Hart
- Loser of the match leaves town (Farris)

Mar 23, 1981: Memphis, TN
& Tommy Rich beat Mr. Onita & Masa Fuchi
- Lawler was a sub for Bill Dundee

wins via Count Out over Terry Funk
- No DQ match

Mar 24, 1981: Louisville, KY
w/Bill Dundee & Dream Machine No Contest
with Dutch Mantell, Jimmy Hart & Tojo
Yamamoto

Mar 25, 1981: Evansville, IN
w/Bill Dundee & Dream Machine No Contest
with Dutch Mantell, Jimmy Hart & Tojo
Yamamoto

Mar 30, 1981: Memphis, TN
won via DQ over Dory Funk Jr.
- Jimmy Hart was suspended above the ring

beat Gypsy Joe & the Angel w/Hart
- Loser leaves town

*Photo Courtesy of Jim Cornette
Jimmy Hart Suspended Above The Ring

Mar 31, 1981: Louisville, KY
w/Dream Machine & Bill Dundee beat Tojo
Yamamoto, Dutch Mantel & Jimmy Hart
- Cage Match

Apr 1, 1981: Evansville, IN
w/Dream Machine & Bill Dundee beat Tojo
Yamamoto, Dutch Mantel & Jimmy Hart

Apr 2, 1981: Nashville, TN
beat Tojo Yamamoto w/Hart
 - If Lawler wins he gets 5 min match vs. Hart

Apr 4, 1981: Nashville, TN
& Plowboy Frazier beat Masa Fuchi & Mr. Onita

Apr 5, 1981: Jackson, TN
won via DQ over Dutch Mantell w/Hart
- Advertised as Lawler vs Billy Robinson w/Hart

Apr 6, 1981: Memphis, TN
& Plowboy Frazier beat Terry & Dory Funk Jr.
- Texas Death Match
- Went 7 falls
- Hart suspended above the ring

*Photo Courtesy of Jim Cornette
Jerry Lawler & Plowboy Frazier

Apr 7, 1981: Louisville, KY
(c) beat Terry Funk w/Hart
- Southern Title Match
- No DQ match

Apr 8, 1981: Evansville, IN
(c) beat Terry Funk w/Hart
- Southern Title Match

April 9, 1981: Lexington, KY
(c) beat Terry Funk w/Hart
- Southern Title Match
- No DQ match

Apr 13, 1981: Memphis, TN
w/Kevin Sullivan No Contest with El Toro, the
Turk & Jimmy Hart
- Sullivan turned on Lawler during the match

*Jerry Lawler vs. Terry Funk: Empty arena match. Another history making event took place on Monday afternoon, April 13, 1981. On the April 11, 1982 Saturday morning Memphis show, Terry Funk sent Jerry Lawler a challenge, via Lance Russell. Jerry accepted the challenge. No one was told what the challenge was. The following Saturday, the fans were shown what happened. With Lance Russell and a camera man the only people present at the Mid-South Coliseum, Jerry Lawler and Terry Funk went to the ring and had an "I Quit" match with no referee. The match went back and forth before Terry had broken off a piece of wood from the ring steps and was using in to try and put out the King's eye. Jerry kicked Terry's arm which sent the wooden spike into Funk's eye. Bloody and screaming, Jerry got Terry to submit. It was an amazing angle and had never been done before, anywhere. It is still talked about today.

Apr 14, 1981: Louisville, KY
& Bill Dundee beat El Toro & the Turk w/Hart

(c) won via DQ over Dutch Mantell w/Hart
- Southern Title Match

Apr 15, 1981: Evansville, In
& Bill Dundee beat El Toro & the Turk w/Hart

(c) won by DQ over Dutch Mantell w/Hart
- Southern Title Match

Apr 20, 1981: Memphis, TN
No Contest with Kevin Sullivan w/Hart

Apr 21, 1981: Louisville, KY
w/Eddie Gilbert & Koko Ware beat the Turk, El Toro & Jimmy Hart

Apr 22, 1981: Evansville, IN
w/Eddie Gilbert & Koko ware beat the Turk, El Toro & Jimmy Hart

April 26, 1981: Memphis, TN
Jerry Lawler beat Kevin Sullivan w/Jimmy Hart
- **Tim McCarver Baseball Stadium, Sunday**

April 28, 1981: Louisville, KY
won via DQ over Kevin Sullivan w/Hart

Apr 29, 1981: Evansville, IN
won via DQ over Kevin Sullivan w/Hart

April 30, 1981: Nashville, TN
won via DQ over Kevin Sullivan w/Hart

May 2, 1981: Nashville, TN
w/ Bill Dundee & Dream Machine vs. Kevin Sullivan, Wayne Farris & Jimmy Hart

May 3, 1981: Jackson, TN
won via DQ over Kevin Sullivan w/Hart

May 4, 1981: Memphis, TN
won via DQ over Crusher Blackwell w/Hart

May 5, 1981: Louisville, KY
beat Crusher Blackwell w/Hart

May 6, 1981: Evansville, IN
beat Crusher Blackwell w/Hart

May 7, 1981: Louisville, KY
beat Kevin Sullivan w/Hart

May 11, 1981: Memphis, TN
won by DQ over Dory Funk, Jr. w/Hart

Jerry Lawler vs. Dory Funk Jr.

May 12, 1981: Louisville, KY
No Contest with Terry Funk w/Hart

May 13, 1981: Evansville, IN
No Contest w/Terry Funk w/Hart

May 15, 1981: Orlando, FL
won via DQ over Don Muraco

May 18, 1981: Memphis, TN
& Jack Brisco lost to Terry & Dory Funk Jr.
w/Hart

May 19, 1981: Louisville, KY
lost to Terry Funk w/Hart
- Cage Match

May 20, 1981: Evansville, IN
lost to Terry Funk w/Hart
- Cage Match

May 25, 1981: Memphis, TN
beat Terry Funk w/Hart

May 26, 1981: Louisville, KY
beat Terry Funk w/Hart
- Texas Death match
- went 5 Falls

May 27, 1981: Evansville, IN
beat Terry Funk w/Hart
- Texas Death Match

May 28, 1981: Nashville, TN
& Dutch Mantell vs Kevin Sullivan & Wayne
Farris(c) w/Hart
- Southern Tag Title Match

May 29, 1981: Orlando, FL
beat via DQ Dory Funk Jr.

May 30, 1981: St. Petersburg, FL
beat via DQ Don Muraco

June 1, 1981: Memphis, TN
w/Dream Machine & Dutch Mantell won via DQ
over Kevin Sullivan, Wayne Farris & the
Nightmares w/Hart

June 2, 1981: Louisville, KY
w/Bill Dundee, Dutch Mantell & Dream Machine
won via DQ over Kevin Sullivan, Wayne Farris &
the Nightmares w/Hart

June 4, 1981: Lexington, KY
beat Terry Funk w/Hart

June 5, 1981: Orlando, FL
beat Hiro Matsuda

June 7, 1981: Jacksonville, FL
lost to Terry Funk

June 8, 1981: Memphis, TN
w/Bill Dundee, Dream Machine & Dutch Mantell
lost to the Nightmares, Kevin Sullivan & Wayne
Farris w/Hart
- No DQ

June 9, 1981: Louisville, KY
w/Bill Dundee, Dream Machine & Dutch Mantell
lost to the Nightmares, Kevin Sullivan & Wayne
Farris w/Hart
- No DQ

June 10, 1981: Evansville, IN
w/Bill Dundee, Dream Machine & Dutch Mantell
lost to the Nightmares, Kevin Sullivan & Wayne
Farris w/Hart
- No DQ

June 11, 1981: Winslow, IN
(c) beat Wayne Farris w/Hart
- Southern Title Match

June 13, 1981: Nashville, TN
w/Plowboy Frazier, Roy Rogers & Dutch Mantell
lost to the Nightmares, Kevin Sullivan & Wayne
Farris w/Hart
- No DQ

(c) beat Wayne Farris w/Hart
- Southern Title Match

June 15, 1981: Memphis, TN
& Dream Machine beat Jimmy Hart &
Nightmares
- Handicap piledriver match

June 16, 1981: Louisville, KY
w/Steve Keirn, Dutch Mantell & Dream Machine
lost to Kevin Sullivan, Wayne Farris & the
Nightmares w/Hart
- No DQ

June 17, 1981: Evansville, IN
w/Steve Keirn, Dutch Mantell & Dream Machine
lost to Kevin Sullivan, Wayne Farris & the
Nightmares w/Hart
- No DQ

beat Nightmare #1 w/Hart

June 19, 1981: Orlando, FL
beat Mr. Pogo

June 21, 1981: Orlando, FL
beat Terry Funk

June 22, 1981: Memphis, TN
w/Bill Dundee, Dutch Mantell & Dream Machine lost to Kevin Sullivan & the Nightmares.
- Winners gets dream match

(c) lost to Jimmy Hart
- Southern Title Match
- Hart Dream Match
- Refs were Wayne Farris & Kevin Sullivan

*Photo Courtesy of Jim Cornette
The King Getting His Hands On Jimmy Hart

June 23, 1981: Louisville, KY
& Dream Machine beat the Nightmares w/Hart
- Piledriver match

June 24, 1981: Evansville, IN
& Dream Machine beat the Nightmares w/Hart
- Piledriver match

June 27, 1981: St. Petersburg, FL
vs. Terry Funk
No DQ match

June 28, , 1981: Orlando, FL
vs. Florida Champ Dory Funk Jr.

June 29, 1981: Memphis, TN
beat Jimmy Hart
- No DQ
- Lawler's Lumberjack Dream Match
- Lawler handpicked the 4 lumberjacks who were around the ring, (Dream Machine, Dutch Mantell, Bill Dundee & Steve Keirn).

June 30, 1981: Louisville, KY
w/Bill Dundee, Dream Machine & Dutch Mantell beat Nightmares, Wayne Farris & Kevin Sullivan w/Hart

July 1, 1981: Evansville, IN
drew with Wayne Farris

w/Steve Keirn, Dutch Mantell & Bill Dundee beat the Nightmares, Wayne Farris & Kevin Sullivan w/Hart
- No DQ match
- Winning team gets Dream Matches

beat Wayne Farris

July 2, 1981: Nashville, TN
w/Steve Keirn, Dutch Mantell & Bill Dundee beat the Nightmares, Wayne Farris & Kevin Sullivan w/Hart
- No DQ match
- Winning team gets Dream Matches

vs. Kevin Sullivan

July 5, 1981: Jackson, TN
w/Bill Dundee, Dutch Mantell & the Dream Machine vs.Kevin Sullivan, the Nightmares & Wayne Farris w/Hart
- No DQ match
-Winning team gets Dream Matches

July 6, 1981: Memphis, TN
& Bill Dundee lost to Wayne Farris & Kevin Sullivan(c) w/Hart
- Southern Tag Title Match

July 9, 1981: Lexington, KY
w/Bill Dundee, Dream Machine & Dutch Mantell beat Wayne Farris, Kevin Sullivan & the Nightmares w/Hart

& Bill Dundee beat Wayne Farris & Kevin Sullivan(c) w/Hart
- Southern Tag Title Match

July 10, 1981: Tupelo, MS
& Steve Keirn lost via DQ with Wayne Farris &
Kevin Sullivan(c) w/Hart
- Southern Title Match

July 11, 1981: Nashville, TN
& Bill Dundee vs. Wayne Farris & Kevin
Sullivan(c) w/Hart
- Southern Title Match

July 13, 1981: Memphis, TN
& Bill Dundee beat Wayne Farris & Kevin
Sullivan(c) w/Hart
- Southern Tag Title Match
- No DQ
- Lawler's hair vs titles

July 14, 1981: Tampa, FL
w/Mike Graham beat Dory Jr. & Terry Funk

July 15, 1981: Miami Beach, FL
vs. Dory Funk Jr.

July 16, 1981: Jacksonville, FL
vs. Dory Funk Jr.

July 17, 1981: Ft. Pierce, FL
beat Assassin III

July 18, 1981: St. Petersburg, FL
DCOR with Hulk Hogan

July 20, 1981: Memphis, TN
Southern Title Tournament
Round 1
lost to Ron Bass w/Hart

July 22, 1981: Miami Beach, FL
lost via DQ to Terry Funk

July 23, 1981
No Contest with the Sheik

July 25, 1981: Memphis, TN - TV Results
beat Ken Wayne

July 25, 1981: Jonesboro, AR
won by DQ over Bugsy McGraw w/Hart

July 27, 1981: Memphis, TN
won via DQ over the Dream Machine w/Hart
- Was originally listed as Lawler & Dream vs
Heartbreakers (Joey Cagle & Rocky Sortar)
w/Hart
- attend. over 9,000

* Photo Courtesy Of Jim Cornette
Jerry Lawler Has The Dream Machine In
Trouble After he Dropped The Strap.

July 28, 1981: Louisville, KY
Southern Title Tournament
Round 1
lost to Bugsy McGraw w/Hart

July 29, 1981: Evansville, IN
Southern Title Tournament
Round 1
lost to Bugsy McGraw w/Hart

July 30, 1981: Nashville, TN
vs. Bugsy McGraw w/Hart

Aug 3, 1981: Memphis, TN
& Jimmy Valiant went to a No Contest with
Dream Machine & Bugsy McGraw w/Hart
- Match was listed as Lawler & mystery partner.
From this point forward Valiant was never used
again as a heel in any of his Memphis
appearances.

Aug 4, 1981: Louisville, KY
& Jimmy Valiant won by DQ over Dream
Machine & Bugsy McGraw w/Hart

Aug 5, 1981: Evansville, IN
& Jimmy Valiant won by DQ over Dream
Machine & Bugsy McGraw w/Hart

Aug 6, 1981: Lexington, KY
& Jimmy Valiant beat Dream Machine & Bugsy
McGraw w/Hart

Aug 7, 1981: Tupelo, MS
won by DQ over the Dream Machine

Aug 8, 1981: Nashville, TN
won by DQ over the Dream Machine

Aug 9, 1981: Louisville, KY
w/Bill Dundee, Dutch Mantell & Steve Keirn won
by DQ over the Nightmares, Bugsy
McGraw & the Dream Machine

won by DQ over the Dream Machine

Aug 10, 1981: Memphis, TN
won by DQ over the Dream Machine

Aug 11, 1981: Tampa, FL
DCOR vs. Terry Funk

Aug 12, 1981: Miami Beach, FL
draw vs. Buzz Sawyer $5000 match

Aug 13, 1981: Jacksonville, FL
beat Jim Kent

Aug 14, 1981: Sarasota, FL
beat Hiro Matsuda

Aug 15, 1981: Key West, FL
beat Hiro Matsuda

Aug 16, 1981: Ft. Myers, FL
vs. Hiro Matsuda

Aug 16, 1981: Orlando, FL
drew with Buzz Sawyer

Aug 17, 1981: Memphis, TN
w/Dutch Mantel, Rick Gibson & Robert Gibson
lost via DQ to the Nightmares, Bugsy McGraw &
Dream Machine w/Jimmy Hart

Aug 18, 1981: Louisville, KY
won by DQ over the Dream Machine

Aug 19, 1981: Evansville, IN
won by DQ over the Dream Machine

Aug 24, 1981: Memphis, TN
beat Dream Machine(c) w/Hart
- Southern Title Match - No DQ
- Loser is tarred & feathered (Dream)

* Photo Courtesy Of Jim Cornette
Dream Machine Is Not Happy About Being
Tarred & Feathered After Loss To Lawler.

Aug 25, 1981: Louisville, KY
w/Steve Keirn, Ricky & Robert Gibson beat the
Dream Machine, the Nightmares & Bugsy
McGraw w/Hart

Aug 26, 1981: Evansville, IN
w/Steve Keirn, Ricky & Robert Gibson beat the
Dream Machine, the Nightmares & Bugsy
McGraw

Aug 27, 1981: Nashville, TN
w/Bill Dundee, Steve Keirn & Roy Rogers beat
Bugsy McGraw, Dream Machine & the
Nightmares w/Hart

Aug 28, 1981: Tupelo, MS
won by DQ over the Dream Machine

Aug 29, 1981: St. Petersburg, FL
No Contest with Terry Funk

Aug 31, 1981: Memphis, TN
& Bill Dundee beat Dream Machine & Jimmy
Hart.
- Loser of fall leaves town (Hart) No DQ

Sep 1, 1981: Louisville, KY
beat Dream Machine(c) w/Hart
- Southern Title Match
- No DQ: Loser is tarred & feathered (Dream)

*Photo Courtesy Of Jim Cornette
Dream Machine VS. Jerry Lawler. The War
Continues.

Sep 2, 1981: Evansville, IN
beat Dream Machine(c) w/Hart
- Southern Title Match
- No DQ
- Loser is tarred & feathered (Dream)

Sep 3, 1981: Lexington, KY
beat Dream Machine(c) w/Hart
- Southern Title Match - No DQ
- Loser is tarred & feathered (Dream)

w/Steve Keirn, Ricky & Robert Gibson beat
Bugsy McGraw, Dream Machine & the
Nightmares

Sep 4, 1981: Tupelo, MS
& Bill Dundee beat Dream Machine & Nightmare
#1 w/Hart

Sep 7, 1981: Memphis, TN
(c) lost to Dream Machine
- Southern Title Match
- Lawler wins, 1st Family leaves town. Dream
wins, Hart returns, Lawler leaves town.
- Koko Ware special ref. Koko turns on Lawler.

Sep 8, 1981: Tampa, FL
w/Charlie Cook vs.Dory Funk Jr. & Assassin #1

Sep 9, 1981: Miami, FL
w/Charlie Cook beat Dory Funk Jr. & Assassin I

Sep 10, 1981: Jacksonville, FL
w/Charlie Cook beat Dory Funk Jr. & Assassin

Sep 11, 1981: Sarasota, FL
vs Terry Funk
- Brass Knucks Match

Sep 12, 1981: Nashville, TN
& Bill Dundee beat the Dream Machine & Jimmy
Hart
- No DQ
- Losers tarred & feathered

Sep 13, 1981: Orlando, FL
beat Bobby Jaggers

Sep 17, 1981: Owensboro, KY, Thursday
beat Dream Machine

Sep 22, 1981: Louisville, KY
won via DQ over Sweet Brown Sugar w/Hart
- Sugar was Koko Ware. Hart renamed him
when he joined the First Family.

Sep 23, 1981: Evansville, IN
won via DQ over Sweet Brown Sugar w/Hart

Sep 26, 1981: St. Petersburg, FL
beat Bobby Jaggers
- Brass Knucks Match

Sep 26, 1981: Memphis, TN
Jimmy Valiant(c) beat Dream Machine
- Southern Title Match
If Valiant wins, Lawler comes back & Valiant
gets Loser Leave Town match with Hart. If
Dream wins, Valiant loses title, hair & leaves
town.

Valiant lost to Jimmy Hart
- Loser Leaves Town - Valiant leaves town.

Sep 29, 1981: Louisville, KY
& Bill Dundee beat the Dream Machine, Sweet
Brown Sugar & Jimmy Hart

Sep 30, 1981: Evansville, IN
& Bill Dundee beat the Dream Machine, Sweet
Brown Sugar & Jimmy Hart

Oct 1, 1981: Irvington, KY
beat Sweet Brown Sugar w/Hart

Oct 5, 1981: Memphis, TN
went to a No Contest with Sweet Brown Sugar
w/Hart

Oct 6, 1981: Louisville, KY
w/Jimmy Valiant & Bill Dundee No Contest
against Jimmy Hart, Sweet Brown Sugar &
Dream Machine

Oct 7, 1981: Evansville, IN
w/Jimmy Valiant & Bill Dundee No Contest
against Jimmy Hart, Sweet Brown Sugar &
Dream Machine

Oct 8, 1981: Lexington, KY
won via a DQ over Sweet Brown Sugar w/Hart

Oct 11, 1981: Jackson, TN
won via a DQ over Sweet Brown Sugar w/Hart

Oct 12, 1981: Memphis, TN
& Jerry Calhoun lost to Sweet Brown Sugar &
Jimmy Hart
- No DQ

Jerry Lawler & Jerry Calhoun

*** Andy Kaufman made his first Memphis
appearance on this card, Kaufman wrestled
4 different woman from the audience,
beating them all.**

Oct 13, 1981: Louisville, KY
won by DQ over Sweet Brown Sugar

Oct 14, 1981: Evansville, IN
beat Sweet Brown Sugar via DQ

Oct 16, 1981: Tupelo, MS
& Rick Morton won by DQ over Stan Lane &
Sweet Brown Sugar w/Hart

Oct 19, 1981: Memphis, TN
won by DQ over Killer Karl Krupp w/Hart

beat Sweet Brown Sugar w/Hart
- Non-Sanctioned, Barbed Wire Match

Oct 26, 1981: Memphis, TN
w/Bill Dundee, Tojo Yamamoto & Steve Keirn
lost to Killer Karl Krupp, Stan Lane, Sweet
Brown Sugar & Jimmy Hart

Oct 27, 1981: Louisville, KY
won by DQ over Killer Karl Kurpp

beat Sweet Brown Sugar w/Hart
- Non-Sanctioned, Barbed Wire Match

Oct 28, 1981: Evansville, IN
won by DQ over Killer Karl Kurpp

beat Sweet Brown Sugar w/Hart
- Non-Sanctioned, Barbed Wire Match

Oct 30, 1981: Tupelo, MS
beat Sweet Brown Sugar w/Hart

Nov 2, 1981: Memphis, TN
lost to Killer Karl Krupp
- No DQ - Jimmy Hart is Special Ref

Nov 3, 1981: Louisville, TN
won by DQ over Killer Karl Krupp

Nov 4, 1981: Evansville, IN
won by DQ over Killer Karl Krupp

Nov 5, 1981: Lexington, KY
w/Bill Dundee, Tojo Yamamoto & Steve Keirn
lost to Killer Karl Krupp, Sweet Brown Sugar,
Jimmy Hart & Stan Lane

beat Sweet Brown Sugar w/Hart
- Non-Sanctioned, Barbed Wire Match

Nov 6, 1981: Tupelo, MS
w/Tojo Yamamoto & Jerry Calhoun beat Killer Karl Krupp, Sweet Brown Sugar & Jimmy Hart

Nov 9, 1981: Memphis, TN
& Tojo Yamamoto beat The Cuban Assassin & Iranian Assassin

beat Killer Karl Krupp w/Hart
- Lumberjack Strap Match

Nov 10, 1981: Louisville, KY
beat Killer Karl Krupp
- Special Ref: Jimmy Hart
- No DQ

Nov 11, 1981: Evansville, IN
lost to Killer Karl Krupp
- Special Ref: Jimmy Hart
- No DQ

Nov 12, 1981: Huntingburg, IN
w/Bill Dundee, Tojo Yamamoto & Steve Keirn beat Killer Karl Krupp, Stan Lane, Sweet Brown Sugar, Jimmy Hart

Nov 16, 1981: Memphis, TN
w/Ricky Morton & Tojo Yamamoto beat Killer Karl Krupp, Nightmare & Speed w/Hart

beat Super Destroyer w/Hart
-if Lawler wins, he gets with Hart

won by DQ over Jimmy Hart

Nov 17, 1981: Louisville, KY
beat Killer Karl Krupp
- Lumberjack match

& Tojo Yamamoto beat the Iranian & Cuban Assassins
Nov 18, 1981: Evansville, IN
beat Killer Karl Krupp
- Lumberjack match

& Tojo Yamamoto beat the Iranian & Cuban Assassins

Nov 19, 1981: Harrodsburg, KY
beat Killer Karl Krupp

& Tojo Yamamoto beat the Iranian & Cuban Assassins

Nov 23, 1981: Memphis, TN
won via DQ over Super Destroyer w/Hart
- Piledriver Legal Match

* Andy Kaufman on the card again. beats first 3 ladies, then the 4th one went to a draw.

*Photo Courtesy of Jim Cornette
Jerry In One Of His Many New Outfits

Nov 24, 1981: Louisville, KY
& Tojo Yamamoto beat the Nightmare & Speed w/Hart

beat Super Destroyer
- Lights Out Match
beat Jimmy Hart

Nov 25, 1981: Evansville, IN
& Tommy Gilbert beat the Nightmare & Speed w/Hart

won by DQ over Jimmy Hart

Nov 27, 1981: Hernando, MS
beat Dream Machine w/Hart

Nov 30, 1981: Memphis, TN
& Bill Dundee lost via DQ to Super Destroyer &
Sweet Brown Sugar w/Hart

*** Andy Kaufman returned. Pinned Foxy, the
lady he went to a draw with the previous
week. Lawler physically, and forcefully
pushed Kaufman away from Foxy after win.
Crowd loved it and wants the King to
destroy Kaufman. This reaction had Jerry
Jarrett's wheels spinning. He knew the
match would have to take place.**

Dec 1, 1981: Louisville, KY
won via DQ over the Super Destroyer w/Hart
Piledriver Legal Match

Dec 3, 1981: Lexington, KY
beat Super Destroyer w/Hart
- If Lawler wins, gets match with Hart

won by DQ over Jimmy Hart

Dec 5, 1981: Memphis, TN - TV results
Memphis, TN tape, Nov 30, 1981: Jerry Lawler
& Bill Dundee vs. Super Destroyer & Sweet
Brown Sugar w/Jimmy Hart

Lance Russell interviews Jerry Lawler & Bill
Dundee

Dec 7, 1981: Memphis, TN
& Bill Dundee beat Super Destroyer & Sweet
Brown Sugar w/Hart
No DQ

Dec 8, 1981: Paragould, AR
vs. Unknown

Dec 9, 1981: Kennett, MS
vs. Unknown

Dec 10, 1981: Clarksdale, MS
vs. Unknown

Dec 12, 1981: Memphis, TN TV results
Memphis, TN tape, Dec 7, 1981: Jerry Lawler &
Bill Dundee vs. Super Destroyer & Sweet Brown
Sugar-Bobby Eaton runs in

1982

Chapter 13

Jan 11, 1982: Memphis, TN
beat the Dream Machine

w/Bill Dundee & Steve Keirn beat Jimmy Hart, the Cuban Assassin & the Iranian Assassin

Jan 16, 1982: St. Petersburg, FL
beat Masa Fuchi

Jan 18, 1982: Memphis, TN
beat Dutch Mantell(c)
- Southern Title Match

Jan 19, 1982: Louisville, KY
w/Bill Dundee & Steve Keirn beat Jimmy Hart, the Iranian Assassin & the Cuban Assassin

beat the Dream Machine w/Hart

Jan 20, 1982: Evansville, IN
w/Bill Dundee & Steve Keirn beat Jimmy Hart, the Iranian Assassin & the Cuban Assassin

beat the Dream Machine w/Hart

Jan 23, 1982: Memphis, TN TV results
beat the Masked Invader

Jan 25, 1982: Memphis, TN
& Tojo Yamamoto lost to the Dream Machine & Sweet Brown Sugar w/Hart

Jan 26, 1982: Louisville, KY
w/Bill Dundee, Ricky & Robert Gibson & Steve Keirn beat the Iranian Assassin, the Nightmares, the Dream Machine & Bobby Eaton

(c) beat Dutch Mantell
- Southern Title Match

Jan 27, 1982: Evansville, IN
(c) beat Dutch Mantell
- Southern Title Match

Jan 31, 1982: Orlando, FL
beat James J Dillon
- Taped Fist Match

& Killer Karl Kox beat Terry Funk & the Iron Sheik

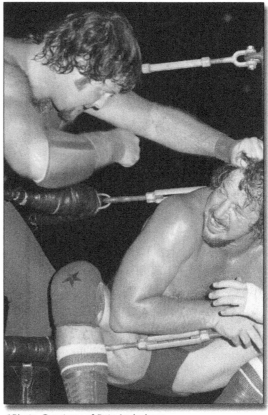

Photo Courtesy of Pete Lederberg
Jerry Lawler vs. Terry Funk

Feb 1, 1982: Memphis, TN
won via DQ over Sweet Brown Sugar w/Hart
Boxing Match

Feb 2, 1982: Louisville, KY
& Tojo Yamamoto lost to Sweet Brown Sugar & the Dream Machine w/Hart

Feb 3, 1982: Evansville, IN
w/Tojo Yamamoto vs. Sweet Brown Sugar & the Dream Machine w/Hart

Feb 4, 1982: Lexington, KY
(c) beat Dutch Mantell
- Southern Title Match

Feb 7, 1982: Memphis, TN
w/Robert Gibson beat Bobby Eaton & Sweet
Brown Sugar w/Hart

(c) lost to Dutch Mantell
- Southern Title Match

From The Programs Sold At The Matches

**Feb 9, 1982: Louisville, KY Gardens,
Tuesday**
won via DQ over Sweet Brown Sugar w/Hart
- Taped Fist Match

Feb 10, 1982: Evansville, IN
won via DQ over Sweet Brown Sugar w/Hart
- Taped Fist Match

Feb 11, 1982: Irvington, KY
beat the Dream Machine w/Hart

Feb 14, 1982: Memphis, TN
(c) lost to Dutch Mantell
-Southern Title Match

Feb 20, 1982: St. Petersburg, FL
w/Don Diamond lost to Terry Funk & Dick
Slater

Feb 22, 1982: Orlando, FL
w/Sweet Brown Sugar & Butch Reed lost to
David Von Erich, Terry & Dory Funk Jr.
- Sweet Brown Sugar, FL version: Skip Young

Feb 23, 1982: Tampa, FL
beat Terry Funk
Brass Knuckles Match
Lights Out Match

Feb 24, 1982: Key West, FL
vs JJ Dillon.
- Battle of the Kings

Feb 25, 1982: Jacksonville, FL
lost to JJ Dillon

Feb 26, 1982: Ft. Myers, FL
beat JJ Dillon
- Brass Knuckles Match
- Also in Battle Royal

Feb 27, 1982: Lakeland, FL
w/Mike Graham beat Iron Sheik & JJ Dillon

Feb 27, 1982: St. Petersburg, FL
beat via DQ Kendo Nagasaki

Feb 28, 1982: Orlando, FL
vs. King James Dillon
- Coal Miner's Glove match

Mar 1, 1982: Memphis, TN
beat Dutch Mantell(c)
- Southern Title Match

Mar 2, 1982: Louisville, KY
(c) lost to Dutch Mantell
- Southern Title Match

Mar 3, 1982: Evansville, IN
(c) lost to Dutch Mantell
- Southern Title Match

Mar 5, 1982: Tupelo, MS
(c) No Contest with Dutch Mantell
- Southern Title Match

Mar 6, 1982: Memphis, TN - TV results
beat Gypsy Joe

Mar 6, 1982: Nashville, TN
(c) No Contest with Dutch Mantell
- Southern Title Match

Mar 7, 1982: Lexington, KY
(c) lost to Dutch Mantell
- Southern Title Match

Mar 8, 1982: Memphis, TN
 (c) beat Norvell Austin
- Southern Title Match

*Photo Courtesy of Jim Cornette
The Southern Champion Once Again.

Mar 9, 1982: Louisville, KY
beat Dutch Mantell(c)
- Southern Title Match

Mar 10, 1982: Evansville, IN
beat Dutch Mantell(c)
- Southern Title Match

Mar 11, 1982: Campbellsburg, IN
won by DQ over Dutch Mantell(c)
- Southern Title Match

Mar 12, 1982: Tupelo, MS
(c)won by DQ over Dutch Mantell
- Southern Title Match

Mar 14, 1982: Louisville, KY
(c) beat Norvell Austin
- Southern Title Match

Mar 15, 1982: Memphis, TN
(c) No Contest with Dutch Mantell
- Southern Title Match

Jerry Lawler vs. Dutch Mantell, The War Continues.

Mar 16, 1982: Springfield, OH
(c) beat Dutch Mantell
- Southern Title Match

Mar 17, 1982: Evansville, IN
 (c) beat Norvell Austin
- Southern Title Match

Mar 19, 1982: Tupelo, MS
& Danny Davis beat Luke Graham & Dream Machine

Mar 21, 1982: Jackson, TN
(c) beat Dutch Mantell
- Southern Title Match

Mar 22, 1982: Memphis, TN
(c) lost to Dutch Mantell
- Southern Title Match - No DQ

Mar 23, 1982: Louisville, KY
(c) No Contest Dutch Mantell
- Southern Title Match

Mar 24, 1982: Evansville, IN
(c) No Contest Dutch Mantell
- Southern Title Match

Mar 29, 1982: Memphis, TN
beat Dutch Mantell(c)
- Southern Title Match
- No DQ - Barbed Wire Match

* Lawler vs. Mantell Feud: End of an amazing babyface feud between these two great talents. One of my favorite feuds of Jerry Lawler's career. Many fans thought Lawler had finally met his match. Both were able to maintain their fans throughout the entire feud. It was done as a slow burn, meaning they two did not face each other every week. It was highly effective in building up the anticipation for this final match. This match of the feud was the best one. It's a wonderful example of telling a story in the ring.

Mar 30, 1982: Louisville, KY
(c) lost to Dutch Mantell
- Southern Title Match

Mar 31, 1982: Nashville, TN
(c) lost to Dutch Mantell
- Southern Title Match
Apr 1, 1982: Lexington, KY
beat Dutch Mantell(c)
- Southern Title Match

Apr 3, 1982: Nashville, TN
beat Dutch Mantell(c)
- Southern Title Match
- No DQ - Barbed Wire Match

Apr 4, 1982: Jackson, TN
 (c) lost to Dutch Mantell
- Southern Title Match

Apr 5, 1982: Memphis, TN
lost via DQ to Andy Kaufman

(c) beat the Monk w/Hart
- Southern Title Match

* Andy Kaufman: What started as a simple comedy gimmick of Kaufman wrestling woman, seemingly culminated on this card when he got in the ring with Jerry Lawler. As the amazing photo shows, the King gave the TV star

Kaufman a piledriver, sending him to the hospital. The following days the video of the piledriver as well as the match were played all over the nation's news shows. It also in all the newspapers. Because of Kaufman's Hollywood ties, this match quickly a big deal, on a national scale. People, inside wrestling and out, were wondering if it was real. One thing is for sure, it raised the Memphis stock in the wrestling world. From this point forward, Memphis Wrestling was a major player. While most thought the Kaufman era was over, the truth was it was just beginning.

*Photo Courtesy of Jim Cornette
Jerry Lawler Giving Andy Kaufman The Piledriver Heard Round The World.

Apr 6, 1982: Louisville, KY
beat Dutch Mantell(c)
- Southern Title Match
- Barbed Wire Match
- No DQ

Apr 7, 1982: Evansville, IN
beat Dutch Mantell(c)
- Southern Title Match
- Barbed Wire Match
- No DQ

Apr 8, 1982: Owensboro, KY
& Jackie Fargo beat Luke Graham & Dream Machine w/Hart

beat Dutch Mantell(c)
- Southern Title Match

Apr 9, 1982: Mt. Sterling, KY
(c) beat Dutch Mantell
- Southern Title Match

Apr 10, 1982: Memphis, TN TV results
Replay of Memphis, TN tape, Apr 5, 1982: Jerry Lawler vs. Andy Kaufman

Apr 12, 1982: Memphis, TN
w/Jackie Fargo beat the Monk & Dream Machine w/Hart

Competed in A Battle Royal

Apr 13, 1982: Louisville, KY
(c) beat the Monk w/Hart
- Southern Title Match

Apr 14, 1982: Evansville, IN
(c) beat the Monk w/Hart
- Southern Title Match

Apr 15, 1982: Tell City, IN
(c) beat Norvell Austin
- Southern Title Match

Apr 17, 1982: Memphis, TN - TV results
beat Masked Invader

Apr 19, 1982: Memphis, TN
(c) beat Sonny King
- Southern Title Match

Apr 22, 1982: Bardstown, KY
(c) beat Norvell Austin
- Southern Title Match

Apr 25, 1982: Orlando, FL
w/Mike Graham lost to David Von Erich & Jim Garvin

Apr 26, 1982: Memphis, TN
& Dutch Mantell beat Dennis Condrey & Norvell Austin (Midnight Express)

Apr 27, 1982: Louisville, KY
(c) beat Sonny King
- Southern Title Match

Apr 28, 1982: Evansville, IN
(c) beat Sonny King
- Southern Title Match

May 1, 1982: Memphis, TN - TV results
& Dutch Mantel beat Ernie Kirkland & Masked Invader

May 2, 1982: Jackson, TN
& Dutch Mantell beat Dennis Condrey & Norvell Austin (Midnight Express)

*Photo Courtesy of Jim Cornette
Jerry Lawler & Dutch Mantell, Teaming Up Right After Their Feud.

May 3, 1982: Memphis, TN
w/Steve Keirn, Dutch Mantell & Bill Dundee lost to Sweet Brown Sugar, Norvell Austin, Dennis Condrey & Bobby Eaton w/Hart

May 4, 1982: Louisville, KY
& Dutch Mantell beat Dennis Condrey & Norvell Austin (Midnight Express)

May 5, 1982: Evansville, IN
& Dutch Mantell beat Dennis Condrey & Norvell Austin (Midnight Express)

May 6, 1982: Lexington, KY
& Dutch Mantell beat Dennis Condrey & Norvell
Austin (Midnight Express)

Competed in A Battle Royal

May 10, 1982: Memphis, TN
beat Jimmy Hart & JR Hart

May 11, 1982: Louisville, KY
w/Steve Keirn, Dutch Mantell & Bill Dundee lost
to Sweet Brown Sugar, Norvell Austin, Dennis
Condrey & Bobby Eaton w/Hart

May 12, 1982: Evansville, IN
w/Steve Keirn, Dutch Mantell & Bill Dundee lost
to Sweet Brown Sugar, Norvell Austin, Dennis
Condrey & Bobby Eaton w/Hart

May 17, 1982: Memphis, TN
w/Dutch Mantell beat Bobby Eaton & Sweet
Brown Sugar
- Lawler & Mantell were subs for Rick & Robert
Gibson.

* Rick Gibson was in a very serious car wreck.

May 18, 1982: Southaven, MS
won via DQ over Iron Sheik
* Show was listed as happening either 5/18 or
5/19.

May 22, 1982: Memphis, TN - TV results
Video is shown of Lawler vs. Kendo Nagasaki
from St. Petersburg, FL. Lawler is shown spitting
up blood at the end of the match. Lance Russell
says that match just took place a few days ago
and Lawler lost the Southern title to Nagasaki in
FL. Reality is the match took place way back in
February, and Lawler didn't drop the Southern
title to Nagasaki. This phantom title change was
used to help build the main event Monday Night
of Lawler vs. Nagasaki for the Southern title.

May 24, 1982: Memphis, TN
beat Kendo Nagasaki(c)
- Southern Title Match
- No DQ

May 25, 1982: Louisville, KY
& Dutch Mantell lost to Bobby Eaton & Sweet
Brown Sugar w/Hart
- Lights Out match

May 26, 1982: Evansville, IN
& Dutch Mantell lost to Bobby Eaton & Sweet
Brown Sugar w/Hart
- Lights out Match

May 28, 1982: Blytheville, AR
vs. Norvell Austin w/Hart

w/Bill Dundee, & Steve Keirn beat Dennis
Condrey, Norvell Austin & the Angel w/Hart

May 29, 1982: Memphis, TN - TV results
won via DQ over Bobby Eaton w/Hart
Video sent from JJ Dillon in FL talking about his
man Kamala that was coming to Memphis to
destroy Jerry Lawler.

May 31, 1982: Memphis, TN
(c) won by DQ over Kamala
- Southern Title Match

Jerry Lawler Getting Pounded By Kamala

June 1, 1982: Louisville, KY
(c)won via DQ over Bobby Eaton w/Hart
- Southern Title Match

June 2, 1982: Evansville, IN
(c) won via DQ over Bobby Eaton w/Hart
- Southern Title Match

June 3, 1982: Lexington, KY
(c) beat Kendo Nagasaki
- Southern Title Match

June 5, 1982: Nashville, TN
(c) won via DQ over Kamala
- Southern Title Match

June 6, 1982: Jackson, TN
& Bill Dundee vs Bobby Eaton & Sweet Brown
Sugar w/Hart
- Lights Out Match

June 7, 1982: Memphis, TN
(c) lost to Kamala
- Southern Title Match
- No DQ

June 8, 1982: Louisville, KY
(c) won via DQ over Kamala
- Southern Title Match

June 9, 1982: Evansville, IN
(c) won via DQ over Kamala
- Southern Title Match

June 10, 1982: Paoli, IN
beat Sweet Brown Sugar w/Hart

June 12, 1982: Memphis, TN - TV results
& Bill Dundee beat beat Tim Hudson & Masked
Invader

June 14, 1982: Memphis, TN
w/Bill Dundee won by DQ over Sweet Brown
Sugar & Bobby Eaton

June 15, 1982: Louisville, KY
(c) lost to Kamala
- Southern Title Match
- No DQ

June 16, 1982: Evansville, IN
 (c) lost to Kamala
- Southern Title Match
- No DQ

June 17, 1982: Jacksonville, FL
& Brian Blair beat Kendo Nagasaki & Derek
Draper

June 19, 1982: Nashville, TN
& Bill Dundee vs. Sweet Brown Sugar & Bobby
Eaton

June 21, 1982: Memphis, TN
& Carl Fergie won via DQ over Midnight
Express - Condrey & Austin(c) w/Hart
- Southern Tag Title Match
- Lawler & Fergie were subs for Steve Keirn &
Roy Rogers.

beat Bobby Eaton & Jimmy Hart
- Handicap Match

June 22, 1982: Louisville, KY
& Bill Dundee won by DQ over Sweet Brown
Sugar & Bobby Eaton w/Hart

June 23, 1982: Evansville, IN
& Bill Dundee won by DQ over Sweet Brown
Sugar & Bobby Eaton w/Hart

June 25, 1982: Blytheville, AR
won via DQ over Kamala

June 26, 1982: Memphis, TN - TV results
w/Bill Dundee, Dutch Mantel & Stan Lane beat
Gypsy Joe, the Angel, Masked Invader & Masked
Executioner

June 28, 1982: Memphis, TN
won via DQ over the iron Sheik
- Lawler wins he gets a Lumberjack Match
w/Hart

lost to Jimmy Hart
-Lumberjack match

June 29, 1982: Louisville, KY
beat Bobby Eaton & Jimmy Hart
- Handicap match

& Carl Fergie won via DQ over the Midnight
Express - Condrey & Austin(c) w/Hart
- Southern Tag Title Match

June 30, 1982: Nashville, TN
beat Bobby Eaton & Jimmy Hart
- Handicap match

& Carl Fergie won via DQ over the Midnight
Express - Condrey & Austin(c) w/Hart
- Southern Tag Title Match

July 1, 1982: Lexington, KY
lost via DQ to Kamala (c)
- Southern Title Match

& Bill Dundee beat Bobby Eaton & Sweet Brown Sugar w/Hart

July 3, 1982: Nashville, TN
& Bill Dundee beat Bobby Eaton & Sweet Brown Sugar w/Hart

July 5, 1982: Memphis, TN
won via Count Out over the Iron Sheik w/Hart
- No DQ
- If Lawler win's gets a Lumberjack match w/Hart

beat Jimmy Hart
- Lumberjack match

The King, Ready To Battle

July 6, 1982: Louisville, KY
won via DQ over the iron Sheik
- Lawler wins he gets a Lumberjack Match w/Hart

lost to Jimmy Hart
-Lumberjack match

July 7, 1982: Evansville, IN
won via DQ over the iron Sheik
- Lawler wins he gets a Lumberjack Match w/Hart

lost to Jimmy Hart
-Lumberjack match

July 8, 1982: Hopkinsville, KY
& Carl Fergie won via DQ over Midnight Express
- Condrey & Austin(c) w/Hart
- Southern Tag Title Match

July 12, 1982: Memphis, TN
lost to the Iron Sheik w/Hart
- Lumberjack Match
- Hart picked all the lumberjacks.

July 13, 1982: Louisville, KY
won via Count Out over Iron Sheik
- No DQ
- If Lawler wins, gets Hart in a Lumberjack Match

won via DQ over Jimmy Hart
- Lumberjack match

July 14, 1982: Evansville, IN
won via Count Out over Iron Sheik
- No DQ
- If Lawler wins, gets Hart in a Lumberjack Match

won via DQ over Jimmy Hart
- Lumberjack match

July 16, 1982: Blytheville, AR
lost to Kamala(c)
- Southern Title Match

July 17, 1982: Memphis, TN - TV results
beat the Invader

July 19, 1982: Memphis, TN
lost to Kamala(c) w/JJ Dillon
- Southern Title Match

July 20, 1982: Louisville, KY
lost to the iron Sheik
- Hart gets a Lumberjack Match w/Lawler, gets to pick lumberjacks

lost to Jimmy Hart
-Lumberjack match

July 21, 1982: Evansville, IN
lost to the Iron Sheik
- Hart gets a Lumberjack Match w/Lawler, gets to pick lumberjacks

lost to Jimmy Hart
-Lumberjack match

The Mouth of the South Baby!

July 22, 1982: Columbia, KY
won via DQ over Kamala(c)
- Southern Title Match

July 24, 1982: Memphis TV results
w/Dutch Mantell & Stan Lane beat Norvell Austin, Dennis Condrey & Sweet Brown Sugar

July 26, 1982: Memphis, TN
lost via DQ to JJ Dillon

July 31, 1982: Nashville, TN
vs. Kamala w/JJ Dillon
- Winner's choice dream match

Aug 2, 1982: Memphis, TN
& Bill Dundee won via DQ over Kamala & JJ Dillon
beat JJ Dillon

Aug 3, 1982: Louisville, KY
beat JJ Dillon

Aug 4, 1982: Evansville, IN
beat JJ Dillon

Aug 5, 1982: Lexington, KY
beat JJ Dillon

won via DQ over Kamala(c) w/JJ Dillon
- Southern Title Match

Aug 7, 1982: Memphis, TN TV results
& Bill Dundee beat the Angel & Sweet Brown Sugar w/Hart

Aug 7, 1982: Nashville, TN
vs. Kamala(c)
- Southern Title Match

Aug 9, 1982: Memphis, TN
beat Kamala(c) w/JJ Dillon
- Southern Title Match - No DQ
- Title vs. Lawler's Hair

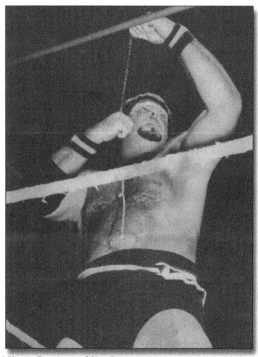

*Photo Courtesy of Jim Cornette
The King Pulls The Chain Out Of His Trunks.

Aug 10, 1982: Louisville, KY
lost via DQ to Kamala(c)
- Southern Title Match

Aug 11, 1982: Evansville, IN
lost via DQ to Kamala(c)
- Southern Title Match

Aug 13, 1982: Blytheville, AR
w/Dutch Mantell & King Cobra beat Kamala, Kim Chee & Dream Machine

Aug 14, 1982: Memphis, TN - TV results
von via Count Out over Ric Flair
- NWA World Title Match

* Was the first (and only) time the NWA World Title had ever been defended on the Sat Morning Memphis Wrestling show. Also the first time the NWA World Title had been defended in Memphis since Dec 19, 1977 (Lawler vs. Harley Race). This was also Ric Flair's first time wrestling in Memphis. What brought all this about? Arguably the Jerry Lawler - Andy Kaufman feud. April 5th was their match and saw Andy taking 2 piledrivers from the King. The next day the footage was on every newscast and the photos were in every newspaper across the country. It didn't end there, in late July, Jerry and Andy had an amazing appearance on David Letterman's Late show. That appearance was capped off with the "slap hear round the world". After being antagonized by the comedian for several minutes, Jerry proceeded to slap Andy so hard it rocked him out of his seat and onto the floor. With Jerry Lawler and Memphis Wrestling on such a national stage, actually twice in under four months, the NWA and more importantly Ric Flair wanted to be close to the action.

Aug 14, 1982 Houston, TX
lost to Bob Sweetan
- Pile Driver match

Aug 15, 1982: Harlingen, TX
vs. Bob Sweetan

Aug 16, 1982: Memphis, TN
& Bill Dundee beat Kamala & Kendo Nagasaki

Aug 17, 1982: Louisville, KY Gardens
(c) w/Hart beat Kamala w/JJ Dillon
- Southern Title Match
- No DQ

Aug 18, 1982: Evansville, IN
(c) w/Hart beat Kamala w/JJ Dillon
- Southern Title Match
- No DQ

Aug 21, 1982: Memphis, TN - TV results
won via DQ over Carl Fergie

Aug 21, 1982: St. Petersburg, FL
w/Butch Reed & Barry Windham won via DQ over John Studd, Bruiser Brody & Dory Funk Jr.

Aug 23, 1982: Memphis, TN
(c) beat Carl Fergie w/Hart
- Southern Title Match

Aug 26, 1982: Owensboro, KY
(c) beat Kamala
- Southern Title Match

Also in a Battle Royal

Aug 28, 1982: Indianapolis, IN - TV results
lost to the Great Kamala
w/Bill Dundee & Stan Lane beat Bobby Eaton, Dennis Condrey & Norvell Austin w/Hart

*There was a short-lived partnership between territory owner Jerry Jarrett & the WWA owned by Dick the Bruiser.

Aug 28, 1982: Booneville, MS
beat Bobby Eaton & Jimmy Hart

Aug 30, 1982: Memphis, TN
(c) won via DQ over Kamala w/Hart
- Southern Title Match

Aug 31, 1982: Louisville, KY
(c) beat Carl Fergie w/Hart
- Southern Title Match

Sep 1, 1982: Nashville, TN
& Jackie Fargo No Contest with Carl Fergie & Jimmy Hart

Sep 2, 1982: Lexington, KY
(c) beat Carl Fergie w/Hart
- Southern Title Match

Sep 4, 1982: Memphis, TN - TV results
beat the Dream Machine

Sep 4, 1982: Jonesboro, AR
(c) beat Kamala w/Hart
- Southern Title Match

Sep 5, 1982: Jackson, TN
(c) beat Carl Fergie w/Hart
- Southern Title Match

Sep 6, 1982: Memphis, TN
won via DQ over Baron Von Raschke
- Southern Title Match

Sep 13, 1982: Memphis, TN
(c) beat Super Destroyer w/Hart
- Southern Title Match

Sep 15, 1982: West Point, MS
(c) beat Kamala w/Hart
- Southern Title Match

Sep 20, 1982: Memphis, TN
& Terry Taylor won via DQ over Sweet Brown
Sugar & Bobby Eaton(c) /Hart
- Southern Tag Title Match
- Lawler was sub for Bill Dundee

& Dutch Mantell lost via DQ to Kamala II &
Crusher Brumfield w/Hart

* Crusher would soon change his name to One
Man Gang. Kamala II was Plowboy Frazier in
Kamala's ring getup & paint.

Sep 21, 1982: Louisville, KY
(c) beat Dutch Mantell
- Southern Title Match

Sep 22, 1982: Evansville, IN
(c) beat Dutch Mantell
- Southern Title Match

Sep 25, 1982: Memphis, TN TV results
beat Masked Enforcer

Sep 25, 1982: Memphis, TN
(c) beat Crusher Broomfield w/Hart
- Southern Title Match
- Title vs. $10,000
- Rare Sat night show

Won M/F Mixed Battle Royal

Sep 28, 1982: Louisville, KY
& Dutch Mantell won via DQ over Bobby Eaton &
Kamala w/Hart

Won Battle Royal

Sep 30, 1982: Tunnelton, IN
(c) beat Carl Fergie w/Hart
- Southern Title Match

Oct 1, 1982 Houston, TX
lost via DQ to Bob Sweetan

Oct 4, 1982: Memphis, TN
(c) won via DQ over Dutch Mantell
- Southern Title Match

Oct 5, 1982: Louisville, KY
(c) beat Kamala II
- Southern Title Match

Oct 7, 1982: Radcliff, KY
vs. Unknown

Oct 9, 1982: Nashville, TN
(c) won via DQ over Dutch Mantell
- Southern Title Match

Oct 10, 1982: Lexington, KY
Won 25-M/F Mixed Battle Royal

& Stan Lane beat Kamala I & Kamala II w/Hart
- Lane was a sub for Dutch Mantell

Oct 11, 1982: Memphis, TN
(c) lost to Nick Bockwinkel
- Southern Title Match

* beginning of a great angle involving Lawler,
Bockwinkel and the World Title. Nick argued he
always came to town and had to defend against
the onslaught of Jerry Lawler. This time he
informed Lance Russell that he was not going to
defend the AWA World Title against Jerry Lawler
because honestly the King had not earned that
title shot. Nick continued and said that he would
be challenging the King for his Southern Title.
Nick win the belt and came back to Memphis
every Monday night for the next month as Jerry
would challenge Nick for the Southern Title.
Eventually Jerry did get the big win against Nick
and showed the Memphis fans he had what it
took to get a clean pinfall win over Nick
Bockwinkel.

Oct 12, 1982: Louisville, KY
(c) won via DQ over Dutch Mantell
- Southern Title Match

Oct 13, 1982: Evansville, IN
(c) won via DQ over Dutch Mantell
- Southern Title Match

Oct 15, 1982: Blytheville, AR
(c) won via DQ over Dutch Mantell
- Southern Title Match

Oct 18, 1982: Memphis, TN Mid-South Coliseum, Monday
lost to Nick Bockwinkel(c)
- Southern Title Match
- Piledriver Legal in this match

Oct 19, 1982: Louisville, KY
won via DQ over Crusher Broomfield w/Jim Cornette

Oct 23, 1982: Savannah, TN
& Dutch Mantell beat the New York Dolls (Rick McGraw & Dream Machine) w/Hart

Oct 25, 1982: Memphis, TN
won via DQ over Nick Bockwinkel
- Southern Title Match

Oct 28, 1982: Nashville, TN Fairgrounds
won via DQ over Crusher Broomfield w/Jim Cornette

Oct 30, 1982: Memphis, TN TV results
& Bill Dundee beat Masked Marauders

*Photo Courtesy of Jim Cornette
Lance Russell Interviews Jerry Lawler

Nov 1, 1982: Memphis, TN
beat the Dream Machine

w/Jackie Fargo, Bill Dundee & The Fabulous Ones (Steve Keirn & Stan Lane) went to a No Contest with Bobby Eaton, Sweet Brown Sugar & New York Dolls: Dream Machine, Rick McGraw & Jimmy Hart
- Elimination Tag Match

Nov 5, 1982: Blytheville, AR
beat Crusher Broomfield w/Jim Cornette

Nov 6, 1982: Atlanta, GA - TV Taping
beat Randy Barber

Nov 7, 1982: Atlanta, GA
No Contest with Tommy Rich
- Due to outside interference.

* Ole Anderson brought in Lawler as a heel to have a feud with Roddy Piper. Their first match was scheduled to take place at the Omni on Nov 7, 1982. The issue was Ole Anderson fired Piper 3 hours before their match. The match was switched to Tommy Rich vs. Jerry Lawler. It was also decided to turn the King into a babyface in Atlanta. During this Omni match between Lawler & Rich, Rich was attacked by Ivan Koloff and Maddog Buzz Sawyer. Lawler quickly helped Rich fight off the sneak attack and turned babyface.

Nov 8, 1982: Memphis, TN
beat Nick Bockwinkel(c)
- Southern Title Match
- No DQ
- Lawler's hair vs. title

Nov 9, 1982: Louisville, KY
w/the Fabulous Ones & Bill Dundee beat Jimmy Hart, Bobby Eaton, Koko Ware & the New York Dolls

Won via DQ over Bobby Eaton

Nov 10, 1982: Evansville, IN
w/Bill Dundee & the Fabulous Ones (Keirn & Lane) beat Jimmy Hart, Bobby Eaton, Sweet Brown Sugar & New York Dolls (McGraw & Dream Machine)
-- Elimination Tag Match

Won via DQ over Bobby Eaton

Nov 15, 1982: Memphis, TN
(c) lost to Sabu (Cocoa Samoa) w/Hart
- Southern Title Match

& Bill Dundee lost to the Sheepherders (Jon Boyd & Luke Williams)

Nov 21, 1982: San Antonio, TX
& Tully Blanchard vs. Bob Sweetan & Scott Casey

Nov 22, 1982: Memphis, TN
& Bill Dundee lost to the Sheepherders

Beat Jimmy Hart & Sweet Brown Sugar
- Handicap match

Nov 23, 1982: Louisville, KY
& Bill Dundee lost via DQ to the Sheepherders

Nov 24, 1982: Evansville, IN
& Bill Dundee lost via DQ to the Sheepherders

Nov 27, 1982: Memphis, TN TV results
& Bill Dundee beat Bobby Eaton & Sweet Brown Sugar w/Hart

Nov 29, 1982: Memphis, TN
& Bill Dundee beat the Sheepherders
- No DQ

Nov 30, 1982: Louisville, KY
w/Bill Dundee lost the Sheepherders

Dec 2, 1982: Lexington, KY
& Bill Dundee lost via DQ to the Sheepherders
- Lights out match

won via DQ over Sabu(c) w/Hart
- Southern Title Match

Dec 3, 1982: Blytheville, AR
& Bill Dundee beat the Sheepherders
- No DQ

Dec 5, 1982: Memphis, TN
& Bill Dundee won via DQ over the New York Dolls(c) w/Hart
- World Tag Title Match

Won 22-Man Battle Royal
(1)Jerry Lawler- WINNER
(2)Adrian Street
(3)Apocalypse
(4)Bill Dundee
(5)Bobby Eaton
(6) Sweet Brown Sugar
(7)Dutch Mantell
(8)Dream Machine
(9)Jacques Rougeau
(10)Steve Keirn
(11)Jon Boyd
(12)Stan Lane
(13)Luke Williams
(14)Bobby Fulton
(15)Rick McGraw
(16)Terry Taylor

(17)Sabu
(18)Jesse Barr
(19)Jimmy Hart
(20)Steve Regal
(21)Spike Huber
(22) Jim Cornette

Dec 7, 1982: Louisville, KY
& Bill Dundee beat the Sheepherders
- No DQ Match

Dec 8, 1982: Evansville, IN
& Bill Dundee beat the Sheepherders
- No DQ Match

Dec 13, 1982: Memphis, TN
beat Jimmy Hart
- Cage Match
- No DQ - No Ref Inside Cage

Dec 18, 1982: Chicago, IL
beat Steve Regal

Dec 20, 1982: Memphis, TN
beat Sabu

Dec 27, 1982: Memphis, TN
beat Nick Bockwinkel (c)
-AWA World Title Match

* Lawler did get the pinfall though Nick's legs were draped over the bottom rope. Dazed ref Jerry Calhoun did not see the Nick's legs over the bottom rope. The AWA World Title was held up and these two would fight for it in Memphis in a few weeks.

Dec 28, 1982: Louisville, KY
& the Fabulous Ones beat the Sheepherders & Sabu w/Hart

1983

Chapter 14

Jan 4, 1983: Louisville, KY
beat Sabu w/Hart

*Photo Courtesy of Jim Cornette
Sabu & Bobby Eaton

Jan 7, 1983: Blytheville, AR
beat Sabu w/Hart

Jan 9, 1983: Jackson, TN 3pm
beat Sabu w/Hart

Jan 10, 1983: Memphis, TN
lost to Nick Bockwinkel
- AWA World Title Held Up.
- Winner of match gets World Title.

*Jimmy Hart seemingly interfered in the match ultimately causing Jerry to lose. Because of Lawler throwing fire at Jimmy Hart weeks earlier, he was wearing sort of a Mummy wrap around his head. As the match ended, Jimmy Hart came out to the ring to congratulate this Mummy headed person. When the person took the Mummy mask off it was revealed it had been Andy Kaufman at ringside the night. This was the first the Memphis fans had seen Kaufman since the incident on the David Letterman Show 6 months earlier. The fans who thought the Lawler-Kaufman feud was over were wrong, it was only just beginning.

Jan 13, 1983: Lexington, KY
beat Sabu w/Hart

Jan 14, 1983: Tupelo, MS
beat Sabu w/Hart

Jan 15, 1983: Memphis, TN - TV results
Jerry Lawler beat Invader

Jan 15, 1983: Chicago, IL
beat Tom Stone

Jan 16, 1983: San Antonio, TX
w/Bob Sweetan lost to Adrian Adonis & Tully Blanchard

Jan 17, 1983: Memphis, TN
& Koko Ware lost via DQ to Sabu & Bobby Eaton - Babyface turn for Sweet Brown Sugar/Koko Ware

*Photo Courtesy of Jim Cornette
Koko Ware & Jerry Lawler

Jan 18, 1983: Louisville, KY
beat Apocalypse w/Jim Cornette

Jan 19, 1983: Evansville, IN
beat Apocalypse w/Jim Cornette

Jan 22, 1983: Memphis, TN - TV results
went to a draw with Sabu w/Hart

Jan 24, 1983: Memphis, TN
& Koko Ware lost to Bobby Eaton & Sabu w/Hart
- No DQ

Jan 25, 1983: Louisville, KY
& Koko Ware lost via DQ to Bobby Eaton & Sabu
/Hart

Jan 26, 1983: Evansville, IN
& Koko Ware lost via DQ to Bobby Eaton & Sabu
w/Hart

Jan 29, 1983: Memphis, TN - TV results
w/Terry Funk & Koko Ware beat the Masked
Marauders & Jesse Barr w/Jim Cornette

Jan 30, 1983: Memphis, TN
w/Terry Funk & Koko Ware beat Carl Fergie,
Bobby Eaton & Sabu w/Hart
- Texas Death Match

Feb 1, 1983: Louisville, KY
& Koko Ware lost to Bobby Eaton & Sabu w/Hart
- No DQ

Feb 2, 1983: Evansville, IN
& Koko Ware lost to Bobby Eaton & Sabu w/Hart
- No DQ

Feb 3, 1983: Lexington, KY
& Koko Ware beat Bobby Eaton & Sabu w/Hart

Feb 4, 1983: Blytheville, AR
& Koko Ware beat Bobby Eaton & Sabu w/Hart

Feb 4, 1983: Jonesboro, AR
& Koko Ware beat Bobby Eaton & Sabu w/Hart

Feb 6, 1983: Jackson, TN 3pm
& Koko Ware beat Bobby Eaton & Sabu w/Hart

Feb 6, 1983: Memphis, TN 7pm
& Koko Ware beat Bobby Eaton & Sabu w/Hart

Feb 7, 1983: Louisville, KY
& Koko Ware beat Bobby Eaton & Sabu w/Hart
- Texas Death Match

Feb 9, 1983: Evansville, IN
& Koko Ware beat Bobby Eaton & Sabu w/Hart
- Texas Death Match

Feb 12, 1983: Chicago, IL
beat Ken Patera

Feb 13, 1983: St. Paul, MN
beat Tom Lintz

Feb 14, 1983: Memphis, TN
No Contest with Nick Bockwinkel(c)
- AWA World Title Match
- No Seconds or Managers

Feb 19, 1983: Memphis, TN - TV results
& Terry Taylor, Koko Ware & King Cobra beat
Masked Invader, Jesse Barr, Masked Marauder &
Masked Destroyer

Feb 20, 1983: Memphis, TN
beat by forfeit with Nick Bockwinkel(c)
- AWA World Title Match
- No DQ

* Bockwinkel could not make it to town because
of bad weather in Minneapolis, MN. Title did not
change hands.

lost to Austin Idol
- No DQ

Feb 22, 1983: Louisville, KY
lost via DQ to Nick Bockwinkel(c)
- AWA World Title Match

Feb 23, 1983: Evansville, IN
lost via DQ to Nick Bockwinkel(c)
- AWA World Title Match

Feb 26, 1983: Milwaukee, WI
beat Sgt. Goulet

Feb 27, 1983: Denver, CO
beat Sgt. Goulet

Mar 1, 1983: Memphis, TN
lost to Austin Idol(c)
- International Title Match

Mar 2, 1983: Evansville, IN
beat Austin Idol(c)
- International Title Match

Mar 3, 1983: Lexington, KY
beat Austin Idol(c)
- International Title Match

Mar 5, 1983: Memphis, TN TV results
beat Pat Hutchinson

Mar 5, 1983: San Francisco, CA
beat John Tolos
Mar 6, 1983: Jackson, TN
beat Austin Idol(c)
- International Title Match

Mar 7, 1983: Memphis, TN
beat Austin Idol(c)
- International Title Match

Jerry Lawler - International Champ

Mar 8, 1983: Salt Lake City, UT
beat John Tolos

Mar 9, 1983: Las Vegas, NV
beat John Tolos
Mar 11, 1983: Tupelo, MS
& Rick Morton lost to Bruise Brothers (Porkchop Cash & Maddog) w/Hart

Mar 13, 1983: Memphis, TN
w/Stagger Lee & Bill Dundee lost to Bobby Eaton & the Bruise Brothers

* Stagger Lee was actually Koko Ware in a mask. Koko had lost a Loser Leaves Town

Match the previous week in Memphis against Bobby Eaton w/Jimmy Hart. It ended up being a great angle for Koko because the Stagger Lee character was hugely popular and over with the fans. The promotion was playing Koko as the huge underdog. Jimmy Hart had booted him out of the First Family and additionally had all those family members out to get Koko. While Koko's loss to Eaton would exile him from Memphis for three months, if Hart's guys unmask Stagger Lee and expose Koko, he will be exiled for a full year.

Mar 15, 1983: Louisville, KY
lost to AWA Champ Nick Bockwinkel
- AWA World Title Match
- No DQ

Mar 16, 1983: Evansville, IN
lost to AWA Champ Nick Bockwinkel
- AWA World Title Match
- No DQ

Mar 17, 1983: Nicholasville, KY
& Rick Morton beat The Bruise Brothers: Porkchop Cash & Troy Graham (Dream Machine) w/Hart

Mar 19, 1983: Memphis, TN - TV results
Jerry Lawler & Stagger Lee beat Rooster Cogburn & Pat Hutchinson

Mar 19, 1983: Helena, AR
& Stagger Lee won via DQ over The Bruise Brothers: Porkchop Cash & Troy Graham (Dream Machine) w/Hart

Also won Battle Royal

Mar 20, 1983: Denver, CO
beat Ken Patera

Mar 21, 1983: Memphis, TN
w/Stagger Lee & Andre the Giant beat the Bruise Brothers (Cash & Graham) & Bobby Eaton w/Hart
*Andre's last Memphis appearance for the Jarrett Promotion

Mar 23, 1983: Southaven, MS
(c) beat Sabu w/Hart
- International Title Match

Won Battle Royal

*Lawler's band played from 7p-8p
Mar 24, 1983: Winnipeg, Manitoba
beat John Tolos

Mar 25, 1983: Milwaukee, WI
beat John Tolos

Mar 26, 1983: Rockford, IL
beat John Tolos

Mar 26, 1983: Green Bay, WI
beat John Tolos

Mar 28, 1983: Memphis, TN
(c) beat Bobby Eaton w/Hart
- International Title Match

Mar 31, 1983: Nashville, TN
& Stagger Lee won via DQ with the Bruise
Brothers w/Hart

Apr 4, 1983: Memphis, TN
lost via DQ to Nick Bockwinkel(c)
- AWA World Title Match

Apr 7, 1983: Lexington, KY
won via DQ over Nick Bockwinkel(c)
- AWA World Title Match

Apr 11, 1983: Memphis, TN
won via DQ over Nick Bockwinkel(c)
- AWA World Title Match
- No Ref inside ring

Apr 12, 1983: Louisville, KY
won via DQ over Nick Bockwinkel(c)
- AWA World Title Match
- No Ref inside ring

Apr 16, 1983: Chicago, IL
lost to Nick Bockwinkel(c)
- AWA World Title Match

Apr 18, 1983: Memphis, TN
(c) beat Duke Myers w/Jim Cornette
- International Title Match

beat Jimmy Hart & Jim Cornette
- Special Challenge Match

Apr 23, 1983: Milwaukee, WI
won via Count Out over Bobby Heenan

Apr 24, 1983: St. Paul, MN
beat John Tolos

Apr 25, 1983: Memphis, TN
(c) beat Tully Blanchard
- International Title Match

Aug 27, 1983: Nashville, TN
(c) vs. Duke Myers
- International Title Match

May 2, 1983: Memphis, TN
beat the Colossus of Death & Andy Kaufman
- Handicap match
- Piledriver Match
- COD was Duke Myers

Jerry Lawler Dropping The Big Fist On The
Colossus Of Death.

May 4, 1983: Evansville, IN
(c) beat Duke Myers w/Jim Cornette
- International Title Match

May 5, 1983: Lexington, KY
won via DQ over Nick Bockwinkel(c)
- AWA World Title Match

May 9, 1983: Memphis, TN
beat Colossus of Death

May 15, 1983: Milwaukee, WI
lost via DQ to Ken Patera

May 16, 1983: Memphis, TN
(c) lost to Ken Patera w/Hart
- International Title Match

Jerry Lawler vs. Ken Patera

May 17, 1983: Louisville, KY
beat the Colossus of Death
- C.o.D. was a sub for Ken Patera

May 21, 1983: Chicago, IL
No Contest with Nick Bockwinkel(c)
- AWA World Title Match

May 23, 1983: Memphis, TN
lost to Ken Patera(c) w/Hart
- International Title Match
- Title vs. Lawler's $5,000

May 24, 1983: Louisville, KY
lost to Ken Patera w/Hart
- International Title Match

May 30, 1983: Memphis, TN
lost to Bill Dundee(c)
- Southern Title Match

May 31, 1983: Louisville, KY
lost to Ken Patera(c) w/Hart
- International Title Match
- Title vs. Lawler's $5,000

June 1, 1983: Evansville, IN
lost to Ken Patera(c) w/Hart
- International Title Match

Ken Patera Has Jerry Lawler In Trouble

June 2, 1983: Lexington, KY
beat Bill Dundee(c)
- Southern Title Match
- No DQ - Loser Leaves Town Match

June 4, 1983: Memphis, TN - TV Taping
beat Jim Jamison

June 4, 1983: Nashville, TN
beat Bill Dundee(c)
- Southern Title Match
- No DQ - Loser Leaves Town Match

June 5, 1983: Jackson, TN
beat Bill Dundee(c)
- Southern Title Match
- No DQ - Loser Leaves Town Match

June 6, 1983: Memphis, TN
beat Bill Dundee(c)
- Southern Title Match
- No DQ - Loser Leaves Town Match

June 7, 1983: Louisville, KY
beat Bill Dundee(c)
- Southern Title Match
- No DQ - Loser Leaves Town Match

June 13, 1983: Memphis, TN
(c) lost to Man Mountain Link w/Hart
- Southern Title Match

June 18, 1983: Chicago, IL
w/Wahoo McDaniel & Dick the Bruiser beat Nick Bockwinkel, Jesse Ventura & Blackjack Lanza

June 20, 1983: Memphis, TN
beat Man Mountain Link(c) w/Hart
- Southern Title Match

won via DQ over Ken Patera(c) w/Hart
- International Title Match

Jerry Lawler Turns The Tide VS. Ken Patera

June 25, 1983: Jonesboro, AR
(c) beat Man Mountain Link w/Hart
- Southern Title Match

June 27, 1983: Memphis, TN
& Austin Idol beat Ken Patera & Man Mountan Link w/Hart

- If Lawler Pins Patera, he gets a future match against Andy Kaufman.

June 29, 1983: Nashville, TN
won via DQ over Man Mountain Link(c) w/Hart
- Southern Title Match

July 1, 1983: Blytheville, AR
won via DQ pver Man Mountain Link(c) w/Hart
- Southern Title Match

July 4, 1983: Memphis, TN
beat Man Mountain Link(c) w/Hart
- Southern Title Match

Won 30-Man Battle Royal - Prize: 1984 Corvette

lost via DQ to Andy Kaufman & Jimmy Hart
- Handicap Match

*Photo Courtesy of Jim Cornette
Andy Kaufman & Jimmt Hart Attacking Jerry Lawler.

July 5, 1983: Louisville, KY Gardens, Tuesday
lost via DQ to Andy Kaufman & Man Mountain Link w/Hart

July 7, 1983: Lexington, KY
beat Ken Patera & Andy Kaufman w/Hart
- Handicap match

July 8, 1983: Oxford, MS
(c) beat Man Mountain Link w/Hart
- Southern Title Match

July 9, 1983: Memphis, TN - TV Taping
beat Jeff Van Camp

w/Austin Idol, Bobby Eaton & Stagger Lee beat
Don Bass, Jimmy Kent, Man Mountain Link &
Duke Myers

July 10, 1983: Jackson, TN
(c) beat Man Mountain Link w/Hart
- Southern Title Match

July 11, 1983: Memphis, TN
& Austin Idol lost to the Bruise Brothers

Jerry Lawler & Austin Idol Form A Tag Team

July 16, 1983: Memphis, TN - TV results
Andy Kaufman asks Jerry Lawler to be his
partner Monday night against Jimmy Hart and
his Assassin. Lawler reluctantly accepts.

July 18, 1983: Memphis, TN
& Andy Kaufman No Contest with Jimmy Hart &
the Assassin

*** The feud between Kaufman & Hart had
been a plan the entire time. Kaufman
turned on Lawler and all three men beat
him up.**

& Austin idol beat the Bruise Brothers (Cash &
Graham) w/Hart

July 25, 1983: Memphis, TN
beat Ken Patera(c) w/Hart
- International Title Match

& Austin Idol beat the Assassins(c) w/Hart
- World Tag Title Match
- Assassins were Roger Smith & Don Bass

*** These "World Tag Titles" were not from
one of the Big 3 (AWA, NWA or WWF).**

They were the ones that Spike Huber &
Steve Regal had originally brought with
them in back in the Fall of 1982 (from Dick
the Bruiser's WWA out of Indianapolis, IN.)
When the deal with Bruiser fell through,
Huber, Regal & the belts stayed. While
Jarrett keep using the belts, he left the
"CWA" off the description.

July 28, 1983: Nashville, TN
& Bobby Eaton beat the Moondogs

Aug 1, 1983: Memphis, TN
& Austin Idol(c) lost to the Assassins w/Hart
- World Tag Title Match

(c) beat Ken Patera w/Hart
- International Title Match
- Lou Thesz was special referee

Aug 4, 1983: Lexington, KY
& Austin Idol(c) lost to the Assassins w/Hart
- World Tag Title Match

Aug 7, 1983: Jackson, TN
& Austin Idol won via DQ over the Assassins(c)
- World Tag Title Match

Aug 8, 1983: Memphis, TN
(c) beat the Prince of Darkness
- International Title Match
- P.o.D. was Duke Myers under a mask

& Austin Idol beat the Assassins(c) w/Hart
- World Tag Title Match

Aug 9, 1983: Louisville, KY
& Austin Idol(c) won via DQ over the Assassins
w/Hart
- World Tag Title Match

Aug 15, 1983: Memphis, TN
& Austin Idol(c) lost to the Assassins w/Hart
- World Tag Title Match
- Titles vs. Hart's Hair Color

(c) lost to Ken Patera w/Hart
- International Title Match

Aug 16, 1983: Louisville, KY
beat the Prince of Darkness
- Prince Of Darkness was Duke Myers

& Austin Idol beat the Assassins(c) w/Hart
- World Tag Title Match
- Titles vs. Lawler's & Idol's Hair Color

Aug 22, 1983: Memphis, TN
w/Austin Idol & Jimmy Valiant lost via DQ to the
Assassins & Ken Patera w/Hart

Ken Patera Is About To Launch Jerry Lawler

Aug 26, 1983: St. Louis, MO
& David Von Erich beat Blackjack Mulligan &
Blackjack Lanza

Aug 29, 1983: Memphis, TN
w/Austin Idol & Jimmy Valiant beat the
Assassins & Ken Patera w/Hart
- No DQ Match

Sep 4, 1983: Memphis, TN - TV
WMC-TV5 debuts The Jerry Lawler Show

Jerry Lawler Gets his Own Show.

Sep 4, 1983: Jackson, TN
vs. Ken Patera(c) w/Hart
- International Title Match

Sep 5, 1983: Memphis, TN
Southern Title Tournament
Round 1
beat Dennis Condrey
Bill Dundee beat Dutch Mantell

Finals
beat Bill Dundee
- Lawler wins Southern Title

The King Reverses A Pin Attempt By Bill
Dundee

Sep 12, 1983: Memphis, TN
(c) lost to Jesse Ventura w/Hart
- Southern Title Match

Sep 13, 1983: Louisville, KY
beat Dennis Condrey w/Hart

Sep 19, 1983: Memphis, TN
lost to Jesse Ventura(c) w/Hart
- Southern Title Match

Sep 20, 1983: Louisville, KY
lost to Jesse Ventura(c) w/Hart
- Southern Title Match

Sep 26, 1983: Memphis, TN
& Austin Idol won via DQ over Stan Hansen &
Jesse Venura w/Hart

Oct 3, 1983: Memphis, TN
w/San Diego Chicken beat Jesse Ventura(c)
w/Hart
- Southern Title Match - No DQ

San Diego Chicken & Jerry Lawler

Oct 6, 1983: Lexington, KY
w/San Diego Chicken beat Jesse Ventura(c)
w/Hart
- Southern Title Match - No DQ

Oct 10, 1983: Memphis, TN
(c) lost to Jesse Ventura w/Hart
- Southern Title Match - No DQ

& Bill Dundee won by DQ over the Bruise
Brothers w/Hart

Oct 15, 1983: Osceola, AR
beat the Russian Invader w/Hart
- Russian Invader was Jerry Novak

Oct 17, 1983: Memphis, TN
w/Roughhouse Fargo, Jimmy Valiant, Austin Idol
& the Fabulous Ones lost to Jesse Ventura,
Buddy Landell, Dennis Condrey, Norvell Austin &
the Masked Assassins w/Hart
- Hospital Elimination Match

& Austin Idol beat the Assassins w/Hart

Oct 18, 1983: Louisville, KY
& Bill Dundee won via DQ the Assassins(c)
w/Hart
- World Tag Title Match

Oct 19, 1983: Evansville, IN
& Bill Dundee vs. the Assassins(c) w/Hart
- World Tag Title Match

Oct 24, 1983: Memphis, TN
& Bill Dundee won via DQ over the Moondogs
w/Hart

Oct 26, 1983: Evansville, IN
& Bill Dundee beat the Bruise Brothers w/Hart

Oct 29, 1983: Nashville, TN
& Bill Dundee won via DQ over the Moondogs
w/Hart

Oct 31, 1983: Memphis, TN
w/Austin Idol & Dutch Mantell beat the
Moondogs & Man Mountain Link.

Nov 1, 1983: Louisville, KY
& Bill Dundee won via DQ over the Moondogs
w/Hart

Nov 3, 1983: Lexington, KY
& Bill Dundee won via DQ over the Moondogs
w/Hart

Nov 6, 1983: Jackson, TN
& Bill Dundee won via DQ over the Moondogs
w/Hart

Nov 7, 1983: Memphis, TN
w/Austin Idol & Dutch Mantell No Contest with
The Moondogs and Man Mountain Link w/Hart
- Falls Count Anywhere

Nov 12, 1983: Memphis, TN - TV Taping
beat Jeff Briggs

Nov 14, 1983: Memphis, TN
lost via DQ to Jimmy Hart & Andy Kaufman
- Handicap Boxing match

Nov 19, 1983: Memphis, TN - TV Taping
won via DQ over Buddy Landell

Nov 19, 1983: Nashville, TN
w/Dutch Mantell & Koko Ware vs. the Moondogs
& Man Mountain Link in An Explosive Match

Nov 19, 1983: Nashville, TN
vs. Man Mountain Link

Nov 21, 1983: Memphis, TN
(c) beat the Russian Invader w/Hart
- Southern Title Match

beat Andy Kaufman w/Hart
- 10 Round Boxing Match

* Last Match For Andy Kaufman. He would occasionally send in some videos to the Memphis Wrestling show and Jerry Lawler show, but this was Andy's last, in ring appearance For Andy in the Jarrett territory. After two years, it was over.

Nov 22, 1983: Louisville, KY
w/Austin Idol & Dutch Mantell beat the Moondogs & Jimmy Hart
- Falls Count Anywhere

Nov 24, 1983: Jackson, TN
beat Bill Dundee
Grudge Match

Nov 28, 1983: Memphis, TN
(c) beat Ken Patera w/Hart
- Southern Title Match

Nov 29, 1983: Louisville, KY
(c) beat Ken Patera w/Hart
- Southern Title Match

(c) beat Russian Invader w/Hart
- Southern Title Match

Dec 4, 1983: Jackson, TN
Jackson Tag Tournament
& Terry Taylor No Contest with Bill Dundee & Russian Invader

Dec 5, 1983: Memphis, TN
(c) won via DQ over Randy Savage
- Southern Title Match

Dec 7, 1983: Shreveport, LA Watt's TV Taping
beat Larry Higgins

Dec 12, 1983: Memphis, TN
won via DQ over Randy savage
- Southern Title Match
- Steel Cage Match

Dec 13, 1983: Louisville, KY
(c) beat Bill Dundee
- Southern Title Match

Dec 19, 1983: Memphis, TN
& Austin Idol won via DQ over Joe Leduc & Randy Savage

Dec 24, 1983: Memphis, TN - TV Taping
& Cowboy Lang beat Plowboy Frazier & Little Tokyo

Dec 26, 1983: Memphis, TN
beat Austin Idol w/Hart
- Winner gets AWA World Title shot
- Hart turned on Idol in the match

1984

Chapter 15

Jan 1, 1984: Memphis, TN
won via DQ over Nick Bockwinkel(c)
- AWA World Title Match

Jan 3, 1984: Louisville, KY
& Austin Idol beat Plowboy Frazier & Sabu
w/Hart

Jan 4, 1984: Evansville, IN
& Austin Idol No Contest with the Road Warriors

Jan 5, 1984: Lexington, KY
& Austin Idol No Contest with the Road Warriors

Jan 7, 1994: Nashville, TN
w/Dutch Mantell beat the Moondogs w/Hart
- Loser Leaves Town Match

Jan 8, 1984: Jackson, TN
(c) beat Joe Leduc w/Hart
- Southern Title Match

Jan 9, 1984: Memphis, TN
lost via reverse decision to Nick Bockwinkel(c)
- AWA World Title Match
- No DQ
- Two ref, one is Austin Idol
- $500 fine for each illegal punch
- Lawler pinned Bockinkel but AWA Pres.
Stanley Blackburn reverses decision and gives
Nick the win,

Jan 10, 1984: Louisville, KY
won via DQ over Nick Bockwinkel(c)
- AWA World Title Match

Jan 11, 1984: Evansville, In
won via DQ over Nick Bockwinkel(c)
- AWA World Title Match

Jan 15, 1984: Atlanta, GA
Double Count Out with Jake Roberts(c)
- National TV Title Match

Jan 16, 1984: Memphis, TN
(c) won via DQ over Killer Karl Krupp w/Hart
- Southern Title Match

Jan 23, 1984: Louisville, KY
lost via reverse decision to Nick Bockwinkel(c)
- AWA World Title Match
- No DQ
- Two ref, one is Austin Idol
- $500 fine for each illegal punch
- Lawler pinned Bockinkel but AWA Pres.
Stanley Blackburn reverses decision and gives
Nick the win.

Jan 24, 1984: Memphis, TN
& Austin Idol won via DQ over Jerry Blackwell &
Ken Patera(c)
- AWA World Tag Title Match

Jan 27, 1984: Cleveland, OH
& Jimmy Valiant lost via DQ to King Kong Bundy
& Bob Roop

Jerry Lawler & Jimmy Valiant

Jan 28, 1984: Memphis, TN - TV results
& Dutch Mantel beat The Street Walkers

Jan 31, 1984: Memphis, TN
& Austin Idol Double DQ with the Road Warriors
- 1st Round - Neither Team Advances
- Southern Tag Title Tournament

Road Warrior Hawk Stalks Jerry Lawler.

Feb 2, 1984: Nashville, TN
(c) vs. Randy Savage
- Southern Title Match

Feb 4, 1984: Memphis, TN - TV Taping
Jerry Lawler, Austin Idol & Dutch Mantel beat
Lou Winston, Pink Panther & the Masked
Marauder

Memphis tape, Jan 31, 1984: Jerry Lawler &
Austin Idol vs. Road Warriors

Feb 5, 1984: Jackson, TN
& Austin Idol beat Joe Leduc & Kong Konga
w/Hart

Feb 6, 1984: Memphis, TN
& Austin Idol beat the Road Warriors
- No DQ

Feb 7, 1984: Louisville, KY
& Austin Idol lost via DQ to the Zambui Express
(Ellijah Akeem & Kareem Muhammad)
- Southern Tag Title Tournament
- Opening Round Match
- Zambui Express won tourny & titles

Feb 8, 1984: Evansville, IN, Wednesday
w/Austin Idol & Dutch Mantel vs. Joe Leduc,
Randy Savage & Jimmy Hart

Lawler & Idol: A Tough Team To Beat.

(c) beat Killer Karl Krupp w/Hart
- Southern Title Match

Feb 11, 1984: Memphis, TN - TV Taping
Lance Russell interviews Jerry Lawler who
introduces Harley Davidson

Feb 18, 1984: Memphis, TN - TV Taping
Lance Russell interviews Jerry Lawler

Jerry Lawler (Southern champ) by DQ beat King
Konga
-Zambui Express runs in, dressing room door
held as Lawler gets pummeled
Feb 19, 1984: Memphis, TN
beat King Konga
Lumberjack Match

& Austin Idol via DQ over Zambui Express (c)
- Southern Tag Title Match

Feb 21, 1984: Louisville, KY
& Austin Idol won via DQ over Joe Leduc &
Randy Savage

Feb 22, 1984: Evansville, IN,
Austin Idol & Jerry Lawler vs. Joe LeDuc &
Randy Savage

Feb 25, 1984: Memphis, TN - TV Taping
Lance Russell interviews Austin Idol and Jerry
Lawler

Feb 28, 1984: Memphis, TN
w/Austin Idol & Tommy Rich won via DQ over
the Zambui Express & King Konga

Feb 29: 1984: Nashville, TN
w/Tommy Rich vs. Zambui Express(c)
- Southern Tag Title Match

Mar 3, 1984: Memphis, TN - TV results
Memphis, TN tape, Feb 28, 1984: Jerry Lawler,
Austin Idol & Tommy Rich vs. Zambui Express
-Joe LeDuc & Jimmy Hart run in to help Lawler

Mar 3, 1984: Nashville, TN
& Dutch Mantell vs. Zambui Express(c) -
Southern Tag Title Match

Mar 4, 1984: Rosemont, IL
& Blackjack Mulligan lost to Ken Patera & Jerry
Blackwell(c)
- AWA World Tag Title Match

Mar 5, 1984: Memphis, TN
& Joe Leduc w/Hart lost via DQ to the Zambui
Express(c)
-Southern Tag Title

Mar 6, 1984: Louisville, KY
& Austin Idol won via DQ over the Zambui
Express(c)
- Southern Tag Title Match

beat King Konga
Lights Out - Lumberjack match

Mar 7, 1984: Evansville, IN
Jerry Lawler (Southern champ) vs. Randy
Savage (Mid-America champ)

Mar 8, 1984: Lexington, KY
drew with Randy Savage

Mar 10, 1984: Nashville, TN
& Joe Leduc vs. the Zambui Express(c)
-Southern Tag Title Match

Mar 12, 1984: Memphis, TN
Joe Leduc & Hart beat the Zambui Express(c)
- Southern Tag Title Match

Strange Tag Team: Lawler & Joe Leduc

Mar 13, 1984: Louisville, KY
& Joe Leduc drew with the Zambui Express(c)
- Southern Tag Title Match

Mar 17, 1984: Nashville, TN
& Joe Leduc vs. the Zambui Express(c)
- Southern Tag Title Match
- No DQ
Mar 18, 1984: Memphis, TN
w/Joe Leduc & Jimmy Hart beat JJ Dillon,
Kareem Muhammad & King Konga
- Leduc & Hart have falling out with Lawler
during match and leave the ring. Lawler wins
match & titles on his own

Mar 20, 1984: Louisville, KY
& Joe Leduc beat the Zambui Express
- Southern Tag Title Match
- No DQ

Mar 26, 1984: Memphis, TN
(c) beat Joe Leduc w/Hart
- Southern Title Match

Mar 31, 1984: Nashville, TN
(c) beat Joe Leduc w/Hart
- Southern Title Match

Apr 1, 1984: Jackson, TN afternoon show
won via DQ over Randy Savage w/Hart
- Lawler's Southern Title vs. Savage's Mid-
America Title.

Apr 1, 1984: Atlanta, GA evening show
& Austin Idol went to a No Contest with the
Road Warriors(c)
- National Tag Title Match

Apr 2, 1984: Memphis, TN
Boogie Jam 84
& JJ Dillon beat Jimmy Hart & Randy Savage
(Savage is sub for Joe Leduc)

Jimmy Valiant beat Assassin II w/Paul Jones
- Hair vs. mask,
- Paul Jones handcuffed to Jerry Lawler
- Assassin unmasked as Ray Hernandez

Apr 3, 1984: Louisville, KY
& JJ Dillon beat Jimmy Hart & Joe Leduc

Apr 9, 1984: Memphis, TN
(c) beat Randy Savage(c) w/Hart
- Lawler's Southern Title vs. Savage's Mid-
America Title

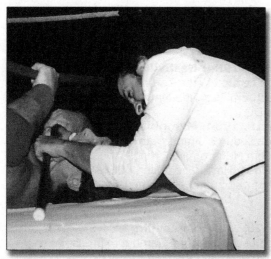

Jimmy Hart Uses His Cane To Choke The
King.

Apr 10, 1984: Louisville, KY, Tuesday
& JJ Dillon beat Joe Leduc & Jimmy Hart

Apr 12, 1984: Lexington, KY, Thursday
(c) beat Randy Savage(c) w/Hart
- Lawler's Southern Title vs. Savage's Mid-
America Title
- Lanny Poffo attacks Lawler after the match

Apr 14, 1984: Nashville, TN
(c) beat Randy Savage(c) w/Hart
- Lawler's Southern Title vs. Savage's Mid-
America Title

Apr 16, 1984: Memphis, TN
(c) lost to Lord Humongous w/Hart
- Southern Title Match
- Ref stopped match because of damage Lawler
sustained.
- Title did not change hands
_ Humongous was Mike Stark

Apr 23, 1984: Memphis, TN
(c) lost to Lord Humongous w/Hart
- Southern Title Match
- No Stopping - No DQ
- Back Alley street fight

Apr 24, 1984: Louisville, KY
(c) won via DQ over Randy Savage w/Hart
- Southern Title Match

Apr 26, 1984: Cleveland, OH
& Austin Idol beat the Road Warriors

Apr 28, 1984: Memphis, TN - TV Taping
& Austin Idol defeated Black Panther and Pink
Panther

Apr 30, 1984: Memphis, TN
(c) won via DQ over Lord Humongous(c) w/Hart
- Lawler's Mid-America Title vs. Humongous'
Southern Title

Lawler Has His Own Mask VS. Humongous

May 1, 1984: Louisville, KY
& Eddie Marlin defeated King Konga and Jimmy
Hart

May 3, 1984: Lexington, KY
Boogie Man Jam
& Jimmy Valiant beat Lanny Poffo & Randy
Savage w/Hart

May 4, 1984: Blytheville, AR
& Eddie Marlin defeated King Konga and Jimmy
Hart

May 5, 1984: Nashville, TN
(c) vs. Lord Humongous(c) w/Hart
Mid-America Title vs. Southern Title

May 5, 1984: Memphis, TN - TV Taping
Lance Russell & Jerry Jarrett
w/Brickhouse Brown & Scott Shannon defeated
Porkchop Cash, Jim Neidhart and Rick Rude

Memphis, TN tape, Apr 30, 1984: Jerry Lawler
vs. Lord Humongus w/Jimmy Hart-Austin Idol
chases Jim Neidhart away, Ox Baker in, Baker
punches Lawler and Eddie Marlin

May 6, 1984: Jackson, TN
& Eddie Marlin won via DQ over Joe Leduc &
Jimmy Hart

May 7, 1984: Memphis, TN
lost via DQ to Lord Humongous w/Hart
- Lawler's Mid-America Title vs. Humongous'
Southern Title

& Eddie Marlin by DQ beat Ox Baker & Jimmy
Hart

May 14, 1984: Memphis, TN
& Junk Yard Dog beat Ox Baker & Joe Leduc

**May 16, 1984: Andy Kaufman passed away
from lung cancer on this day.**

*** For true Memphis Wrestling fans, Andy
Kaufman will always hold a special place in
their hearts. While he was always a bad
guy, he certainly helped the promotion get
national coverage. He also was able to
make the fans laugh. His character was
amusing and always generated good heat.
Andy's passing was a sad day for true
Memphis Wrestling fans.**

Jerry Lawler & Andy Kaufman

May 20, 1984: Atlanta, GA
w/Austin Idol lost to Ted Dibiase & the Spoiler

May 21, 1984: Memphis, TN
beat Humongous(c) w/Hart
- Southern Title Match

The King Finally Gets The Hockey Mask Off
Humongous And The Fists Start Flying.

May 28, 1984: Memphis, TN
(c) beat King Kong Bundy w/Hart
- Southern Title Match

June 2, 1984: Memphis, TN - TV Taping
w/Johnny Wilhoit & Bart Batten defeated
Nightmare #2, Norvell Austin and Koko Ware

June 4, 1984: Memphis, TN
(c) won via Count Out over Kamala w/Hart
- Southern Title Match

June 6, 1984: Evansville, IN
(c) vs. Humongous w/Hart
- Southern Title Match

June 7, 1984: Lexington, KY
(c) beat Humongous w/Hart
- Southern Title Match

June 9, 1984: Baltimore, MD
& Austin Idol Double DQ with the Road Warriors

June 10, 1984: Jackson, TN
beat the Animal w/Hart
- Not Road Warrior Animal

June 11, 1984: Memphis, TN
(c) lost to Rick Rude w/Hart & Angel
- Southern Title Match

June 12, 1984: Louisville, KY
beat the Animal w/Hart
- Not Road Warrior Animal

June 18, 1984: Memphis, TN
& the Fabulous Ones (Keirn & Lane) beat Rick
Rude & PYT Express (Norvell Austin & Koko
Ware)

June 21, 1984: Henderson, TN
won via DQ over Rick Rude w/Hart & Angel
- Southern Title Match

June 23, 1984: Blytheville, AR
& Jimmy Valiant beat the Assassins

June 24, 1984: Louisville, KY
& the Fabulous Ones (Keirn & Lane) beat Rick
Rude & PYT Express (Norvell Austin & Koko
Ware)

June 24, 1984: Memphis, TN - TV show
Featuring co-host Jerry Clower, Jimmy Valiant,
Ace Cannon, the Fabulous Ones: Steve Keirn &
Stan Lane, Weird Al Yankovic, Hawk & Animal:
the Road Warriors, Playboy Playmate Gayle
Stanton, the Rock N Roll Express: Robert Gibson
& Ricky Morton, the Klassy Kats Breakdancers,
the San Diego Chicken, Zippy the Wrestling
Chimp, Dana Kirk, Keith Lee, Marv Thornberry,
more.

*This episode was a two hour prime time special
broadcast at 8 PM CT on WMC-TV in competition
against a WWF house show card in town on this
night

June 25, 1984: Memphis, TN
Star Wars 84
& Austin Idol won via DQ over the Road
Warriors(c)
- National Tag Title Match

June 28, 1984: Nashville, TN
vs. Rick Rude(c) w/Hart & Angel
- Southern Title Match

June 30, 1984: Miami, FL
won via DQ over One Man Gang

July 1, 1984: Jackson, TN
vs. Rick Rude(c) w/Hart & Angel
- Southern Title Match

w/Austin Idol, Dutch Mantell & Porkchop Cash
vs. PYT Express, Rick Rude & Oriental
Connection w/Hart

July 2, 1984: Memphis, TN
won via DQ over Rick Rude(c) w/Hart & Angel
- Southern Title Match
- Also won a Battle Royal

July 7, 1984: Nashville, TN
vs. Rick Rude(c) w/Hart & Angel
- Southern Title Match

July 9, 1984: Memphis, TN
& the Fabulous Ones (Keirn & Lane) beat Jimmy
Hart, Rick Rude, the Animal, Jim Neidhart &
Angel

* The Animal individually listed in this record
book is not Road Warrior Animal. The Road
Warriors are in this book, but only listed as the
Road Warriors, since neither wrestled in singles
matches against Jerry Lawler in the territory.

July 16, 1984: Memphis, TN
lost to King Kong Bundy w/Hart
- Lawler gets $1000 per minute he lasts.
- Match lasted: 6:29

Jerry Lawler & Ron Mikolajczyk went to a No Contest with Ric Rude & Jim Neidhart w/Hart & Angel

*During the 1970s & 80s, Ron Mikolajczyk was football player in the NFL (NY Giants). He also played for both Memphis WFL & USFL football teams: the Memphis Grizzlies and the Memphis Showboats. While in Memphis he became friends with Jerry Lawler and this led to his trying his hand in Memphis Wrestling.

July 22, 1984: Louisville, KY
w/Ron Mikolajzcyk drew with Rick Rude & Jim Neidhart

lost to King Kong Bundy w/Hart
- bodyslam challenge

July 23, 1984: Memphis, TN
lost via DQ to Rick Rude w/Hart & Angel
- Loser gets 10 lashes
- Angel gave Lawler 10 lashes

Jerry Lawler VS. Rick Rude. Lawler Wins & Rude Valet Angel Jumps On His Back.

July 30, 1984: Memphis, TN
beat Rick Rude w/Hart & Angel
- Pole-Strap Match
- Lawler gave piledriver to Angel

July 31, 1984: Louisville, KY
lost via DQ to Rick Rude w/Hart & Angel
- Loser gets 10 lashes

Aug 5, 1984: Jackson, TN
& Bill Dundee vs. Phil Hickerson & the Spoiler(c)
- Southern Title Match
- Spoiler was Frank Morrell

Aug 6, 1984: Memphis, TN
Tag Tournament
<u>1st Round</u>
& Jimmy Valiant beat Randy Savage & Lanny Poffo

<u>2nd Round</u>
& Jimmy Valiant beat Phil Hickerson & the Spoiler

<u>Semi-Finals</u>
& Jimmy Valiant beat Masao Ito & the Animal

<u>Finals</u>
& Jimmy Valiant beat Rick Rude & King Kong Bundy

- Tournament winners will go to Japan for a yearly tag tournament.

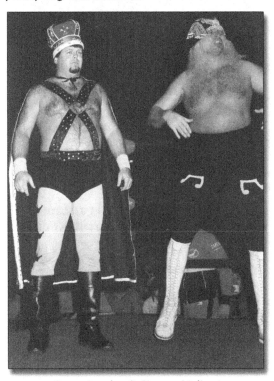

Jerry Lawler & Jimmy Valiant

Aug 7, 1984: Louisville, KY
Tag Tournament
<u>1st Round</u>
& Jimmy Valiant beat Randy Savage & Lanny Poffo

<u>2nd Round</u>
Jerry Lawler & Jimmy Valiant beat Masao Ito & the Animal

Semi-Finals
Jerry Lawler & Jimmy Valiant beat Phil Hickerson & Masked Spoiler

Finals
& Jimmy Valiant beat Rick Rude & King Kong Bundy

- Tournament winners will go to Japan for a yearly tag tournament.

Aug 9, 1984: Lexington, KY
lost to King Kong Bundy w/Hart
Bodyslam challenge

& Jimmy Valiant beat Rick Rude & King Kong Bundy

Jerry Has King Kong Bundy Trapped In A Headscissors.

Aug 11, 1984: Memphis, TN - TV results
No Contest with Rick Rude(c) w/Hart & Angel
- Southern Title Match

-Ric Rude takes a baseball bat to Jerry's Car.

Aug 13, 1984: Memphis, TN
lost via DQ to Rick Rude(c) w/Hart & Angel
- Southern Title Match
- Rude was injured by Lawler

Aug 14, 1984: Louisville, KY
beat Rick Rude w/Hart & Angel
- Grudge Match

Aug 17, 1984: Milan, TN
beat Rick Rude w/Hart & Angel
- Grudge Match

Aug 18, 1984: Memphis, TN - TV results
Memphis, TN TV show tape: Lance Russell interviews Jimmy Hart-Rick Rude, Angel come out then Jerry Lawler then King Kong Bundy

Aug 18, 1984: Nashville, TN
vs. King Kong Bundy(c) w/Hart
- Southern Title Match

Aug 20, 1984: Memphis, TN
(c) won via DQ Rick Rude
- Mid-America Title Match

Aug 25, 1984 in Memphis, TN - TV Results
Memphis, TN tape, Aug 20, 1984: Jerry Lawler vs. Rick Rude w/Jimmy Hart
- the Animal, Masked Spoiler, the Nightmares, King Kong Bundy, Kurt Von Hess, Masao Ito, Phil Hickerson all get involved then Dutch Mantel and Eddie Marlin come in

Memphis tape: Road Warriors w/Paul Ellering vs. Jerry Lawler & Austin Idol

Aug 26, 1984: Louisville, KY
(c) won via DQ over Rick Rude
- Mid-America Title Match

Aug 27, 1984: Memphis, TN
beat Ric Rude w/Hart & Angel
- Cage match
- No DQ

Aug 29, 1984: Evansville, IN, Wednesday
won via DQ over Rick Rude w/Hart & Angel

w/Mantell No Contest Jimmy Hart w/Rude

Aug 30, 1984: Nashville, TN
won via DQ over Rick Rude w/Hart & Angel

w/Mantell No Contest Jimmy Hart w/Rude

Sep 1, 1984: Memphis, TN - TV Taping
Jerry Lawler by DQ beat Eddie Gilbert-Rick Rude and Jimmy Hart ran in

Sep 2, 1984: Jackson, TN
w/Tommy Rich & Jimmy Valiant vs. Rick Rude, Eddie Gilbert & King Kong Bundy

vs. Rick Rude w/Hart & Angel

Sep 3, 1984: Memphis, TN
lost to King Kong Bundy w/Hart
- Round one of Cadillac tournament

Sep 4, 1984: Louisville, KY
& Jimmy Valiant beat King Kong Bundy & Rick Rude

Sep 6, 1984: Lexington, KY
lost to King Kong Bundy w/Hart
- Round one of Cadillac tournament

Sep 8, 1984: Memphis, TN - TV Taping
over Keith Roberson

Rude & Bundy attack Randy Savage in his match.

Jerry Lawler won by DQ over Rick Rude w/Jimmy Hart- King Kong Bundy jumps in, then Dirty White Boys jump in, then Randy Savage in to help Lawler.

* Dirty White Boys are Tony Anthony & Len Denton. Had wrestled recently in Memphis as the masked Grapplers.

Sep 10, 1984: Memphis, TN
& Randy Savage lost via DQ to Rick Rude & King Kong Bundy w/Hart & Angel

Jerry Lawler & Randy Savage

Sep 11, 1984: Louisville, KY
won via DQ over King Kong Bundy w/Hart

Sep 15, 1984: Memphis, TN TV results
& Rock n Roll Express (Ricky Morton & Robert Gibson) won by DQ over Kurt Von Hess, King Kong Bundy & Rick Rude w/Hart
-Nightmares and Jimmy Hart interfere

Sep 16, 1984: Louisville, KY
lost to King Kong Bundy w/Hart

beats King Kong Bundy to win
20-Man, 2-Ring Battle Royal

Sep 17, 1984: Memphis, TN
& Randy Savage lost to Rick Rude & King Kong Bundy w/Hart
- No DQ

Sep 18, 1984: Memphis, TN
Pro Wrestling USA TV Taping
& Tommy Rich beat the Dirty White Boys
& Tommy Rich beat the Nightmares
beat Eddie Gilbert

Sep 22, 1984: Memphis, TN - TV results
King Kong Bundy & Rick Rude attack promoter Jerry Jarrett leading to a brawl w/Jerry Lawler & Randy Savage

Sep 23, 1984: Memphis, TN
& Randy Savage lost to Rick Rude & King Kong Bundy w/Hart

Sep 24, 1984: Jackson, TN
w/Jimmy Valiant & Randy Savage vs. King Kong Bundy, Rick Rude & Kurt Von Hess w/Hart

Sep 25, 1984: Louisville, KY
& Randy Savage lost to Rick Rude & King Kong Bundy w/Hart

Sep 26, 1984: Evansville, IN, Wednesday
& Randy Savage lost to Rick Rude & King Kong Bundy w/Hart

Sep 27, 1984: Nashville, TN
& Randy Savage vs. Rick Rude & King Kong Bundy

Oct 1, 1984: Memphis, TN
w/Jimmy Valiant & Randy Savage beat King Kong Bundy, Rick Rude & Jimmy Hart

Oct 3, 1984: Evansville, IN, Wednesday
& Randy Savage vs. King Kong Bundy & Rick Rude w/Hart

Oct 4, 1984: Lexington, KY
& Randy Savage vs. King Kong Bundy & Rick Rude w/Hart

Jerry Lawler About To Eat The Turnbuckle VS. King Kong Bundy.

Oct 5, 1984: Booneville, MS
& Randy Savage vs. King Kong Bundy & Rick Rude w/Hart

Oct 6, 1984: Memphis, TN - TV results
Video: "Wimpbusters" by Jerry Lawler

Oct 15, 1984: Memphis, TN
w/Jimmy Valiant & Randy Savage beat Phil Hickerson & the Dirty white Boys
- Phil Hickerson is sub for Jimmy Hart

Oct 17, 1984: Atlanta, GA - TV Taping
w/Tommy Rich & Jerry Oates drew with Bob Roop, Ted Oates & Rip Rogers

Oct 20, 1984: Memphis, TN - TV results
Jerry Lawler beat Dr. Detroit

Oct 20, 1984: Nashville, TN
w/Randy Savage & Tommy Rich vs. King Kong Bundy, Rick Rude & Dutch Mantell

Oct 22, 1984: Memphis, TN
& Randy Savage won via DQ over the Dirty White Boys w/Hart

Jerry Lawler VS. Dirty White Boy Tony Anthony, Randy Savage Wants In.

Oct 23, 1984: Spartanburg, SC
Pro Wrestling USA TV Taping
w/Tommy Rich beat Randy Barber & Don Sanders
Oct 24, 1984: Evansville, IN, Wednesday
vs. King Kong Bundy(c) w/Hart
- Southern Title Match

Jerry Going Against King Kong Bundy

Oct 27, 1984: Miami Beach, FL
& Dusty Rhodes beat the Purple Haze & Kevin Sullivan

Oct 29, 1984: Memphis, TN
& Jimmy Valiant beat Dirty White Boys w/Hart

Oct 31, 1984: Atlanta, GA - TV Taping
w/Tommy Rich & Jerry Oates beat Bob Roop,
Ted Oates & Rip Rogers

won via DQ over Bob Roop

Nov 1, 1984: Lexington, KY
w/Jimmy Valiant & Randy Savage beat King
Kong Bundy, Korchenko & Dr. Detroit

(c) beat King Kong Bundy w/Hart
- Southern Title Match

Nov 2, 1984: Blytheville, AR
w/Jimmy Valiant & Randy Savage vs Dirty White
Boys & Jimmy Hart

Nov 3, 1984: Memphis, TN - TV results
& Jimmy Valiant beat the Destroyers w/Hart

Rick Rude vs. King Kong Bundy w/Hart. the
Dirty White Boys (Len Denton & Tony Anthony)
attack Rude. Jerry Lawler & Jimmy Valiant run
in but were tarred & feathered.

Nov 4, 1984: Jackson, TN
w/Jimmy Valiant & Randy Savage vs King King
Bundy, Eddie Gilbert & Kurt Von Hess w/Hart
- Lawler's Team vs. Hart's Team
- Losers will have eggs thrown at them by fans.

Nov 5, 1984: Memphis, TN
w/Jimmy Valiant & Rick Rude lost to the Dirty
White Boys & King Kong Bundy w/Hart

Nov 6, 1984: Louisville, KY
& Jimmy Valiant beat the Dirty White Boys

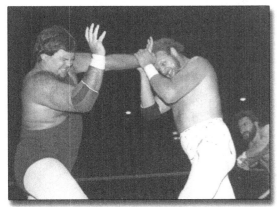
Jerry Lawler VS. Dirty White Boy Tony
Anthony, as DWB - Len Denton Watches.

Nov 11, 1984: Louisville, KY
& Ric Rude & Randy Savage DDQ with the Dirty
White Boys & King Kong Bundy w/Hart

Jerry Lawler & Rick Rude

Nov 12, 1984: Memphis, TN
beats King Kong Bundy(c) w/Hart
- Southern Title Match
- Lawler's hair vs. Title
- Special Ref = Rick Rude

Jerry Lawler VS. King Kong Bundy
Special Ref: Rick Rude

Nov 13, 1984: Union City, TN
& Jimmy Valiant vs. the Dirty White Boys w/Hart

Nov 14, 1984: Atlanta, GA - TV Taping
& Jimmy Valiant beat George South & Italian
Stallion

Nov 15, 1984: Sumter, SC
Pro Wrestling USA TV Taping
w/Brian Adidas beat Randy Barber & Paul Kerry

w/Brian Adidas lost to the Long Riders (Bill & Scott Irwin)

beat Mike Favier

Nov 17, 1984: Memphis, TN - TV results
Jerry Lawler says if he doesn't win a world title in 1985, he will retire.

* According to Jerry Jarrett he had a handshake deal to let Jerry Lawler win the NWA World Title from Ric Flair, and then drop it back to Ric within a few weeks . It would help the promotion by having Jerry win an actual World Title, (which he had been chasing for a decade) and the fans would get the payoff of having their hometown hero with the NWA World Title. Unfortunately, the deal fell through and 1985 passed with Jerry not winning a World Title.

THE CROWNING OF A KING

The Illustrated Story of Professional Wrestling's JERRY LAWLER
By Jim Barron

Nov. 1984 Saw This Book Came Out In The Memphis Area Book Stores.

Nov 17, 1984: Nashville, TN
& Jimmy Valiant vs. the Dirty White Boys

Nov 18, 1984: Atlanta, GA
& Jimmy Valiant beat Ox Baker & Mr. Ito

& Jimmy Valiant won via DQ to the Road Warriors

& Jimmy Valiant lost to the Long Riders

Nov 19, 1984: Memphis, TN Mid-South Coliseum, Monday
(c) lost via DQ to Mike Sharpe w/Hart
- Southern Title Match

Nov 20, 1984: Louisville, KY
w/Rick Rude & Jimmy Valiant lost to Jimmy Hart & the Dirty White Boys

Nov 22, 1984: Jackson, TN
& Rick Rude vs. the Dirty White Boys w/Hart

Nov 25, 1984: Louisville, KY
(c) No Contest with Korstia Korchenko w/Hart
- Southern Title Match

Nov 27, 1984: Memphis, TN
(c) beat Korstia Korchenko w/Hart
- Southern Title Match

Won 21 Man Elimination Match

Nov 29, 1984: Nashville, TN
& Jimmy Valiant vs. the Dirty White Boys w/Hart
- Loser Gets Tarred & Feathered Match

Dec 1, 1984: Nashville, TN
w/Jimmy Valiant & Jackie Fargo vs. Mike Sharpe, Korchenko & Jimmy Hart

Dec 2: Atlanta, GA
Southern Champ beat Jason via DQ

Dec 3, 1984: Memphis, TN
(c) won via DQ over Bob Roop
- Southern Title Match

Rick Rude beat King Kong Bundy w/Hart
- Loser Leaves Town
- No DQ
- Special Ref: Jerry Lawler

Dec 4, 1984: Louisville, KY
(c) beat Mike Sharpe
- Southern Title Match

Dec 7, 1984:
beat Bob Roop

Dec 8, 1984: Nashville, TN
(c) won via DQ over Rick Rude
- Southern Title Match

Dec 9, 1984: Jackson, TN
& Jimmy Valiant vs. the Interns(c) w/Troy
Graham
- Southern Tag Title Match

**Dec 10, 1984: Memphis, TN Mid-South
Coliseum, Monday**
(c) won via DQ over Rick Rude
- Southern Title Match

Dec 11, 1984: Louisville, KY
(c) won via DQ over Rick Rude
- Southern Title Match

Dec 12, 1984: Evansville, IN
(c) won via DQ over Rick Rude
- Southern Title Match

Dec 15, 1984: Nashville, TN
(c) vs. Rick Rude
- Lumberjack Match
- Southern Title Match

Dec 17, 1984: Memphis, TN
w/Randy Savage & Jimmy Valiant won via DQ
over the Interns & Plowboy Frazier w/Troy
Graham
- Plowboy was sub for Rick Rude

Dec 27, 1984: Lexington, KY
& Jimmy Valiant beat the Dirty White Boys
w/Hart

won via DQ over Eddie Gilbert

**Dec 28, 1984: Memphis, TN Mid-South
Coliseum, Friday**
won via DQ over Adrian Street
- Southern Title Match

Dec 29, 1984: Nashville, TN
(sc) No Contest with Eddie Gilbert(ic) w/Hart
- Southern Title vs. International Title Match

Dec 30, 1984: Jackson, TN Afternoon
& Jimmy Valiant vs. the Interns(c) w/Troy
Graham
- Southern Tag Title Match

Dec 30, 1984: Jonesboro, AR Evening
(sc) won via DQ over Eddie Gilbert(ic) w/Hart
- Southern Title vs. International Title Match

Dec 31, 1984: Memphis, TN
(sc) went to a No Contest with Eddie Gilbert(ic)
w/Hart
- Southern Title vs. International Title Match

Iron Mike Sharpe(c) beat Jimmy Valiant w/Jerry
Lawler
-Mid-America Title Match

1985

Chapter 16

Jan 1, 1985: Louisville, KY
(c) won via DQ over Adrian Street
- Southern Title Match

Jan 5, 1985: Memphis, TN - TV Taping
beats the Inferno

Jan 6, 1985: Louisville, KY
went to a No Contest with Eddie Gilbert

Jan 7, 1985: Memphis, TN
(c) beat Eddie Gilbert
- Southern Title Match
- Barb Wire Match

Jan 11, 1985: Mayland, TN
(c) vs. Eddie Gilbert
- Southern Title Match

Jan 14, 1985: Memphis, TN
& Johnny Wilhoit drew with Eddie Gilbert & Mike Sharpe
- Round 1 Southern Title Tournament
- Gilbert & Sharpe won a coin toss to advance

Jan 15, 1985: Louisville, KY
 (c) beat Eddie Gilbert
- Southern Title Match
- Barb Wire Match

Jan 21, 1985: Memphis, TN
vs. Eddie Gilbert
- Cancelled because of ice

Jan 22, 1985: Louisville, KY
& Jimmy Valiant lost to Eddie Gilbert & Mike Sharpe
- Texas Tornado Death Match

Jan 27, 1985: Memphis, TN
(c) No Contest with Eddie Gilbert
- Southern Title Match
- Texas Death Match
- Title held up

* Back on Aug 6, 1984, Jerry Lawler and Jimmy Valiant won the tournament to represent the Jarrett promotion in the AJPW (All Japan Pro Wrestling) Tag Tournament. The tournament started on Jan 30, 1985 and concluded Feb 5, 1985.

Jan 30, 1985: Otaru, Japan
& Jimmy Valiant beat Killer Kahn & Kiroku Eigan

Jan 31, 1985: Tomakomai, Japan
& Jimmy Valiant beat Takeshi Ishikawa & the Magic Dragon

Feb 1, 1985: Sapporo, Japan
& Jimmy Valiant lost to Killer Kahn & Masa Saito

Feb 2, 1985: Memphis, TN - TV results
Memphis, TN tape, Jan 27, 1985: Texas death match: Jerry Lawler vs. Eddie Gilbert w/Jimmy Hart

Feb 2, 1985: Muroran, Japan
& Jimmy Valiant Double Count Out with Mighty Inoue & Akio Sato

Feb 3, 1985: Kitami, Japan
& Jimmy Valiant beat Nobuo Honaga & Fumihiro Nikura

Feb 4, 1985: Obihiro, Japan
& Jimmy Valiant lost to Killer Kahn & Animal Hamiguchi

Feb 5, 1985: Tokyo, Japan
& Jimmy Valiant lost to the Great Kabuki & Takashi Ishikawa

Feb 9, 1985: Memphis, TN - TV results
Lance Russell interviews Jerry Lawler and Jimmy Valiant about their trip to Japan.

Music video: "Famous Final Scene" featuring Jerry Lawler & Jimmy Hart

Feb 10, 1985: Memphis, TN - The Jerry Lawler Show
Japan tape: Jimmy Valiant & Jerry Lawler vs. Masa Saito & Killer Khan

Feb 10, 1985: Jackson, TN
vs. Eddie Gilbert(c)
- Southern Title Match

Feb 11, 1985: Memphis, TN
beats Eddie Gilbert(c)
- Southern Title Match
- If Gilbert loses, Hart leaves Memphis
- Hart had already left Memphis and was replaced at ringside by a look-alike. Jimmy w afraid Jerry would possible break his jaw with an errant punch, (which had happened before).
- Jimmy went to the WWF.

* This was truly the end of an era. Jimmy Hart had started as Jerry Lawler's manager in the fall of 1979 and for nearly 6 straight years been a huge part of the Jarrett promotion. When Jerry Lawler went down with a broken leg back in Jan of 1980, it was Hart that emerged as the territory's top heel and helped keep the promotion's head above water until the King returned in Dec 1980. Also during 1980, Hart initiated a feud with Jerry Lawler that was second to none. Batman had the Joker as his nemesis and Jerry Lawler had Jimmy Hart as his. It just worked and over the years and never grew old.

Feb 12, 1985: Louisville, KY
lost via DQ to Eddie Gilbert(c)
- Southern Title Match

Feb 16, 1985: Memphis, TN - TV results
Lance Russell interviews Jerry Lawler and shows the Memphis, TN tape, Feb 11, 1985: Jerry Lawler vs. Eddie Gilbert

Jerry Lawler by DQ beat Jerry Bryant-Eddie Gilbert & Playboy Frazier run in

Feb 18, 1985: Memphis, TN
(c) beat Eddie Gilbert
- Southern Title Match

Feb 19, 1985: Louisville, KY
beat Eddie Gilbert (c)
- Southern Title Match
- Hart or Lawler will leave town for 1 year

Feb 23, 1985: Memphis, TN - TV results
Lance Russell interviews Jerry Lawler
Jerry Lawler & Lanny Poffo beat Playboy Frazier & Eddie Gilbert

Feb 24, 1985: East Rutherford, NJ
Pro Wrestling USA
& Baron Von Raschke lost the Road Warriors(c) with Paul Ellering

- AWA World Tag Title Match

& Baron Von Raschke also competed in a tag team Battle Royal

Feb 25, 1985: Memphis, TN
& Abdullah the Butcher beat the Interns

& Steve Keirn beat Harley Hogg & JR Hogg
- Jerry was a sub for Stan Lane.

Feb 28, 1985: Nashville, TN
& Randy Savage vs. Eddie Gilbert & Iron Mike Sharpe w/Tommy H

The King & The Macho Man, Unlikely Allies.

Mar 2, 1985: Memphis, TN - TV result
Music video montage to the Queen song "We Are The Champions" featuring Jerry Lawler vs. Nick Bockwinkel.

Lance Russell interviews Jerry Lawler

Jerry Lawler beat Mad Dog
- Tux Newman comes out

Mar 4, 1985: Memphis, TN
No Contest with Nick Bockwinkel(c)
- AWA World Title Match
- Even though Rick Martel was the current AWA World Champ. Lawler & Jerry Jarrett felt the fans would not be behind Martel as they would for Nick. The fans truly bought Bockwinkel as the "World Champ".

The King

Mar 7, 1985: Lexington, KY
& Randy Savage beat Mike Sharpe & Eddie Gilbert

Mar 10, 1985: Jackson, TN
& Joe Lightfoot vs. Eddie Gilbert & Mr. Wrestling

Mar 11, 1985: Memphis, TN
lost to Nick Bockwinkel(c)
- AWA World Title Match
- Texas Death Match
- Randy Savage turned on Lawler, causing loss

Mar 18, 1985: Memphis, TN
(c) lost to Randy Savage w/Tux Newman
- Southern Title Match

Mar 19, 1985: Louisville, KY
lost to Eddie Gilbert
- Texas Death Match

Mar 20, 1985: Evansville, IN
& Dutch Mantell vs. Mike Sharpe & Eddie Gilbert

Mar 21, 1985: Owensboro, KY, Thursday
& Dutch Mantell vs. Mike Sharpe & Eddie Gilbert

Mar 24, 1985: Cape Girardeau, MO
beat Randy Savage

Mar 25, 1985: Memphis, TN
won via DQ over Randy Savage w/Tux Newman
- Southern Title Match
- Savage piledrives Lawler who is carried out on a stretcher.

Mar 30, 1985: Memphis, TN - TV results
Memphis, TN tape, Mar 25, 1985: Jerry Lawler vs. Randy Savage with Tux Newman- Savage piledrives Lawler several times including once on a curved title plate, Lawler is carted off on a stretcher

Apr 22, 1985: Memphis, TN
went to a No Contest with Randy Savage(c) w/Tux Newman
- Southern Title Match

Apr 23, 1985: Louisville, KY
went to a No Contest with Randy Savage(c) w/Tux Newman
- Southern Title Match

Apr 29, 1985: Memphis, TN
beat Randy Savage w/Tux Newman

Apr 30, 1985: Louisville, KY
won via DQ over Randy Savage w/Tux Newman
2 out of 3 falls match

May 4, 1985: Memphis, TN - TV Taping
& the Fabulous Ones (Stan & Steve) beat Bobby Colt, Jr Hogg & Billy Travis

May 5, 1985: Jackson, TN
& the Fabulous Ones (Stan & Steve) went to a DDQ with Randy Savage, Lanny Poffo & David Schultz

May 6, 1985: Memphis, TN
& Bruiser Brody went to a DCO with Randy Savage & David Schultz

May 7, 1985: Louisville, KY
went to a No Contest with Randy Savage w/Tux Newman
- Chain Match

May 9, 1985: Lexington, KY
lost to Randy Savage w/Tux Newman

May 11, 1985: Memphis, TN - TV Taping
beat Lou Winston

May 13, 1985: Memphis, TN
& Bill Dundee went to a DCO with Kareem
Muhammad & Bruiser Brody

May 20, 1985: Memphis, TN
won via DQ over Bruiser Brody

May 21, 1985: Louisville, KY
No Contest with Bruiser Brody

May 24, 1985: Waverly, TN
vs. Kareem Muhammad

May 27, 1985: Memphis, TN
& Austin Idol beat Bruiser Brody & Kareem
Muhammad

May 28, 1985: Louisville, KY
won via DQ over Bruiser Brody
- No ref in ring

June 2, 1985: Jackson, TN
beat Kareem Muhammad

June 3, 1985: Memphis, TN
beat Randy Savage(c)
- Southern Title Match
- Cage Match, No DQ
- Savage Manager Tux Newman was eliminated
in an earlier Cage Match vs. Jackie Fargo.
Lawler loses, he retires. Savage loses, he leaves

June 4, 1985: Louisville, KY
& Jay Youngblood won via DQ over Bruiser
Brody & Kareem Muhammad

June 5, 1985: Evansville, IN
beat Randy Savage(c)
- Southern Title Match
- Lawler Retires If He Loses

June 6, 1985: Lexington, KY
beat Randy Savage(c)
- Southern Title Match
- Loser Leaves Town

June 8, 1985: Nashville, TN
beat Randy Savage(c)
- Southern Title Match
- Loser Leaves Town

June 10, 1985: Memphis, TN
(c) lost via DQ over Bruiser Brody
- Southern Title Match

June 11, 1985: Louisville, KY
& Tojo Yamamoto lost via Count Out to PYT
Express

June 12, 1985: Evansville, IN
& Tojo Yamamoto lost via Count Out to the PYT
Express

Jerry Lawler & Tojo Yamamoto About To
Tag Up In A Match.

June 15, 1985: Nashville, TN
& Tojo Yamamoto vs. PYT Express
Southern Tag Title Match

June 17, 1985: Memphis, TN
Southern Tag Title Tournament
Round 1
& Nick Bockwinkel beat PYT's (Norvell Austin &
Koko Ware)

Round 2
& Nick Bockwinkel lost via DQ to Billy Travis &
Ron Sexton
- Questionable DQ by ref Tom Branch

June 18, 1985: Louisville, KY
& Tojo Yamamoto lost to PYT Express
- Falls Count Anywhere

June 19, 1985: Evansville, IN
& Tojo Yamamoto lost to PYT Express
- Falls Count Anywhere

June 24, 1985: Memphis, TN
(c) lost to Bota the Witch Doctor
- Southern Title Match

- ref Jerry Calhoun goes down, ref Tom Branch comes in and quick counts Lawler.
- Bota was Tio Taylor, one of the original Gulas-TN Samoans from a decade earlier

Jerry Lawler In Trouble Against Bota The Witch Doctor.

June 25, 1985: Louisville, KY
w/Tojo Yamamoto & Jeff Jarrett beat PYT Express & Tom Branch
- Jarrett & Branch were both refs for the promotion.

June 26, 1985: Evansville, IN
w/Tojo Yamamoto & Jerry Jarrett beat PYT Express & Tom Branch

June 29, 1985: Memphis, TN - TV results
Lance Russell interviews Jerry Lawler who recalls his problems with referee Tom Branch.

Memphis, TN tape: Jerry Lawler vs. Bruiser Brody-ref Tom Branch hinders Lawler

Memphis, TN tape: June 17, 1985: Jerry Lawler & Nick Bockwinkel vs. Ron Sexton & Billy Travis with Buddy Wayne-Branch DQs Lawler & Bockwinkel

Memphis, TN tape: June 24, 1985: Jerry Lawler vs. Bota the Witch Doctor with Leslie Floyd Creachman, III - ref Jerry Calhoun goes down, Branch comes out and quick counts Lawler

Lance Russell interviews Jerry Lawler and (in another studio) Tom Branch

June 29, 1985: Nashville, TN
vs. Bota the Witch Doctor(c)
- Southern Title Match

July 1, 1985: Memphis, TN
beat Tom Branch & Phil Hickerson
- Handicap Match

Phil Hickerson Giving Jerry Lawler A Big Piledriver.

July 5, 1985: Lexington, KY
won via DQ over Bota the Witch Doctor(c)
- Southern Title Match

July 6, 1985: Memphis, TN - TV results
Memphis, TN tape, July 1, 1985: Phil Hickerson & Tom Branch vs. Jerry Lawler

July 6, 1985: Nashville, TN
beat Tom Branch & Phil Hickerson
- Handicap Match

July 7, 1985: Jackson, TN
won via DQ over Bota the Witch Doctor(c)
- Southern Title Match

July 8, 1985: Memphis, TN
beat Tom Branch
- First Blood match

July 9, 1985: Louisville, KY
won via DQ over Bota the Witch Doctor(c)
- Southern Title Match

beat Tom Branch
- Special Challenge Match

July 10, 1985: Evansville, IN
won via DQ over Bota the Witch Doctor(c)
- Southern Title Match

beat Tom Branch
- Special Challenge Match

July 13, 1985: Nashville, TN
beat Tom Branch
- First Blood Match

July 15, 1985: Memphis, TN
beat Man Mountain Link(c)
- Mid-America Title Match

& Tojo Yamamoto beat the Nightriders

July 16, 1985: Louisville, KY
& Jerry Jarrett beat Bota the Witch Doctor &
Tom Branch

July 17, 1985: Evansville, IN
& Jerry Jarrett beat Bota the Witch Doctor &
Tom Branch

July 22, 1985: Memphis, TN
won via DQ over Bota the Witch Doctor(c)
- Southern Title Match

July 23, 1985: Louisville, KY
w/Jerry Jarrett & Big John Harris beat Bota the
Witch Doctor, Tom Branch & Phil Hickerson

July 24, 1985: Evansville, IN
w/Jerry Jarrett & Big John Harris beat Bota the
Witch Doctor, Tom Branch & Phil Hickerson

July 29, 1985: Memphis, TN
beat Bota the Witch Doctor(c)
- Southern Title Match

July 30, 1985: Louisville, KY
won via DQ over Bota the Witch Doctor(c)
- Southern Title Match

Aug 1, 1985: Nashville, TN
w/Jerry Jarrett & Jackie Fargo beat Bota, Tom
Branch & Phil Hickerson

Aug 3, 1985: Memphis, TN - TV results
Memphis, TN tape, July 29, 1985: Michael
Hayes vs. Tom Branch, Bota the Witch Doctor
in, Jerry Lawler makes the save.

Memphis, TN tape, July 29, 1985: Bota the
Witch Doctor with Tom Branch lost to Jerry
Lawler-Michael Hayes in, Lawler accidently
burns Hayes with a fireball.

Aug 4, 1985: Jackson, TN
won via DQ over Bota the Witch Doctor(c)
- Southern Title Match

Aug 5, 1985: Memphis, TN
& Austin Idol went to a No Contest with the
Fabulous Freebirds (Michael Hayes & Terry
Gordy).

Aug 6, 1985: Louisville, KY
beat Bota the Witch Doctor(c)
- Southern Title Match
- No DQ

Aug 7, 1985: Evansville, IN
& Big John Harris beat Bota the Witch Doctor &
Tom Branch
- Hospital Elimination Match

Aug 9, 1985: Booneville, MS
(c) beat Bota the Witch Doctor w/Tom Branch
- Southern Title Match

Aug 10, 1985: Memphis, TN TV results
Memphis, TN tape, Aug 5, 1985: Jerry Lawler &
Austin Idol vs. The Fabulous Freebirds: Terry
Gordy & Michael Hayes

Aug 10, 1985: Nashville, TN Sports Arena
(c) beat Bota the Witch Doctor
- Southern Title Match

Aug 12, 1985: Memphis, TN
& Austin Idol won via Count Out over the
Fabulous Freebirds

Aug 13, 1985: Louisville, KY
& Koko Ware went to a No Contest with the
Fabulous Freebirds

Aug 16, 1985: Selmer, TN
(c) lost to Taras Bulba
- Southern Title Match

Jerry Lawler Making A Comeback Against Taras Bulba.

Aug 17, 1985: Memphis, TN - TV results
Memphis, TN tape, Aug 12, 1985: Terry Gordy & Michael Hayes vs. Jerry Lawler & Austin Idol

Aug 19, 1985: Memphis, TN
won via DQ over Taras Bulba(c)
- Southern Title Match

Aug 20, 1985: Louisville, KY
beat Bota the Witch Doctor
- Piledriver Match

Aug 23, 1985: Mayland, TN
won via DQ over Taras Bulba(c)
- Southern Title Match

Aug 24, 1985: Memphis, TN - TV results
Lance Russell interviews Jerry Lawler, who is having trouble finding a partner to face the Freebirds - Phil Hickerson makes his plea.

Selmer, TN tape, Aug 16, 1985: Taras Bulba beat Jerry Lawler for Southern title- masked man looking like Michael Hayes attacks Lawler, causing loss.

Memphis, TN TV show tape: Ron Sexton, Billy Travis, Masked Spoiler & Phil Hickerson with Buddy Wayne lose to Jerry Lawler, Koko Ware, Jerry Jarrett & Tojo Yamamoto

Jerry Lawler in then the Sheepherders: Jonathan Boyd & Rip Morgan in then Phil Hickerson makes the save.

Aug 26, 1985: Memphis, TN
& Phil Hickerson went to a No Contest with the Fabulous Freebirds

Jerry Lawler & Phil Hickerson About To Take On The Freebirds (Hayes & Gordy).

Aug 31, 1985: Memphis TV results
Jerry Lawler beats Bota the Witch Doctor w/Tom Branch - Michael Hayes in after match and hits Lawler with a garbage can.

Sep 1, 1985: Jackson, TN
won via Count Out over Taras Bulba(c)
- Southern Title Match

Sep 2, 1985: Memphis, TN
& Phil Hickerson beat the Fabulous Freebirds (Buddy Roberts & Terry Gordy)
- Taped Fist Match

Sep 3, 1985: Louisville, KY
won via Count Out over Taras Bulba(c)
- Southern Title Match

Sep 5, 1985: Lexington, KY
lost via Count Out to Ric Flair(c)
- NWA World Title Match

Sep 6, 1985: Martin, TN
beat Taras Bulba(c)
- Southern Title Match

Sep 9, 1985: Memphis, TN
w/Mongolian Stomper & Phil Hickerson went to a No Contest with the Fabulous Freebirds (Hayes, Gordy & Roberts).
- Stomper turned on Lawler & Hickerson

Sep 10, 1985: Louisville, KY
& Phil Hickerson lost to the Fabulous Freebirds (Gordy & Roberts)

Sep 14, 1985: Memphis, TN TV results
Memphis, TN tape, Sep 9, 1985: The Fabulous Freebirds: Buddy Roberts, Terry Gordy & Michael Hayes vs. Mongolian Stomper, Jerry Lawler & Phil Hickerson - Stomper turns on Lawler.

Sep 14, 1985: Corinth, MS
(c) beat Taras Bulba
- Southern Title Match

Sep 16, 1985: Memphis, TN
went to a No Contest with the Mongolian Stomper

Sep 17, 1985: Louisville, KY
& Phil Hickerson went to a No Contest with Buddy Roberts & Terry Gordy
- Bad Street Match

Sep 23, 1985: Springfield, TN
& Bota the Witch Doctor vs. the Fabulous Freebirds

Sep 24, 1985: Louisville, KY
went to a No Contest with the Mongolian Stomper

Sep 25, 1985: Evansville, IN
went to a No Contest with the Mongolian Stomper

Sep 30, 1985: Memphis, TN
Great American Bash
lost via DQ to NWA World Champ Ric Flair
- NWA World Title Match
- In Conjunction with Jim Crockett Promotions

Oct 1, 1985: Louisville, KY
& Bill Dundee went to a No Contest with the Sheepherders (Rip Morgan & Jonathon Boyd)

Oct 6, 1985: Jackson, TN
won via DQ over Harley Race

Oct 7, 1985: Memphis, TN
(c) went to a No Contest with Bill Dundee
- Southern Title Match

Oct 12, 1985: Memphis, TN - TV Taping
& Bill Dundee won via DQ over Tom Prichard & Pat Rose
- 2 out of 3 falls

Oct 12, 1985: Nashville, TN
lost via DQ to Rick Martel(c)
- AWA World Title Match

Jerry Lawler Waiting For His Opponent.

Oct 13, 1985: Louisville, KY
(c) went to a No Contest with Bill Dundee
- Southern Title Match

Oct 14, 1985: Memphis, TN
& Bill Dundee beat Mongolian Stomper & Taras Bulba

Oct 16, 1985: Evansville, IN
(c) went to a No Contest with Bill Dundee
- Southern Title Match

Oct 19, 1985: Memphis, TN - TV results
(c) lost to Bill Dundee
- Southern Title Match

Oct 21, 1985: Memphis, TN
won via DQ over Bill Dundee(c)
- Southern Title Match

Bill Dundee Choking Jerry Lawler.

Oct 26, 1985: Cleveland, OH
beat Tony Viccaro
- For Jim Crockett Promotions

Oct 28, 1985: Memphis, TN
beat Tom Renesto

Oct 29, 1985: Louisville, KY
No Contest with Bill Dundee(c)
- Southern Title Match

Oct 30, 1985: Evansville, IN
No Contest with Bill Dundee(c)
- Southern Title Match

Nov 3, 1985: Jackson, TN
& the Fabulous Ones (Stan & Steve) beat the
Sheepherders & Bill Dundee

Nov 4, 1985: Memphis, TN
beat Tom Branch

the Hawaiian Flash won via DQ over Bill
Dundee(c)
- Southern Title Match

*** Hawaiian Flash was Jerry Lawler. Dundee
was ducking Jerry Lawler and refused to
give him a title shot at the Southern belt.
On the Sat morning Memphis show (Nov
2), the Hawaiian Flash was Jerry Jarrett in
a masked and Dundee accepted the
challenge. After the contract was signed
Jerry Jarrett came out and a masked
Lawler, in the Hawaiian Flash mask came
out, which caused Dundee to go crazy.**

Nov 6, 1985: Evansville, IN
beat Tom Renesto

Nov 10, 1985: Louisville, KY
the Hawaiian Flash won via DQ over Bill
Dundee(c)
- Southern Title Match

Nov 11, 1985: Memphis, TN
beat Tom Branch(c)
- Mid-America Title Match
-Lawler's hair vs. title

Nov 13, 1985: Honolulu, HI
beat Anoaro Atisanoe

Nov 17, 1985: Lexington, KY
w/Dusty Rhodes & Magnum TA beat Tully
Blanchard, Arn & Ole Anderson
- Bunkhouse Match
- Anything Goes, No DQ

Nov 18, 1985: Memphis, TN
w/Dusty Rhodes & Magnum TA beat Tully
Blanchard, Arn & Ole Anderson
- Bunkhouse Match
- Anything Goes, No DQ

Nov 19, 1985: Louisville, KY
(c) beat Tom Branch
- Mid- America Title Match

Nov 20, 1985: Evansville, IN
w/Tojo Yamamoto & Jerry Jarrett beat the
Sheepherders

Nov 25, 1985: Memphis, TN
beat the Guru
- Guru was Jerry Grey

& Eddie Marlin lost to Bill Dundee & Tom
Renesto

Battle Royal: won by Lawler
- 1st man eliminated was tarred & feathered:
Tony Falk

Nov 30, 1985: Nashville, TN
& Eddie Marlin beat Bill Dundee & Tom Renesto

Dec 2, 1985: Memphis, TN
beat Tony Falk
- Loser Gets Diapered Match

Dec 3, 1985: Louisville, KY
& Eddie Marlin beat Bill Dundee & Tom Renesto

Big Punch From Jerry Lawler Puts Bill
Dundee Down.

Dec 4, 1985: Evansville, IN
& Eddie Marlin beat Bill Dundee & Tom Renesto

Dec 9, 1985: Memphis, TN
& Austin Idol beat Bill Dundee & Dutch
Mantel(c)
- Southern Tag Title Match

Dec 10, 1985: Louisville, KY
beat Tony Falk
- Loser Gets Diapered Match

Dec 14, 1985: Nashville, TN
& Koko Ware vs. Bill Dundee & Dutch Mantell(c)
- Southern Tag Title Match
- Special ref: Eddie Marlin

Dec 15, 1985: Jackson, TN
beat the Guru

Dec 16, 1985: Memphis, TN
& Austin Idol(c) beat the Freedom Fighters -
Southern Tag Title Match
- Freedom Fighter Justice was Jim Hellwig
- Freedom Fighter Flash was Steve Borden

*** While rookies at this point, Hellwig would
go on to become the Ultimate Warrior and
Borden would become Sting. Both are now
WWE HOF'ers. Being rookies, both were
incredibly green. Both had amazing
physiques so they tried to use them in the
territory. It was definitely the era of the
body builder physiques and these two were
second to none in that aspect.
Unfortunately their rig work was limited to
clothlines, bodyslams & punches. Jerry
Jarrett decided to put them in programs
with Lawler & Idol, then Lawler &
Hickerson to protect them and make them
entertaining, or at least attempt to.**

Lawler & Idol Double Team Freedom Fighter
Justice, (Jim Hellwig - Ultimate Warrior).

Dec 18, 1985: Honolulu, HI
beat Mr. Wrestling II

Dec 21, 1985: Memphis, TN
beat Bill Dundee(c)
- Southern Title Match
- Dundee's title vs. Lawler's wife's hair (Paula)

The King Piledriving Bill Dundee.

Dec 22, 1985: Louisville, KY - Afternoon
& Phil Hickerson beat Freedom Fighter (Hellwig & Borden)

The King Dropping A Big Fist on Freedom Fighter Flash (Steve Borden - Sting).

Dec 22, 1985: Nashville, TN Sports Arena
& Phil Hickerson beat the Freedom Fighters (Hellwig & Borden)

Dec 27, 1985: Houston, TX
beat Masked Superstar
- ref overturns the decision, giving Lawler the win.

Dec 28, 1985: Memphis, TN - TV Taping
beat Tony Falk

The King Being Interviewed By Lance Russell.

Dec 28, 1985: Jackson MS
beat Masked Superstar

Dec 30, 1985: Memphis, TN
(c) lost to Bill Dundee
- Southern Title Match
- Title & Leaving Town vs. both Bill & his wife's hair.

* Greatly executed match. This was one of those angles that took Lawler (and the fans) where they had never gone before. Earlier that night, Tony Falk had thrown ink into the face of Jerry Lawler, blinding him temporarily in one eye. The King would wear a bandage around his head (for a visual effect) but still fought Dundee while at a disadvantage. Nearing the end of the match, when Jerry FINALLY dropped the strap and was making a huge comeback, Falk went to ringside and put something in

Dundee's hand. As Lawler was about to resume his attack, Bill threw it into Jerry's good eye. Bill was able to pin the King and send him packing. For the first time ever, Jerry Lawler would actually be gone from the territory. Memphis Wrestling & Jerry Jarrett were always willing to think outside the box. It's one of the things that made it so great

1986

Chapter 17

Jan 2, 1986: Lexington, KY
(c) lost to Bill Dundee
- Southern Title Match
- Title & Leaving Town vs. both Bill & his wife's hair.

Jan 4, 1986: Nashville, TN
(c) lost to Bill Dundee
- Southern Title Match
- Title & Leaving Town vs. both Bill & his wife's hair.

Jan 6, 1986: Hopkinsville, KY
beat Buddy Landell

Jan 7, 1986: Louisville, KY
(c) lost to Bill Dundee
- Southern Title Match
- Title & Leaving Town vs. both Bill & his wife's hair.

Jan 8, 1986: Evansville, IN
(c) lost to Bill Dundee
- Southern Title Match
- Title & Leaving Town vs. both Bill & his wife's hair.

Jan 25, 1986: Singapore
beat Lars Anderson(c)
- Polynesian Pacific Title Match

Feb 13, 1986: San Jose, CA
(c) lost via DQ to Lars Anderson
- Polynesian Pacific Title Match
- Buddy Wolfe interfered on behalf of Lawler

Feb 14, 1986: San Luis Obispo, CA
(c) beat Jimmy Snuka
- Polynesian Pacific Title Match

Feb 15, 1986: Los Angeles, CA
(c) lost via DQ to Lars Anderson
- Polynesian Pacific Title Match
- Buddy Wolfe interfered on behalf of Lawler

Mar 1, 1986: Memphis, TN - TV Taping
Bill Dundee & Buddy Landell beat David Johnson & Jim Jamison
- After the match Landell and Dundee attack referee Jeff Jarrett (son of promotion owner Jerry Jarrett). Jerry Jarrett runs to his son's aid, but eventually gets laid out as well. As Dundee and Landell try to take out Jerry's good eye, Jeff fights back, then Dutch Mantell runs in to makes the save.

Interview of Jerry Jarrett - Jerry tries to speak but can't stop crying so Lance Russell walks him off the set.

Interview: Eddie Marlin comes out and announces he's too old to get in the ring with Dundee & Landell. Jerry Jarrett's eyes won't allow him to be in a match with the two. Jeff is just a boy. One thing Eddie can do is bring someone to Memphis who can deal with Dundee & Landell, someone who isn't afraid to face them. Marlin announces as booker he is lifting the current ban on him and bringing back Jerry Lawler. Dundee and Landell run out claiming Marlin can't do that. Marlin says he can and if they don't like it they can sue him.

Interview: Lance Russell, Dutch Mantel & Eddie Marlin call Jerry Lawler on a speaker phone at the announce desk. Eddie tells Jerry what's happened, tell him his 90 ban is lifted and asks Jerry Lawler to return to Memphis. To help gain control of Memphis Wrestling and revenge for the Jarrett family, Lawler accepts.

Mar 3, 1986: Memphis, TN
& Dutch Mantell beat Bill Dundee & Buddy Landell
- Legit Sell-out of the Mid-South Coliseum, attendance of 11,300.

* Amazing Memphis angle. Jerry Lawler had honored the Loser-Leaves-Town agreement and was having a wonderful time in Hawaii. With Bill Dundee and Buddy Landell running over all the competition the fans were getting frustrated. It was time for the King to come back. As you read the Memphis TV Taping info from March 1, it's so easy to see how great things were handled. You have the top two bad guys in Memphis, Dundee & Landell beat us a 170 lbs kid in Jeff Jarrett. Then you have them beat his nearly blind father, Jerry Jarrett, who comes in to help. Jerry

comes on TV and cries because he can't save his son from the beat down. Real issues made the fans care in Memphis. This angle fired up the people watching at home. We know the payoff is there when Eddie Marlin comes in and makes that call to Lawler. The fans remember two months ago when he was cheated by Dundee and made to leave town. With Marlin lifting that ban, the fans know the King, (along with Dutch Mantell as his partner), is the one guy who can stop Dundee and Landell. This was a huge match for the fans. The Mid-South Coliseum sold all 11,300 tickets. Beyond that, over 3,000 people were turned away. This was a huge success for the Jarrett Promotion.

Mar 8, 1986: Memphis, TN - TV Taping
Taped interview with Jerry Lawler

At the end of the show, Bill Dundee gets into it with Lance Russell and slaps him. Lance gets mad and drops the mic and walks off the set.

Mar 8, 1986: Nashville, TN
& Dutch Mantell beat Bill Dundee & Buddy Landell

Mar 9, 1986: Memphis, TN
& Dutch Mantell beat Bill Dundee & Buddy Landell
- Injuries to Dundee & Landell forced the ref to stop the match and award it to Lawler & Mantell

Jerry Lawler Letting Dundee & Landell Know Their War Is Far From Over.

Mar 11, 1986: Louisville, KY
& Dutch Mantell beat Bill Dundee & Buddy Landell

Mar 15, 1986: Memphis, TN - TV Taping
In the aftermath of Bill Dundee slapping Lance Russell, the show starts with Bill Dundee and Buddy Landell having taken over the show. The duo has set up a new announce table with their names on it. It says the "Bill & Buddy Show". The duo gets thru a match or two when Jerry Lawler & Dutch Mantell storm the set and destroy Dundee & Landell. After they have fled to the back, Lawler & Mantell destroy the Bill & Buddy table. At that point Lance Russell & Dave Brown come out and take their spots behind their old announce table.

* This is one of the most remembered angles that was played out on the Saturday Morning show. The funny thing is the "Bill & Buddy Show" angle only lasted part of one episode of the show. Many people think it lasted for weeks, when it didn't.

Mar 17, 1986: Memphis, TN
& Dutch Mantell beat Bill Dundee & Buddy Landell

The War Continues.

Mar 18, 1986: Louisville, KY
& Dutch Mantell vs. Bill Dundee & Buddy Landell

Mar 21, 1986: Booneville MS
& Dutch Mantell No Contest with Bill Dundee & Buddy Landell

Mar 24, 1986 Memphis, TN
& Dutch Mantell beat Bill Dundee & Buddy Landell
- Texas Death Match
- 26 falls

Lawler & Mantell Want More Of Dundee & Landell.

Mar 26, 1986: Honolulu, HI
(c) lost to SuperFly Tui Selinga
- Polynesian Pacific Title Match

Mar 28, 1986: Jackson, TN
& Dutch Mantell beat Bill Dundee & Buddy Landell

Mar 29, 1986: Nashville, TN
& Dutch Mantell beat Bill Dundee & Buddy Landell
- Texas Death Match

Mar 31, 1986: Memphis, TN
& Dutch Mantell lost to Bill Dundee & Buddy Landell
- Texas Death Elimination Match
- 13th fall

Apr 4, 1986: Nashville, TN
& Dutch Mantell beat Bill Dundee & Buddy Landell
- Texas Death Match

Apr 5, 1986: Memphis, TN - TV Taping
beat Pat Rose

Apr 5, 1986: Nashville, TN
& Dutch Mantell lost to Bill Dundee & Buddy Landell
- Texas Death Elimination Match
- 13th fall

Apr 7, 1986: Memphis, TN
beat Bill Dundee(c)
- Southern Title Match
- NO DQ Cage Match

Jerry Lawler Is Once Again The Southern Champ.

Apr 9, 1986: Evansville, IN
& Dutch Mantell lost to Bill Dundee & Buddy Landell
- Texas Death Elimination Match

Apr 10, 1986: Morengo, IN
vs. Buddy Landell

Apr 11, 1986: Jackson, TN
& Dutch Mantell lost to Bill Dundee & Buddy
Landell
- Texas Death Elimination Match

Apr 12, 1986: Nashville, TN
beat Bill Dundee(c)
- Southern Title Match

Apr 14, 1986: Memphis, TN
(c) beat Tony Falk
- Southern Title Match
-Falk was a sub for Nord the Barbarian who no
showed.

*** Jerry Lawler said he would fight anyone
on the card that the fans wanted. Falk got
the most applause. The fans still
remembered how Tony had thrown ink into
Lawler's eyes and helped cause him to lose
the Loser Leave Town matchto Dundee
back in late Dec. 1985.**

Apr 19, 1986: Memphis, TN TV results
Lance Russell interviews Jerry Lawler Memphis,
TN tape, Apr 14, 1986: Jerry Lawler vs. Tony
Falk - Bill Dundee, Buddy Landell run in
Memphis, TN tape, Apr 14, 1986: Joe Leduc &
Jeff Jarrett vs. Bill Dundee & Buddy Landell-

Apr 19, 1986: Nashville, TN
& Jeff Jarrett beat Tony Falk & Abdul Gaddafi

Apr 21, 1986: Memphis, TN
w/Joe Leduc & Jeff Jarrett beat Bill Dundee,
Buddy Landell & Tony Falk

Joe Leduc, Jeff Jarrett & Jerry Lawler

Apr 23, 1986: Oxford, MS
(c) beat MasterBlaster
- Southern Title Match

Jerry Lawler & Billy Travis beat Memphis Vice:
Jerry Bryant & Lou Winston

Apr 25, 1986: Jackson, TN
& Jeff Jarrett beat Tony Falk & Abdul Gaddafi

Jerry Lawler Teaming Up With Jeff Jarrett.

Apr 26, 1986: Memphis, TN - TV Taping
Memphis, TN tape, Apr 21, 1986: Jerry Lawler,
Joe Leduc & Jeff Jarrett vs. Bill Dundee, Buddy
Landell & Tony Falk-JD Costello runs in then out
comes Eddie Marlin
Lance Russell interviews Jerry Lawler & Joe
Leduc
Memphis, TN tape: Leduc, Lawler

Apr 28, 1986: Memphis, TN
& Joe Leduc won via DQ over Bill Dundee &
Buddy Landell

May 2, 1986: Jackson, TN
(c) lost to Bill Dundee
- Southern Title Match

May 3, 1986: Memphis, TN - TV taping
An announcement is made that Bill Dundee has regained the Southern title from Jerry Lawler with the help from referee Jesse Allen. This particular referee would then become suspended from duty.

Interview: JD Costello-Costello offers his managerial services to Jerry Lawler plus $100000, Jerry Lawler comes out declines the offer, Costello slaps Lawler, Lawler runs Costello into the ring and strips him revealing ladies lingerie

wins by DQ over Abdul Gaddafi with Tony Falk
-MOD Squad: Basher & Spike, JD Costello out then Dutch Mantel, Eddie Marlin out
-Costello burns Lawler

May 3, 1986: Nashville, TN
& Joe Leduc vs. Bill Dundee & Buddy Landell

Jerry Lawler Backs Buddy Landell Into A Corner.

May 5, 1986: Memphis, TN
& Dutch Mantell lost to the MOD Squad

May 6, 1986: Louisville, KY
& Joe Leduc beat Bill Dundee & Buddy Landell

May 9, 1986: Jackson, TN
went to a No Contest with Bill Dundee
-Thunder Dome 1986

May 10, 1986: Nashville, TN
& Dutch Mantell lost to the MOD Squad

May 12, 1986: Memphis, TN
Winners to represent Memphis in World Tag Champions next year in Japan
Rd 1
& Austin Idol beat the MOD Squad

Semi-finals
& Austin Idol beat the Hunters

Finals
& Austin Idol beat Bill Dundee & Buddy Landell

May 13, 1986: Louisville, KY
& Dutch Mantell lost to the MOD Squad w/JD Costello

May 15, 1986: Tuckerman, AR
& Dutch Mantell won by DQ over the Mod Squad

May 17, 1986: Memphis TN - TV Taping
Interview: Jerry Lawler & Giant Hillbilly Memphis, TN tape, May 12, 1986: Bill Dundee & Buddy Landell vs. Jerry Lawler & Austin Idol-Dundee & Landell split after their loss

Jerry Lawler & Giant Hillbilly vs. EZ Ryder & Keith Eric

Giant Hillbilly & Jerry Lawler

May 17, 1986: Nashville, TN
& Giant Hillbilly vs. the MOD Squad(c)
- Southern Tag Title Match
- Giant Hillbilly is Plowboy Frazier

May 19, 1986: Memphis, TN
& Giant Hillbilly won via DQ over the MOD Squad(c)
- Southern Tag Title Match

May 20, 1986: Louisville, KY
Winners to represent Memphis in World Tag
Champions next year in Japan
Rd 1: & Austin Idol beat the MOD Squad

Semi-finals: & Austin Idol beat the Hunters

Finals: & Austin Idol beat Bill Dundee & Buddy
Landell

May 23, 1986: Amory, MS
& Dutch Mantell won via DQ over the MOD
Squad

May 26, 1986: Memphis, TN
& Giant Hillbilly beat the MOD Squad & JD
Costello
- Handicap 2 on 3 Match

Won Thunderdome 85 Battle Royal
- those eliminate... Abdul Gaddafi, Baron Von
Brauner, Basher, Bill Dundee, Buddy Landel,
Danny Fargo, Dutch Mantell, Giant Hillbilly, JD
Costello, Jeff Jarrett, Joe Leduc, Billy Travis,
Paul Diamond, Pat Rose, Pat Tanaka, Tracy
Smothers, Rip Rogers, Spike, Tojo Yamamoto,
Strong Machine, & Tony Falk,

ThunderDome 85: Jerry Lawler (masked)
Attacking Hustler Rip Rogers

May 27, 1986: Louisville, KY
& Giant Hillbilly vs. the MOD Squad(c) & JD
Costello
- Southern Tag Title Match

Giant Hillbilly & Jerry Lawler

May 29, 1986: Kansas City, MO
beat Kevin Kelly

June 9, 1986: Memphis, TN
w/Austin Idol & Giant Hillbilly beat the MOD
Squad & JD Costello
- Stretcher match

June 10, 1986: Louisville, KY
w/Austin Idol & Giant Hillbilly vs. Mod Squad &
JD Costello

Jerry Lawler Escaping Basher From (Mod
Squad).

June 11, 1986: Evansville, IN
& Giant Hillbilly vs. the MOD Squad(c)
- Southern Tag Title Match

June 14, 1986: Memphis, TN - TV Taping
& Giant Hillbilly beat The Libyan and Strong
Machine

June 16, 1986: Memphis, TN
went to a No Contest with Bill Dundee
- Southern Title Tournament
- Round 1

& Giant Hillbilly won via DQ over the MOD
Squad(c)
- Southern Tag Title Match

June 23, 1986: Memphis, TN
& Giant Hillbilly beat the MOD Squad(c)
- Southern Tag Title Match
June 30, 1986: Memphis, TN
w/Giant Hillbilly(c) won via DQ over the
Nightmares
- Southern Tag Title Match
- Mod Squad interfere on behalf of Nightmares,
who don't like it and start fighting with the MOD
Squad.

July 5, 1986: Memphis, TN - TV Taping
Jerry Lawler & The Giant Hillbilly beat Rough &
Ready with Boss Winters- 0:22
Lance Russell announces Lawler's match went
:22, this brings out Bam Bam Bigelow who says
he will beat that time
Bam Bam Bigelow beat Mike Murphy- 0:13

July 7, 1986: Memphis, TN
lost to Bill Dundee(c)
- International Title Match

w/Austin Idol & Giant Hillbilly lost to Bam Bam
Bigelow, Fire & Flame
- Fire & Flame are Don Bass & Dirty Rhodes

7/10 ?
w/Giant Hillbilly Elmer beat Bam Bam Bigelow &
Larry Sharpe

July 12, 1986: Memphis, TN - TV Results
Fire & Flame vs. the Nightmares when a female
in the crowd gets involved with Fire & Flame.
They proceed to Suplex the lady at ringside.
Totally unscripted. Lance announces the match
is over, Randy Hales & Jerry Lawler come out
and run off Fire & Flame as they cut to an
unplanned commercial break. Apparently the
female was a friend of Bass & Rhodes (Fire &
Flame) and they planned the whole thing, but
the promotion had no idea it was going to
happen, nor did they condone it. When they

came back after the commercial break the
match the match was changed to the MOD
Squad vs the Nightmares and no mention was
made of it. This was only seen on the live
Memphis feed of this episode. The other cities in
the promotion were shown the MOD Squad vs.
Nightmares match only. Weird piece of Memphis
Wrestling history.

July 14, 1986: Memphis, TN
beat Bill Dundee(c)
- International Title Match
- Loser Leaves Town
- No DQ

Bill Dundee Has The Upper Hand.

July 15, 1986: Louisville, KY
beat Bill Dundee
- Loser Leaves Town
- No DQ

July 18, 1986: Jackson, TN
& Giant Hillbilly(c lost to Fire & Flame
- Southern Tag Title Match

July 19, 1986: Memphis, TN - TV Taping
Jackson, TN tape, July 18, 1986: Fire & Flame
with Billy Spears beat Jerry Lawler & Giant
Hillbilly (Southern tag champs) to win titles

Jerry Lawler & JT Southern vs. Keith Eric & Don
Donovan

July 19, 1986: Nashville, TN
beat Bill Dundee(c)
- International Title Match
- Loser Leaves Town
- No DQ

July 21, 1986: Memphis, TN
lost to Nick Bockwinkel(c)
- AWA World Title Match

July 22, 1986: Louisville, KY
lost to Nick Bockwinkel(c)
- AWA World Title Match

July 25, 1986: Memphis, TN
Jerry Lawler & company play softball
@ Tim McCarver Stadium (same fairgrounds
area as the Mid-South Coliseum, where UWF
had their card.)
Attendance: 7000
- This was to counter a UWF card in Memphis,
TN on this date which drew 2000.

July 26, 1986: Memphis, TN
& Giant Hillbilly lost to Memphis Vice (Jerry
Bryant & Big Lew Winston)

July 28, 1986: Memphis, TN
In Battle Royal for Southern Title
- won by Bam Bam Bigelow

(c) won by DQ over Bam Bam Bigelow
- International Title Match

July 29, 1986: Louisville, KY
w/Giant Hillbilly vs. Fire & Flame(c)
- Southern Tag Title Match

July 31, 1986: Nashville, TN
w/Giant Hillbilly vs. Fire & Flame(c)
- Southern Tag Title Match

Aug 2, 1986: Memphis, TN - TV Taping
beat Juicy Johnny

Aug 2, 1986: Nashville, TN
won via DQ over Bam Bam Bigelow w/Larry
Sharpe
- Lawler's International Title vs. Bigelow's
Southern Title.

Aug 4, 1986: Memphis, TN
won via DQ over Bam Bam Bigelow w/Larry
Sharpe
- Lawler's International Title vs. Bigelow's
Southern Title.

Aug 5, 1986: Louisville, KY
(c) won via DQ over Bam Bam Bigelow w/Larry
Sharpe
- International Title Match

In 20-Man Battle Royal
- Winner gers Southern Title
- won by Bam Bam Bigelow

Aug 6, 1986: Evansville, IN
won via DQ over Bam Bam Bigelow w/Larry
Sharpe
- Lawler's International Title vs. Bigelow's
Southern Title.

Aug 8, 1986: Birmingham, AL
won via DQ over Stan Hansen

Aug 9, 1986: Honolulu, HI
beat Super Samoan Sakalia

Aug 16, 1986: Nashville, TN
w/Jeff Jarrett & Pat Tanaka beat Tojo
Yamamoto, Akio Sato & Tarzan Goto

Aug 25, 1985: Memphis, TN
& the Killer lost to Bam Bam Bigelow & Larry
Sharpe
- Killer is the Snowman Eddie Crawford

Aug 28, 1986: Kansas City, KS
lost to Sam Houston

Aug 30, 1986: Nashville, TN
& Giant Hillbilly vs. Memphis Vice

Sep 1, 1986: Memphis, TN
& the Killer lost to Bam Bam Bigelow & Larry
Sharpe
- Double Elimination death match

Sep 2, 1986: Louisville, KY
& the Killer vs. Bam Bam Bigelow & Larry
Sharpe

Sep 4, 1986: Lexington, KY
w/Jeff Jarrett & Pat Tanaka vs. Akio Sato,
Tarzan Goto & the Great Kabuki w/Tojo
Yamamoto

Sep 8, 1986: Memphis, TN
beat Bam Bam Bigelow(c) w/Larry Sharpe
- Southern Title Match

Sep 9, 1986: Louisville, KY

vs. Bam Bam Bigelow w/Larry Sharpe
- Texas Death Match

Sep 15, 1986: Memphis, TN
& Bam Bam Bigelow beat Man Mountain Link & Larry Sharpe

Sep 20, 1986: Memphis, TN - TV Taping
beat Larry Wright

beat Flame

lost to Fire
-Tommy Rich was late to the TV Taping so Lawler took on Fire & Flame individually. Flame interfered in the

Sep 26, 1986: Memphis, TN
& Tommy Rich beat Fire & Flame
- Loser Leaves town vs.Masks
- Fire & Flame unmasked as Dirty Rhodes & Don Bass
- Rare Friday Night Card, because of Mid-South Fair at the Fairgrounds

Sep 27, 1986: Memphis, TN - TV results
Lance Russell announces that Lawler & Rich have defeated Fire & Flame earlier in the week in a hair vs. masks match. Fire was unmasked to be Dirty Rhodes, Flame was Don Bass and Torch was Larry Wright.
Lawler is scheduled to wrestle Keith Eric but is not in the dressing room. Randy Hales announces the match is postponed. Interview: Dirty Rhodes, Don Bass & Larry Wright Interview-Rhodes claims they have taken out Lawler and shows Lawler's car keys are now in his possession.
Tommy Rich vs. Keith Roberson when Don Bass, Dirty Rhodes & Larry Wright attack Rich. the 3 on 1 leaves Tommy bloody in the ring. All 3 go to Lance at the announcer table and say that they left Lawler the same as Rich before the show started. A few minutes later Don Bass & Dirty Rhodes are being interviewed by Lance Russell when Jerry Lawler & Tommy Rich storm the set and Lawler busts a coke bottle over Dirty Rhodes's head. Rich attacks Bass and then quickly takes Larry Wright out of the picture. Lawler, Rich, Bass & Rhodes are left bloody.

Sep 29, 1986: Memphis, TN
& Tommy Rich went to a No Contest with Dirty Rhodes & Don Bass(c)
- Southern Tag Title Match

Oct 1, 1986: Evansville, IN
& Tommy Rich vs. Dirty Rhodes & Don Bass(c)
- Southern Tag Title Match

Oct 4, 1986: Memphis, TN - TV Taping
beat Nikita Mulkavich

Oct 4, 1986: Nashville, TN
& Tracey Smothers went to a No Contest with Don Bass & Dirty Rhodes(c)
- Southern Tag Title Match

Oct 6, 1986: Memphis, TN
(c) won via DQ over Dirty Rhodes
- Southern Title Match

& Jeff Jarrett beat Tarzan Goto, Akio Sato & Tojo Yamamoto

Won 20-Man Battle Royal
- Wins a 1986 4x4 Truck

Oct 13, 1986: Memphis, TN
w/Jeff & Jerry Jarrett won via DQ over Akio Sato, Tarzan Goto & Tojo Yamamoto

& Austin Idol won via DQ over Dirty Rhodes & Don Bass

Oct 20, 1986: Memphis, TN
w/Austin Idol, Tommy Rich, Jeff & Jerry Jarrett lost to Tarzan Goto, Akio Sato, Tojo Yamamoto, Don Bass & Dirty Rhodes
- Hospital Elimination Match

Oct 27, 1986: Memphis, TN
(c) won via DQ over Dirty Rhodes
- Southern Title Match

Nov 1, 1986: Memphis, TN - TV Taping
beat Bubba Monroe

won a 20 -Man Battle Royal

Nov 3, 1986: Memphis, TN
& Big Bubba beat Don Bass & Dirty Rhodes(c)
- Southern Tag Title Match

(c) beat Dirty Rhodes
- Southern Title Match

Nov 4, 1986: Louisville, KY
(c) vs. Dirty Rhodes
- Southern Title Match

Nov 10, 1986: Memphis, TN
Southern Tag Title Toournament
& Tommy Rich beat Ninja & Boy Tony

& Tommy Rich drew with the Sheepherders
- Sheepherders were Jon Boyd & Big Foot
- Sheepherders moved on via a coin toss

won via DQ over Big Bubba w/Downtown Bruno
Lights Out Match

Nov 11, 1986: Evansville, IN
& Big Bubba vs. Don Bass & Dirty Rhodes
- Bubba turned on Lawler

(c) beat Dirty Rhodes
- Southern Title Match

Nov 15, 1986: Nashville, TN
vs. Big Bubba w/Downtown Bruno

Nov 17, 1986: Memphis, TN
lost via DQ to Big Bubba w/Downtown Bruno

Jerry Lawler Has Big Bubba In The Corner.

Nov 18, 1986: Louisville, KY
(c) vs. Big Bubba w/Downtown Bruno
- Southern Title Match

Nov 19, 1986: Honolulu, HI
w/ Kini Popo I & Fallen Angel vs. Uncle Elmer,
Superfly Tui & Mystery Lady

Nov 23, 1986: Memphis, TN
beat Big Bubba w/Downtown Bruno
- Hair Match

Dec 1, 1986: Memphis, TN
lost to Big Bubba w/Downtown Bruno
- Throw in the towel match

Jerry Giving Big Bubba A Leg Drop In The
Last Place He Would Want It.

Dec 8, 1986: Memphis, TN
beat The Great Kabuki

Jerry Lawler Used His Own Face Make-up
Going Against Kabuki.

Dec 10, 1986: Evansville, IN
vs. Big Bubba w/Downtown Bruno

Dec 15, 1986: Memphis, TN
lost to Kabuki
- Barbed Wire Match

Dec 17, 1986: Evansville, IN
& Lew Winston vs. Big Bubba & Goliath
w/Downtown Bruno

Dec 20, 1986: Nashville, TN
w/Memphis Vice vs. Big Bubba, Goliath &
Downtown Bruno

Dec 22, 1986: Memphis, TN
DDQ with Tommy Rich

Dec 27, 1986: Memphis, TN - TV Taping
beat Keith Eric

Dec 29, 1986: Memphis, TN
beat Tommy Rich

1987

Chapter 18

Jan 4, 1987: Memphis, TN
drew with Nick Bockwinkel(c)
- AWA World Title Match
- Went to a 60 Minute draw

Jan 7, 1987: Evansville, IN
vs. Tommy Rich

Jan 10, 1987: Memphis, TN - TV results
Memphis Tape: Jerry Lawler vs. Tommy Rich from Dec match
Interview with Nick Bockwinkel about 3-Man tournament to decide who gets the next AWA World Title Match in Memphis.

Jan 11, 1987: Memphis, TN
lost via DQ to Tommy Rich

Jerry Lawler won via DQ over Austin Idol

* Tommy Rich came out during the Lawler-Idol match and caused the DQ of Idol. Both men then preceded to pummel Jerry for a few minutes. Idol & Rich then dragged Jerry to one of the ring corners, jumped out of the ring, each grabbed a leg and pulled the King into the corner posts. It wasn't pretty. Just to make sure they got the job done, they did it again. Jerry was stretchered out of the ring that night. On the following Saturday morning's TV show, the fans were told the King suffered a ruptured testicle and would be out of action indefinitely, until he healed. The fans were stunned. Tommy Rich's & Austin Idol's conversion to the area's top heels was complete as the fans HATED them now.

The reality of the situation, which was usually different from what was shown on the TV show or in the ring, was that Jerry Lawler had a vasectomy and needed time to recover. This angle gave Jerry the month off he needed to get recover and also gave the fans incentive to hate Idol & Rich.

Jan 17, 1987: Memphis, TN - TV results
Memphis Tape> Jan 10, 1987 Recap of Lawler vs. Rich & then Idol. Showing the posting of Lawler. Lance explains Lawler has a ruptured testicle and will be out for a month.

Lance interviews Austin Idol & Tommy Rich, who gloat about putting Lawler out of wrestling.

Feb 2, 1987: Memphis, TN
* Tournament was held for the Southern Heavyweight Title. Jerry Lawler was stripped of it because he failed to defend it in 30 days. The finals of the tournament saw Austin Idol defeat Soul Train Jones to win the title.

Feb 9, 1987: Memphis, TN
Soul Train Jones & the Killer went to a No Contest with Austin Idol & Tommy Rich
- Killer was Eddie Crawford

* After the match ended Idol & Rich attempted to run the Killer into the corner post just as they had done to the King in January. Out of nowhere, Jerry Lawler ran from the back of the Coliseum and made the save. The fans went crazy.

Feb 14, 1987: Memphis, TN - TV Taping
Recap of the Lawler posting incident.
Lance interviews the returning Jerry Lawler. Jerry explains he knows Idol & Rich are a serious threat. He went to find the toughest guy he knew which explains why his partner is Nick Bockwinkel.

Interview tape of Nick Bockwinkel. Nick says he doesn't like Lawler but admits Lawler is an honorable man. He talks about the match he had few weeks earlier in Memphis, defending his AWA World title against Austin Idol and how Tommy Rich interfered and attempted to seriously hurt him. He says he would normally not team with Lawler but because of the lack of honor of Idol & Rich, he will team with him.

Feb 15, 1987: Jackson, TN
& the Fabs (Keirn & Lane) beat Jonathon Boyd & the Sheepherders (Luke Williams & Butch Miller)

- First match back for Lawler, after corner posting incident.

Feb 16, 1987: Memphis, TN
& Nick Bockwinkel win via DQ over Tommy Rich
& Austin Idol

Jerry Lawler Teaming Up With Nick
Bockwinkel.

Feb 17, 1987: Evansville, IN
lost via DQ to Tommy Rich

Feb 21, 1987: Memphis, TN - TV Taping
Interview: Jerry Lawler, Nick Bockwinkel

Feb 21, 1987: Blytheville, AR
& Soul Train Jones beat Tojo Yamamoto &Akio
Sato

Feb 23, 1987: Memphis, TN
Nick Bockwinkel & Jerry Lawler beat Humongous
& Austin Idol
- At the end of the match Lawler accidently
punched Bockwinkel who left the ring and let
Idol & Humongous beat up Jerry.
- Looks like Humongous was a young Sid Eudy
(Sid Vicious).

Feb 24, 1987: Evansville, IN
& Nick Bockwinkel vs. Austin Idol & Tommy Rich

Mar 2, 1987: Memphis, TN
& Bam Bam Bigelow lost via DQ to Tommy Rich
& Austin Idol
-Lawler & Bigelow hit the ring and the match
never really started. The duo obliterated Idol &
Rich. The fans loved every minute of it.

Mar 4, 1987: Evansville, IN
& Bam Bam Bigelow lost via DQ to Tommy Rich
& Austin Idol

Mar 7, 1987: Nashville, TN
won via DQ over Austin Idol(c)
- Southern Title Match

Mar 8, 1987: Jackson, TN
won via DQ over Austin Idol(c)
- Southern Title Match

Mar 9, 1987: Memphis, TN
& Bam Bam Bigelow beat Austin Idol & Tommy
Rich

Mar 11, 1987: Evansville, IN
& Bam Bam Bigelow beat Tommy Rich & Austin
Idol

Mar 14, 1987: Memphis, TN - TV Taping
& Bam Bam Bigelow beat The Medics

Mar 14, 1987: Nashville, TN
& Bam Bam Bigelow No Contest with Big Bubba
& Goliath(c) w/Downtown Bruno
- Southern Tag Title Match

Mar 16, 1987: Memphis, TN
went to a No Contest with Austin Idol(c)
- Southern Title Match

Austin Idol vs. Jerry Lawler

Feb 17, 1987: Evansville, IN
went to a No Contest with Austin Idol(c)
- Southern Title Match

Mar 20, 1987: Lewisburg, TN
drew with Nick Bockwinkel(c)
- AWA World Title Match

Mar 21, 1987: Blytheville, MS
lost via Count Out to Lord Humongus

Battle Royal. Winner: Jerry Lawler

Mar 22, 1987: Jackson, TN - Afternoon card
& Bam Bam Bigelow won via Count Out over Austin Idol & Lord Humongous W/Paul E. Dangerly
- Paul E. Dangerly was originally brought in to manage Humongous but was switched over to Austin Idol (and Tommy Rich).

Mar 22, 1987: Memphis, TN, Evening
& Bam Bam Bigelow beat Austin Idol & Tommy Rich
- Texas Death Match

* Lawler got revenge as he & Bigelow were able to pull Tommy Rich onto the corner post (the same way Lawler had been done back in January.)

Mar 28, 1987: Memphis, TN - TV Taping
Interview with Jerry Lawler: Lawler explains that he and Bigelow were both fined for their posting of Tommy Rich in the Mar 22 Memphis match. He paid his fine but Bam Bam Bigelow refused to, so Bam Bam was suspended by Eddie Marlin.
Lance explains that Tommy Rich is now out with an injury after the posting by Lawler & Bigelow. Monday night match will feature Lawler vs. Idol in a singles match

Mar 30, 1987: Memphis, TN
won via DQ over Austin Idol w/Paul E. Dangerly
- Card was cancelled because of snow.

Apr 5, 1987: Jackson, TN
vs. Humongous w/Paul E. Dangerly

Apr 6, 1987: Memphis, TN, Monday
went to a No Contest with Austin Idol w/Paul E. Dangerly

Apr 7, 1987: Louisville, KY
won via DQ over Austin Idol w/Paul E. Dangerly
- Strap Match

Apr 11, 1987: Chattanooga, TN
lost via DQ to Austin Idol(c) w/Paul E. Dangerly
- Southern Title Match
- No Referee in Ring

Apr 12, 1987: Nashville, TN
lost via DQ to Austin Idol(c) w/Paul E. Dangerly
- Southern Title Match
- No Referee in Ring

Apr 13, 1987: Memphis, TN
Lost to Austin Idol(c) w/Paul E. Dangerly
- Southern Title Match

Apr 18, 1987: Nashville, TN
Jeff Jarrett w/Jerry Lawler beat Pat Tanaka & Paul Diamond
- $10,000 vs. Travis coming back
- Tanaka & Diamond must win in ten minutes:

Apr 20, 1987: Memphis, TN
beat Austin Idol(c) w/Paul E. Dangerly
- Southern Title
- No DQ Chain Match

* Both men connected to an 8 foot chain. Referee Jerry Calhoun attaches the chain to Lawler first, who then stands in the corner waiting for Idol to be attached. Idol doesn't want to be attached and grandstands outside the ring until Calhoun gives him a 10-count to be attached or he will award the Southern Title to Jerry Lawler. As Calhoun reaches the 7 count Idol just back in the ring. Calhoun attaches the chain to Idol, who is still belly-aching. Calhoun calls for the bell and the match is underway. At that point Lawler walks across the ring without the chain attached to his wrist. In all of Idol's carrying on, the King had unattached the chain and re-attached it to the top rope. As Paul E. Dangerly has hopped on the ring to complain and Idol is frantically trying to unhook his chain, Lawler pulls his own smaller chain out of his trunks, wraps it around his fist and knocks Idol out. Jerry drops down and pins Idol. 1-2-3. In under a minute the King got the win and his Southern Title back. Jerry asks for the ringside microphone and announces to Idol, "Idol, that's what you call a Memphis Chain Match!"

Apr 27, 1987: Memphis, TN, Monday
(c) lost Southern Title to Austin Idol w/Paul E. Dangerly

- Southern Title Match
- hair match
- If Idol loses, will payback everyone's ticket cost.
- reposted Lawler
- gone a month for hair to grow back some.

May 4, 1987: Memphis, TN
Bill Dundee & Rocky Johnson won by DQ over Tommy Rich & Austin Idol w/Paul E. Dangerly

* Dundee & Johnson won when Pat Tanaka, Paul Diamond & Downtown Bruno interferred in the match. At that point it was 6 on 2. As Bruno & Dangerly were about to cut Dundee's hair, a masked man ran out from the dressing room area and made the save. The masked man threw a fireball at Dangerly and then started cutting Bruno's hair. This masked man looked suspiciously like Jerry Lawler.

May 23, 1987: Memphis, TN - TV Taping
A female fan at ring side asked Tommy Rich to sign her photo and Tommy obliged. As he was doing it the lady attacked Tommy. The "female" was Jerry Lawler in drag and he laid into Tommy as the fans cheered.

May 24, 1987: Jackson, TN
& Bill Dundee beat Tommy Rich & Moondog Spot

May 25, 1987: Memphis, TN, Monday
lost via DQ to Tommy Rich
-after the match Austin Idol ran in, followed by Bill Dundee.

May 26, 1987: Louisville, KY, Tuesday
& Bill Dundee went to a Double Count Out with Tommy Rich & Austin Idol

May 30, 1987: Memphis, TN - TV Taping
& Bill Dundee beat Chick Donavon & Jack Hart(c)
- Non Title Match
- Donavon & Hart were Southern Tag champs

June 1, 1987: Memphis, TN, Monday
& Bill Dundee lost to Austin Idol & Tommy Rich - First Blood Match

Jerry Lawler & Bill Dundee: Looking For Revenge.

June 3, 1987: Evansville, IN
beat Tommy Rich

June 5, 1987: Florence, AL
beat Tommy Rich

Jerry Lawler, Bill Dundee, Rocky Johnson, Memphis Vice (Bryant & Winston) vs. Tommy Rich, Chick Donovan, Jack Hart & the Assassins
- Elimination Match

June 6, 1987: Memphis, TN - TV Taping
Interview: Paul E. Dangerly re: Dangerly claims to be Dundee's new manager but the Superstar disagrees. Paul gives Dundee his credit card for a month which the Superstar takes. Eventually Jerry Lawler comes out and holds Paul E. while Dundee strips him down to his underwear

June 8, 1987: Memphis, TN
beat Austin Idol(c) w/Paul E. Dangerly
- Southern Title Match
- New Ref: Brickhouse Brown
- Brown clotheslines Lawler and leaves ring. Lawler makes a comeback and Jerry Calhoun runs out and makes the 3-count.

& Bill Dundee lost via DQ to Phil Hickerson & Mr. Shima
- Round 1: Southern Tag Title Tournament
- Ref: Brickhouse Brown gets into it with Jerry Lawler after DQ'ing him & Dundee

June 13, 1987: Memphis, TN - TV Taping
With Jerry Lawler present, recap of Ref Brickhouse Brown and his mishandling of 3 different matches the previous Monday Night. Randy Hales comes out and fires ref Brickhouse Brown.
Interview: Bill Dundee & Jerry Lawler
& Bill Dundee beat Rough & Ready with Boss Winters

June 13, 1987: Nashville, TN
& Bill Dundee lost via DQ to Goliath& Mr. Shima
- Round 1: Southern Tag Title Tournament

June 15, 1987: Memphis, TN
& Bill Dundee beat Tommy Rich & Austin Idol
- Scaffold Match
- Tommy Rich breaks wrist in fall off the scaffold

June 22, 1987: Memphis, TN
& Bill Dundee beat Austin Idol & Brickhouse Brown

June 29, 1987: Memphis, TN
(c) won via DQ over Brickhouse Brown
- Southern Title Match

July 1, 1987: Evansville, IN
won via DQ over Brickhouse Brown
- Southern Title Match

July 4, 1987: Memphis, TN - TV Taping
beat Keith Roberson

July 6, 1987: Memphis, TN
(c) lost to Brickhouse Brown
- Southern Title Match

July 8, 1987: Evansville, IN
(c) lost to Brickhouse Brown
- Southern Title Match

July 11, 1987: Nashville, TN
won via DQ over Brickhouse Brown(c)
- Southern Title Match
- Title vs. Crown & a shoe shine

July 12, 1987: Jackson, TN
won via DQ over Brickhouse Brown(c)
- Southern Title Match

July 13, 1987: Memphis, TN
beat Brickhouse Brown(c)
- Southern Title Match

July 14, 1987: Louisville, KY
won via DQ over Brickhouse Brown(c)
- Southern Title Match
- Title vs. Crown & a shoe shine

July 15, 1987: Evansville, IN
won via DQ over Brickhouse Brown(c)
- Southern Title Match
- Title vs. Crown & a shoe shine

July 18, 1987: Nashville, TN
beat Brickhouse Brown(c)
- Southern Title Match
- Title & Crown vs. shoe shine

July 20, 1987: Memphis, TN
(c) beat Brickhouse Brown
- Southern Title Match

July 22, 1987: Evansville, IN
beat Brickhouse Brown(c)
- Southern Title Match

July 27, 1987: Memphis, TN,
beat Nick Bockwinkel
- Winner gets shot at new AWA World Champ, Curt Hennig.

Jerry Lawler: Determined To Win.

July 28, 1987: Louisville, KY
beat Nick Bockwinkel
- Winner gets shot at new AWA World Champ,
Curt Hennig.

Bockwinkel Punches Lawler

July 29, 1987: Evansville, IN
beat Nick Bockwinkel
- Winner gets shot at new AWA World Champ,
Curt Hennig.

July 31, 1987: Columbus, MS
(c) beat Brickhouse Brown
- Southern Title Match

Aug 3, 1987: Memphis, TN
& Rocky Johnson lost to Don Bass & Brickhouse
Brown
- Big Bubba Special Ref
- Dream Match
- If Lawler is pinned, loses Southern title to
whoever pins him.
-If Johnson is pinned, he loses hair
-If Bass is pinned, he loses hair
-If Brown is pinned, he tosses $5,000 to fans
- Lawler pinned by Bass, Bass new Southern
champ
-Big Bubba turned on Lawler causing loss.

Aug 8, 1987: Nashville, TN
& Rocky Johnson lost to Don Bass & Brickhouse
Brown
- Big Bubba Special Ref
- Dream Match
- If Lawler is pinned, loses Southern title to
whoever pins him.
-If Johnson is pinned, he loses hair
-If Bass is pinned, he loses hair
-If Brown is pinned, he tosses $5,000 to fans
- Lawler pinned by Bass, Bass new Southern
champ
-Big Bubba turned on Lawler causing loss.

Sunday Aug 10: Memphis, TN
lost to Curt Hennig(c)
- AWA World Title Match

Aug 15, 1987: Nashville, TN
beat Big Bubba

Aug 16, 1987: Jackson, TN
beat Big Bubba

Aug 17, 1987: Memphis, TN
No Contest with Don Bass(c)
- Southern Title Match
- Title held up
Aug 23, 1987: Marietta, GA
lost to Curt Hennig(c)
- AWA World Title Match

Aug 24, 1987: Memphis, TN
lost to Don Bass
- Southern Title Match - Belt is held up

Aug 29, 1987: Nashville, TN
lost to Don Bass
- Southern Title Match - Belt is held up

Aug 31, 1987: Memphis, TN
beat Don Bass(c)
- Southern Title Match
- Steel Cage Match
- Lawler's hair vs. Title

Sep 7, 1987: Memphis, TN
lost to Brickhouse Brown

Sep 14, 1987: Memphis, TN
beat the Black Prince
- Black Prince was Brickhouse Brown

Sep 20, 1987: Jackson, TN
beat the Black Prince

Sep 21, 1987: Memphis, TN
& Bill Dundee went to a No Contest with Carl
Fergie & Don Bass

Sep 26, 1987: Memphis, TN - TV Taping
& Bill Dundee beat Keith Eric & Keith Roberson

Sep 30, 1987: Evansville, IN
& Bill Dundee lost to Carl Fergie & Don Bass

Oct 5, 1987: Memphis, TN
& Bill Dundee lost to Carl Fergie & Don Bass

Oct 7, 1987: Evansville, IN
& Bill Dundee won via DQ over Carl Fergie &
Don Bass

Oct 10, 1987: Nashville, TN
& Bill Dundee beat Don Bass & Carl Fergie
in An Explosive match

Oct 11, 1987: Memphis, TN
w/Bill Dundee & Steve Keirn lost to Carl Fergie,
Black Prince & Don Bass

& Bill Dundee beat Soldat Ustinovs.& Doug
Somers(c)
- AWA World Tag Title Match
- Lawler & Dundee were the AWA World Tag
Champs.

Jerry Lawler & Bill Dundee: AWA World Tag
Team Champions

Oct 14, 1987: Evansville, IN
& Bill Dundee beat Carl Fergie & Don Bass
- Falls Count Anywhere

Oct 18, 1987: Jackson, TN
& Bill Dundee(c) beat Don Bass & Carl Fergie
- AWA World Tag Title Match

beat Steve Keirn

Oct 19, 1986: Memphis, TN
& Bill Dundee(c) lost to Hector Guerrero & Dr. D
- AWA World Tag Title Match
- Dr. D was Carl Styles

beat Steve Keirn

Oct 24, 1987: Huntingdon, TN
beat Don Bass

Oct 26, 1987: Memphis, TN
& Bill Dundee beat Hector Guerrero & Dr. D(c) -
- AWA World Tag Title Match

Oct 29, 1987: Nashville, TN
& Bill Dundee(c) beat Hector Guerrero & Dr. D
- AWA World Tag Title Match

won via DQ over Steve Keirn

Oct 30, 1987: Milwaukee, WI
& Bill Dundee beat Mike Richards & Rick Gantner

& Bill Dundee(c) lost to Dennis Condrey & Randy
Rose w/Paul E.Dangerly
- AWA World Tag Title Match

Nov 1, 1987: Jackson, TN
& Bill Dundee won via DQ over Steve Keirn &
Jimmy Jack Funk

Nov 2, 1987: Memphis, TN
won via DQ over Bobby Jaggers(c)
- Southern Title Match

won a 20-Man Battle Royal

Nov 4, 1987: Evansville, IN
& Bill Dundee won via DQ over Steve Keirn &
Hector Guerrero

Nov 7, 1987: Memphis, TN - TV Taping
beat the Blue Knight

Nov 9, 1987: Memphis, TN
lost to Bobby Jaggers(c)
- Taped Fist Match
- Southern Title Match

Nov 11, 1987: Louisville, KY
won via DQ over Bobby Jaggers(c)
- Southern Title Match

Nov 16, 1987: Memphis, TN
lost to Steve Keirn

Nov 22, 1987: Memphis, TN
beat Bobby Jaggers(c)
- Southern Title Match

& Jeff Jarrett went to a No Contest with Steve Keirn & Jimmy Jack Funk

Nov 24, 1987: Louisville, KY
won via DQ over Steve Keirn

Nov 28, 1987: Memphis, TN - TV Taping
& Jeff Jarrett beat the Rock n Roll RPM's
- RPM's were Mike Davis & Tommy Lane

Nov 30, 1987: Memphis, TN
& Jeff Jarrett won via DQ over Steve Keirn & Jimmy Jack Funk

Dec 1, 1987: Louisville, KY
& Jeff Jarrett beat Steve Keirn & Jimmy Jack Funk

Dec 2, 1987: Evansville, IN
& Jeff Jarrett beat Steve Keirn & Jimmy Jack Funk

Dec 6, 1987: Jackson, TN
& Jeff Jarrett beat Steve Keirn & Jimmy Jack Funk

Dec 7, 1987: Memphis, TN
(SC) beat Jeff Jarrett(MAC)
- Southern Title vs. Mid-American Title
- Unification Match

(SC & MAC) beat Manny Fernandez(IC)
- Southern & Mid-American Title vs. International Title
- Unification Match of all 3 Memphis singles titles.

Jeff Jarrett lost to Curt Hennig(c)
- AWA World Title Match
- Lawler injured arm vs. Fernandez, asked Jeff to take his place.

* After 6 years, the promotion was eliminating some of their titles. It had always had the Southern Title. In 1981 it brought aboard the Mid-America Title followed by the International Title in 1983. Now the idea was to merge all three into the CWA Title. Not the same as the 1979 CWA World Title, which had been created specifically for Jerry Lawler. This CWA title would continue to be used until October

1989 when the CWA would go away and in its place the USWA would come into existence. At that point the CWA title would become the USWA Southern Title.

Dec 9, 1987: Evansville, IN
& Jeff Jarrett beat Steve Keirn & Jimmy Jack Funk

Dec 14, 1987: Memphis, TN
beat Curt Hennig(c)
- Non-title match
- Hennig was the AWA World Champ

Dec 21, 1987: Memphis, TN
beat Jimmy Jack Funk
- Quarter-final
- Lord of the Ring Tournament Match

Dec 27, 1987: Jackson, TN
(c) beat Manny Fernandez
- CWA Title Match

Dec 28, 1987: Memphis, TN
Lord of the Ring Tournament
Semi-finals:
beat Scott Hall
Bill Dundee beat Jeff Jarrett

Finals:
beat Bill Dundee

* Pro Wrestling Illustrated 1987 Awards

1987 Feud of the Year:
2nd Runner up: Jerry Lawler vs. Austin Idol & Tommy Rich

1988

Chapter 19

Jan 2, 1988: Memphis, TN - TV Taping
& Bill Dundee lost to Manny Fernandez and Jeff Jarrett

Jan 2, 1988: Nashville, TN
(c) beat Jimmy Jack Funk
- CWA Title Match

Jan 4, 1988: Memphis, TN
won via DQ over Bill Dundee
- Lawler's Lord of the Ring vs. Dundee's $5,000

Jan 7, 1988: Louisville, KY
lost to Bill Dundee

Jan 10, 1988: Jackson, TN
(c) beat Hector Guerrero
- CWA Title Match

Jan 11, 1988: Memphis, TN
went to a NO Contest with Bill Dundee
- Lawler's Lord of the Ring vs. Dundee's $5,000
- Ref ruled a NC b/c Terry Taylor attacked both.

Jan 15, 1988: Evansville, IN
won via DQ over Bill Dundee

Jan 18, 1988: Memphis, TN
lost to Curt Hennig(c)
Lawler's ring vs. AWA World Title

Jan 23, 1988: Jonesboro, AR
beat Terry Taylor

Jan 27, 1988: Memphis, TN
& Bill Dundee lost via DQ to the Midnight Rockers(c)
- AWA World Tag Title Match

Feb 1, 1988: Memphis, TN
& Bill Dundee lost via DQ to Don Bass & Carl Fergie
- Round 1: CWA Tag Title Tournament

Feb 3, 1988: Evansville, IN
& Bill Dundee won via DQ over the Midnight Rockers(c)
- AWA World Tag Title Match

Feb 6, 1988: Jonesboro, AR
(c) won via DQ over Max Pain
- CWA Title Match - Barbed Wire Match

Feb 8, 1988: Memphis, TN
(c) lost to Max Pain
- CWA Title Match

Feb 13, 1988: Nashville, TN
(c) lost to Max Pain
- CWA Title Match

Feb 15, 1988: Memphis, TN
won via DQ over Tommy Rich

Feb 16, 1988: Louisville, KY
lost to Tommy Rich
- Loss was via a ref's reverse decision

Feb 19, 1988: Las Vegas, NV
lost via DQ to Curt Hennig(c)
- AWA World Title Match

Feb 20, 1988: Memphis, TN - TV Taping
beat the Choir Boy I

Studio 5 Wrestling At WMC TV Station

Feb 22, 1988: Memphis, TN
won via DQ over Tommy Rich
- DQ was due to Eddie Gilbert interference

Feb 22, 1988 Nashville, TN
vs. Max Pain for CWA Title

Mar 5, 1988: Jonesboro, AR
won via DQ over Eddie Gilbert

Mar 14, 1988: Memphis, TN
lost via DQ to Eddie Gilbert

Mar 19, 1988: Nashville, TN
lost to Eddie Gilbert

Mar 21, 1988: Memphis, TN
lost to Eddie Gilbert

Rallying The Crowd

Mar 22, 1988: Louisville, KY
lost to Eddie Gilbert

Mar 23, 1988: Evansville, TN
lost to Eddie Gilbert

Mar 28, 1988: Memphis, TN
beat Eddie Gilbert

Jerry Working His Way To The Ring.

Mar 29, 1988: Louisville, KY
lost via DQ to Eddie Gilbert

Mar 30, 1988: Evansville, TN
lost via DQ to Eddie Gilbert

Apr 2, 1988: Memphis, TN - TV Taping
beat Tommy Punk

Apr 4, 1988: Memphis, TN
lost to Curt Hennig
- Stretcher Match

Apr 5, 1988: Louisville, KY
beat Eddie Gilbert

Apr 6, 1988: Evansville, TN
beat Eddie Gilbert

Apr 8, 1988: Bolivar, TN
beat Eddie Gilbert

Apr 9, 1988: Memphis, TN - TV Taping
beat Scotty the Body

Apr 11, 1988: Memphis, TN
won via Count Out over Dory Funk Jr.

Apr 16, 1988: Nashville, TN
& Eddie Marlin beat Tommy & Doug Gilbert
- Texas Death Match

Apr 18, 1988: Memphis, TN
lost to Max Pain(c)
- CWA Title Match

lost via DQ to Ernest Angel
- Ref: Max Pain

Apr 19, 1988: Louisville, KY
lost to Max Pain(c)
- CWA Title Match

Apr 20, 1988: Evansville, IN
lost to Max Pain(c)
- CWA Title Match

Apr 25, 1988: Memphis, TN
beat Robert Fuller

Apr 27, 1988: Evansville, IN
beat Robert Fuller

Apr 30, 1988: Jonesboro, AR
& Eddie Marlin won via DQ over Tommy & Doug Gilbert

May 2, 1988: Memphis, TN
lost to Eddie Gilbert

May 9, 1988: Memphis, TN
beat Curt Hennig(c)
- AWA World Title Match
- Title vs. Lawler Retiring
- Special Ref: Jackie Fargo
- Memphis Mayor Named May 9, 1988 Jerry Lawler day In Memphis And Given Key To The City.
- Gate: $52,000

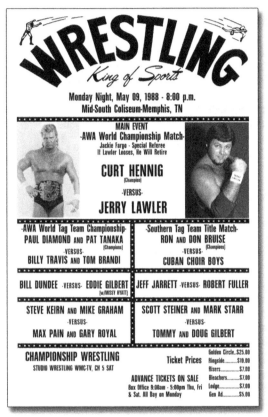

Jerry Put It All On The Line.

* Easily One Of The Most Remembered Matches In Memphis Wrestling History. It was a magical night as Jerry Lawler finally fulfilled his dream of becoming a World Champion. There was no false finish, no taking the title back, etc. Jerry Lawler got a clean pinfall over Curt Hennig and was now the AWA World Heavyweight Champion.

For many of the fans, they never thought this day would happen. Everyone wondered what would happen next, as we were used to Jerry Lawler always being in Memphis. Would this continue, would a whole new array of wrestling stars come to Memphis

to challenge Jerry for the title? After all these years of watching Jerry Lawler & Memphis Wrestling, they were about to flip things on their head yet again. And it would be amazing to watch.

Press Conference After Beating Curt Hennig For AWA World Title, Mid-South Coliseum.

May 14, 1988: Las Vegas, NV - AWA TV Taping
& Greg Gagne won via DQ over Riki Choshu & Mr. Saito

beat Dennis Stamp

beat Daryl Nickel

May 16, 1988: Memphis, TN
(c) beat Bill Dundee
- AWA World Title Match

May 17, 1988: Louisville, KY
(c) beat Dutch Mantell
- AWA World Title Match

May 18, 1988: Evansville, IN
(c) beat Bill Dundee
- AWA World Title Match

May 21, 1988: Nashville, TN
 (c) beat Bill Dundee
- AWA World Title Match

May 29, 1988: Memphis, TN
(c) beat Dutch Mantell
- AWA World Title Match

June 4, 1988: Memphis, TN - TV Taping
Interview with Jerry Lawler

June 4, 1988: Nashville, TN
(c) lost via DQ to Curt Hennig
- AWA World Title Match

June 6, 1988: Memphis, TN
(c) won via DQ over Curt Hennig
- AWA World Title Match

AWA World Champ: Jerry Lawler

June 11, 1988: Memphis, TN - TV Taping
Memphis, TN tape, June 6, 1988: Jerry Lawler
vs. Curt Hennig
Interview with Jerry Lawler
Interview with Curt Hennig

June 12, 1988: Las Vegas, NV - AWA TV Taping
(c) beat Soldat Ustinov
- AWA World Title Match

June 13, 1988: Memphis, TN
(c) beat Curt Hennig
- AWA World Title Match

June 15, 1988: Evansville, IN
(c) beat Curt Hennig
- AWA World Title Match

June 16, 1988: Louisville, KY
(c) beat Curt Hennig
- AWA World Title Match

June 17, 1988: Dallas, TX
(c) beat Terry Taylor
- AWA World Title Match

June 18, 1988: Memphis, TN - TV Taping
Interview with Jerry Lawler (taped)
Interview with Iceman Parsons (taped)

June 18, 1988: San Antonio, TX
(c) beat Iceman King Parsons
- AWA World Title Match

June 19, 1988: Mesquite, TX
(c) beat Iceman King Parsons
- AWA World Title Match

June 20, 1988: Memphis, TN
(c) beat Iceman King Parsons
- AWA World Title Match
June 24, 1988: New Haven, CT
(c) beat Curt Hennig
- AWA World Title Match

June 25, 1988: Memphis, TN - TV Taping
Interview with Jerry Lawler (taped)
Interview with Kerry Von Erich (taped)

June 25, 1988: Jersey City, NJ
(c) beat Curt Hennig
- AWA World Title Match

June 27, 1988: Memphis, TN
(c) Double Count Out with Kerry Von Erich
- AWA World Title Match

July 2, 1988: Dothan, AL
(c) lost via DQ to Austin Idol
- AWA World Title Match

(c) beat Ken Wayne
- AWA World Title Match

July 3, 1988: Memphis, TN
& Jeff Jarrett won via DQ over Robert Fuller &
Jimmy Golden w/Bruno & Sylvia
- Sylvia was Fuller's wife and Bruno was
Downtown Bruno.

July 9, 1988: Memphis, TN - TV Taping
Memphis, TN tape, July 3, 1988: Jerry Lawler &
Jeff Jarrett vs. Robert Fuller & Jimmy Golden-
Tojo Yamamoto & Great Sensei interfere, Jimmy
Valiant makes save

July 9, 1988: Nashville, TN
& Jeff Jarrett went to a Double DQ with Robert
Fuller & Jimmy Golden w/Bruno & Sylvia

July 11, 1988: Memphis, TN
w/Jimmy Valiant & Jeff Jarrett won via DQ over
Robert Fuller, Jimmy Golden & the Great Sensei
w/Bruno & Sylvia

July 14, 1988: Anaheim, CA
(c) beat Curt Hennig
- AWA World Title Match

July 16, 1988: Las Vegas, NV
(c) lost via DQ to Curt Hennig
- AWA World Title Match

July 16, 1988: Memphis, TN TV results
Memphis, TN tape, July 11, 1988: Robert Fuller,
Jimmy Golden & Great Sensei vs. Jerry Lawler,
Jimmy Valiant & Jeff Jarrett
Tape: Jerry Lawler vs. Kerry Von Erich
Tape: Lawler interview

July 18, 1988: Memphis, TN
(ac) won via DQ over Kerry Von Erich(wc)
- AWA World Title vs. World Class World Title
Unification Match

July 21, 1988: Johnson City, TN
(c) beat Wendell Cooley
- AWA World Title Match

July 22, 1988:Knoxville, TN
(c) won via DQ over Doug Furnas
- AWA World Title Match

July 25, 1988: Memphis, TN
(ac) 60 min draw Kerry Von Erich(wc)
- AWA World Title vs. World Class World Title
Unification Match

July 29, 1988: Columbus, MS
(c) lost via DQ to Eddie Gilbert
- AWA World Title Match

July 30, 1988: Memphis, TN - TV Taping
Interview with Jerry Lawler (taped)

July 30, 1988: Tampa, FL
(c) lost via DQ to Kerry Von Erich
- AWA World Title Match

Aug 1, 1988: Memphis, TN
(c) beat Buddy Landell
- AWA World Title Match

Aug 6, 1988: Memphis, TN - TV Taping
interview with Jerry Lawler

Aug 7, 1988: Jackson, TN
& Jeff Jarrett won via DQ over Robert Fuller &
Jimmy Golden w/Bruno & Sylvia
- Tennessee Street Fight

Aug 8, 1988: Memphis, TN
(c) lost via DQ to Austin Idol
- AWA World Title Match

Aug 13, 1988: Memphis, TN - TV Taping
Interview with Jerry Lawler (taped) & Kerry Von
Erich(taped) about Monday Night Match

**Aug 13, 1988: Las Vegas, NV - AWA TV
Taping**
(c) lost via DQ to Curt Hennig
 - AWA World Title Match

Aug 15, 1988: Memphis, TN
(c) beat Kerry Von Erich
- AWA World Title Match

Aug 16, 1988: Louisville, KY
(c) beat Kerry Von Erich
- AWA World Title Match

Aug 17, 1988: Evansville, IN
(c) beat Kerry Von Erich
- AWA World Title Match

**Aug 20, 1988: Las Vegas, NV - AWA TV
Taping**
(c) beat Teijo Khan

Aug 22, 1988: Memphis, TN
(c) lost via DQ to Tommy Rich
- AWA World Title Match

Aug 29, 1988: Memphis, TN
& Kerry Von Erich beat Tommy Rich & Buddy Landell

Aug 30, 1988: Owensboro, KY
(c) won via DQ over Tommy Rich
- AWA World Title Match

Sep 3, 1988: Memphis, TN - TV Taping
Memphis, TN, tape, Aug 29, 1988: Jerry Lawler & Kerry Von Erich vs. Tommy Rich & Buddy Landell

Sep 3, 1988: Medina, OH
(c) beat Wahoo McDaniel
- AWA World Title Match

Sep 5, 1988: Memphis, TN
& Jimmy Valiant beat Tommy Rich & Buddy Landell

Sep 7, 1988: Owensboro, KY
(c) beat Tommy Rich
- AWA World Title Match

Sep 9, 1988: Dallas, TX
(c) won via DQ over Kerry Von Erich
- AWA World Title Match

Sep 10, 1988: Memphis, TN - TV Taping
Interview with Jerry Lawler

Sep 12, 1988: Memphis, TN
& Kerry Von Erich won via Count Out over Tommy Rich & Buddy Landell

Sep 14, 1988: Evansville, IN
& Jimmy Valiant won via Count Out over Tommy Rich & Buddy Landell

Sep 17, 1988: Memphis, TN - TV Taping
Interview with Jerry Lawler

Sep 17, 1988: Nashville, TN
(ac) No Contest with Kerry Von Erich(wc)
- AWA World Title vs. World Class World Title Unification Match

Sep 18, 1988: Louisville, KY
& Jimmy Valiant No Contest with Kerry Von Erich & Michael Hayes

beat Terry Adonis

* Regular card & AWA TV Taping combined

Sep 19, 1988: Memphis, TN
- Renegades Mayhem in Memphis
 (ac) No Contest with Kerry Von Erich(wc)
- AWA World Title vs. World Class World Title Unification Match

* Regular card & AWA TV Taping combined

Going After The World Class World Title.

Sep 24, 1988: Dallas, TX
(ac) No Contest with Kerry Von Erich(wc)
- AWA World Title vs. World Class World Title Unification Match

Sep 30, 1988: Memphis, TN
(c) won via DQ over Ronnie Garvin
- AWA World Title Match

*Mid-South Fair was going on, rare Friday card

Oct 1, 1988: Jackson, TN
(c) beat Buddy Landell
- AWA World Title Match

Oct 2, 1988: Marietta, GA
(c) won via DQ over Tommy Rich
- AWA World Title Match

Oct 3, 1988: Memphis, TN
(c) lost via DQ to Ronnie Garvin
- AWA World Title Match

Jerry In His Role As World Champion

Oct 8, 1988: Memphis, TN - TV results
beat Terry Adonis

Oct 10, 1988: Memphis, TN
w/Jeff Jarrett, Eddie Marlin & Bill Dundee lost to
Kevin & Kerry Von Erich, Steve Cox & Frank
Dusek
- TX/TN Shootout

Oct 15, 1988: Memphis, TN - TV Taping
Interview: Lawler via phone call
Tape: Tatsumi Fujinami beats Jimmy Snuka

Oct 15, 1988: Dallas, TX
(c) lost to Kerry Von Erich(c)
- AWA World Title vs. World Class World Title
- Texas Death Match
- Match was later reviewed and win by Von Erich
was overturned, both men kept titles.
- World Class Cotton Bowl Extravaganza '88

Oct 17, 1988: Memphis, TN
(c) won by DQ over Tatsumi Fujinami
- AWA World Title Match

Oct 21, 1988: Dallas, TX
& Jimmy Jack Funk went to a Double DQ with
Kerry Von Erich & Michael Hayes.

Oct 23, 1988: Memphis, TN
(ac) beat Kerry Von Erich(wc)
- AWA World Title vs. World Class World Title

Oct 26, 1988: Evansville, IN
(c) beat Dutch Mantell
- AWA World Title Match

Oct 29, 1988: Memphis, TN - TV Taping
& Jeff Jarrett beat Tim Woodard & Keith Eric

Oct 31, 1988: Memphis, TN
& Jeff Jarrett No Contest with Kerry Von Erich &
Michael Hayes

Jerry Teamng With Jeff Jarrett.

Nov 4, 1988: Dallas, TX
(c) lost to Kerry Von Erich
- World Class World Title Match
- AWA World Title not on the line

Nov 7, 1988: Memphis, TN
& Jeff Jarrett No Contest with Kerry Von Erich &
Michael Hayes

Nov 11, 1988: Dallas, TX
w/Jeff Jarrett, Bill Dundee & Eddie Marlin lost to
Frank Dusek, Steve Cox, Kevin & Kerry Von
Erich

Nov 12, 1988: Las Vegas, NV
(c) won via DQ over Wahoo McDaniel
- AWA World Title Match

Nov 14, 1988: Memphis, TN
(c) beat Botswana Beast
- AWA World Title Match

Nov 18, 1988: Jackson, TN
(c) beat Kerry Von Erich
- AWA World Title Match

Nov 19, 1988: Nashville, TN
(c) beat Buddy Landell
- AWA World Title Match

Nov 20, 1988: Memphis, TN
(c) beat the Pit Viper
- AWA World Title Match

Nov 24, 1988: Jackson, TN
(c) beat Kerry Von Erich
- AWA World Title Match

Nov 25, 1988: Dallas, TX
lost to Kerry Von Erich(c)
- World Class World Title Match
- Steel Cage Match

Nov 26, 1988: Minneapolis, MN
(c) won via DQ over Wahoo McDaniel
- AWA World Title Match

Nov 26, 1988: Bloomington, IN
(c) won via DQ over Wahoo McDaniel
- AWA World Title Match

Nov 28, 1988: Memphis, TN
w/Bill Dundee & Rick Casey beat Robert Fuller,
Jimmy Golden & Sid Vicious

Dec 2, 1988: Oshkosh, WI
(c) lost via DQ to Greg Gagne
- AWA World Title Match

Dec 5, 1988: Memphis, TN
(c) won via DQ over Jimmy Garvin
- AWA World Title Match

Dec 7, 1988: Memphis, TN
w/Bill Dundee & Rick Casey beat Robert Fuller,
Jimmy Golden & Sid Vicious

Dec 10 Nashville, TN
(c) beat Kamala
- AWA World Title Match

Dec 12, 1988: Memphis, TN
(c) won by DQ over Kamala
- AWA World Title Match

Dec 13, 1988: Chicago, IL
Super Clash III - PPV
beat Kerry Von Erich
- Match was stopped because Kerry was
bleeding too bad. Lawler declared winner.
- AWA World Champ beat World Class World
Champ to merge both belts into the Unified
World Champ.

SuperClash III
AWA Vs. WCCW - Lawler Vs. Von Erich

* **The whole Super Clash III story was
almost out of a Hollywood screenplay.
Rumor abound that the WWF was going to
make public the fact that Kerry had lost his
foot in his motorcycle accident 2 years
earlier. The Illinois Athletic Commission
would not allow a wrestler with one foot,
leg, etc to wrestle. This was the one reason**

the announcement for the main event participants was held off. Another reason was Jerry Jarrett was heavily trying to get another big name to fight Jerry Lawler for the AWA World Title in the main event. Both of those factors never materialized and the Lawler-Von Erich match ended up being the main event.

An incident did take place in the dressing room before the main event. Kerry Von Erich had taped a piece of a razor blade to one of his fingers so he could blade during the match. Rumor has it Kerry was pretty out of it in the dressing room and forgot about the razor blade. Later, his arm started itching and he instinctively scratched it, with the razor bladed finger, in turn shredding his arm. There was a major effort backstage to try and control the bleeding. As they say, the match must go on.

Dec 19, 1988: Memphis, TN
lost to Dutch Mantell
- Non-Title Match

Dec 26, 1988: Memphis, TN
(c) No Contest with Dutch Mantell
- World Unified Title Match

20-Man Battle Royal won by Jerry Lawler

Jerry & Dutch Mantell Discussing Their Impending Match.

* Pro Wrestling Illustrated 1988 Awards

1988 Wrestler of the year:
1st Runner Up: Jerry Lawler

1988 Match of the Year:
2nd Runner Up: Jerry Lawler beats Curt Hennig For AWA World Title

1988 Feud of the Year:
2nd Runner up: Jerry Lawler vs. Kerry Von Erich

1988 Inspirational Wrestler of the year:
Winner: Jerry Lawler

1989

Chapter 20

* After SuperClash III on Dec 13, 1988, the merged AWA, CWA & World Class World Titles were referred to in Memphis as the "World Unified Title".

World Unified Champ: Jerry Lawler

Jan 1, 1989: Nashville, TN
(c) No Contest with Dutch Mantel
- World Unified Title Match

Jan 2, 1989: Memphis, TN
(c) No Contest with Dutch Mantel
- World Unified Title Match

Jan 10, 1989: Memphis, TN
(c) lost to Dutch Mantel
- World Unified Title Match

Jerry Lawler Lets Out A Primal Scream VS. Dutch Mantell.

Jan 14, 1989: Hammond, IN
(c) won via DQ over Kerry Von Erich
- World Unified Title Match

Jan 16, 1989: Memphis, TN
& Wendell Cooley lost to Dutch Mantell & Ricky Morton

Jan 18, 1989: Jonesboro, AR
won via DQ over Dutch Mantel(c)
- World Unified Title Match

* On Jan 20, 1989, the AWA stripped Jerry Lawler of the AWA World Heavyweight Title. The issue between the AWA, CWA, Verne Gagne (AWA owner), Jerry Jarrett (CWA owner) & Jerry Lawler, started the previous month on December 13, 1988 at Super Clash III. At the end of the event, none of Jerry Jarrett's guys got paid. Now, were not talking about the PPV money, which took months to come in (cable customers had to be billed, then pay their cable company, then the cable company had to pay had to pay Verne, etc). Verne

took in money for 1,500 tickets sold. That's the money Jerry Jarrett felt that should have at least helped pay his trope he brought up from TN & TX. Jerry Jarrett went ahead and out of his pocket paid 21 of the wrestlers he brought to SuperClash III. Jerry Lawler was co-owner of the Memphis promotion and the AWA World champ, so Jarrett did not pay him. Lawler took his grievance straight to Verne Gagne and demanded payment. Gagne said he would not pay him. On top of that, he told Jerry that he was no longer the AWA World champ and to send the AWA World Title back to him. Jerry informed Gagne that he needed to pay him. Gagne still refused and threatened to sue Jerry to get back his belt. Lawler laughed and said as far as suing him, good luck trying that in Memphis. He also let Verne know that he was going to sell the AWA World Title and that would be the money Verne owed him from the SuperClash III PPV.

That's how it ended. Lawler sold the belt and got his money, Verne never did sue the King. Jerry Jarrett never got a single dollar from Verne for the PPV and broke ties with the AWA.

Jan 21, 1989: Memphis TN - TV Taping
& Wendell Cooley won via DQ over Beauty & the Beast

Jan 21, 1989: Nashville, YN
& Wendell Cooley vs. Dutch Mantell & Ricky Morton

Jan 28, 1989: Memphis TN - TV Taping
beat Keith Eric

Jan 29, 1989: Jackson TN
& Bill Dundee Double Count Out with Ricky Morton & Dutch Mantel

Jan 30, 1989: Memphis, TN
(c) lost via DQ to Ricky Morton
- World Unified Title Match

Feb 3, 1989: Dallas, TX
& Gary Royal lost to Kevin & Kerry Von Erich

Feb 4, 1989: Nashville, YN
vs. Master of Pain

Feb 7, 1989: Memphis, TN
(c) won via DQ over Master of Pain
- World Unified Title Match

* Master of Pain was a rookie named Mark Calaway. in a very short time Calaway would go on to become the Undertaker in the WWF/WWE, one of pro wrestling's biggest stars.

Feb 11,1989 Nashville, TN
& Bill Dundee vs. Dutch Mantell & Master of Pain

Feb 13, 1989: Memphis, TN
& Robert Gibson went to a No Contest with Ricky Morton & Master of Pain
- Gibson turned on Lawler

Feb 20, 1989: Memphis, TN
& Bill Dundee won via DQ against the Rock n' Roll Express

Feb 27, 1989: Memphis, TN
& Jimmy Valiant beat Tommy Rich & Austin Idol

Mar 5, 1989: Jackson, TN
(c) won via DQ over Master of Pain
- Unified World Title Match

Mar 6, 1989: Memphis, TN
(c) won via DQ over Tommy Rich
- Unified World Title Match

Mar 10, 1989: Kurashiki, Okayama, Japan
& Ron Starr defeated George Takano and Tatsumi Fujinami
- NJPW Big Fight Series - Day 10

Mar 11, 1989: Niiza, Saitama, Japan
& Mark Fleming lost to Hiroshi Hase and Riki Choshu
- NJPW Big Fight Series - Day 11

Mar 12, 1989: Tokyo, Japan
& Ron Starr defeated Kengo Kimura and Tatsumi Fujinami
- NJPW Big Fight Series - Day 12

Mar 14, 1989: Nagoya, Aichi, Japan
lost via DQ to Riki Choshu
- NJPW Big Fight Series - Day 14

Mar 16, 1989: Yokohama, Kanagawa, Japan
lost to Tatsumi Fujinami(c)
- IWGP Title Match
- NJPW Big Fight Series - Day 15

Mar 20, 1989: Memphis, TN
beat Master of Pain
- Non-Title Match

(c) won via DQ over Tommy Rich
- World Unified Title Match

Mar 25, 1989: Jonesboro, AR
(c) lost via DQ to Master of Pain
- World Unified Title Match

The King

Mar 27, 1989: Memphis, TN
(c) beat Boy Gone Bad
- World Unified World Title Match
- Boy Gone Bad was Joe Daniels

Mar 29, 1989: Evansville, IN
(c) won via DQ over Master of Pain w/Ronnie P. Gossett
- Unified World Title Match

Apr 1, 1989: Memphis, TN - TV Taping
(c) lost to Master of Pain w/Ronnie P. Gossett
- Unified World Title Match

Apr 3, 1989: Memphis, TN
won via DQ over Master of Pain(c) w/Ronnie P. Gossett
- Unified World Title Match

Apr 7, 1989: Dallas, TX
(c) drew with Kerry Von Erich
- Unified World Title Match
- Title Held Up

Apr 8, 1989: Nashville, TN
lost via DQ to Master of Pain(c) w/Ronnie P. Gossett
- Unified World Title Match

Apr 10, 1989: Memphis, TN
w/Brian Lee, Lord Humongous, Jeff Jarrett & John Paul beat Detroit Demolition, Robert Fuller, Dutch Mantell, Action Jackson & Master of Pain
- Rage in the Cage

beat Action Jackson

Apr 12, 1989: Owensboro, KY
lost via DQ to Master of Pain(c) w/Ronnie P. Gossett
- Unified World Title Match

Apr 14, 1989: Dallas, TX
beat Kerry Von Erich
- Unified World Title Match
Apr 15, 1989: Memphis, TN - TV Taping
beat Keith Eric

Apr 15, 1989: Nashville, TN
beat Action Jackson

w/Jeff Jarrett, Tracey Smothers, John Paul & Scott Steiner vs. Robert Fuller, Master of Pain, Dutch Mantell, Action Jackson & Detroit Demolition
- Rage in the Cage

Apr 17, 1989: Memphis, TN
beat Austin Idol

Apr 19, 1989: Owensboro, KY
beat Action Jackson

w/Jeff Jarrett, Humongous, Tracy Smothers & John Paul beat Robert Fuller, Dutch Mantell, Action Jackson, Master of Pain & Detroit Demolition w/Ronnie P. Gossett
- Rage In A Cage

* In April 1989, Jerry Jarrett and his group left Evansville and moved that weekly show to Owensboro, KY. Lack of ticket sales and the Evansville Coliseum being an older building (with no heat or air

conditioning) played into the decision. The Sportscenter in Owensboro was a more modern facilty.

Apr 22, 1989: Jonesboro, AR
w/Jeff Jarrett, Lord Humongous, Scott Steiner & Chris Adams lost to Master of Pain, Dutch Mantel, Detroit Demolition, Robert Fuller & Brian Lee
- Rage in the Cage

won via DQ over Master of Pain(c) w/Ronnie P. Gossett
- Unified World Title Match

Apr 23, 1989: Jackson, TN
w/Jeff Jarrett, Lord Humongous, Scott Steiner & Chris Adams lost to Master of Pain, Dutch Mantel, Detroit Demolition, Robert Fuller & Brian Lee
- Rage in the Cage

won via DQ over Master of Pain(c) w/Ronnie P. Gossett
- Unified World Title Match

Apr 24, 1989: Memphis, TN
beat PY Chu HI
beat Samurai
beat Mr. Devastation
beat Master of Pain(c) w/Ronnie P. Gossett
- Unified World Title
- Lawler had to win all the gauntlet matches to get title shot.
- PY Chu HI was Phil Hickerson

May 25, 1989: Jackson, TN
& Austin Idol beat PY Chu Hi & Mr. Devastation w/Ronnie P. Gossett

Apr 28, 1989: Dallas, TX
(c) beat Matt Borne
- Unified World Title Match

May 5, 1989: Dallas, TX
(c) beat Matt Borne
- Unified World Title Match

May 12, 1989: Dallas, TX
lost to Matt Borne
- Non Title Match

May 22, 1989: Memphis, TN
& Austin Idol beat Shogun & PY Chu HI

May 29, 1989: Memphis, TN
& Austin Idol beat PY Chu Hi & Master of Pain w/Ronnie P. Gossett

May 31, 1989: Henderson, KY
& Austin Idol beat PY Chu Hi & Master of Pain w/Ronnie P. Gossett

June 2, 1989: Dallas, TX
(c) beat Al Perez
- Unified World Title Match

June 3, 1989: Nashville, TN
& Austin Idol beat Master of Pain & PY Chu Hi

June 5, 1989: Memphis, TN
& Freddie beat PY Chu Hi & Master of Pain w/Ronnie P. Gossett
- Freddie was a replacement for Austin Idol
- Freddie was Doug Gilbert

June 10, 1989: Memphis, TN - TV Taping
& Frankie Lancaster won by DQ over Mr Devastation & Keith Roberson

June 10, 1989: Nashville, TN
& Bill Dundee won via DQ over Master of Pain & Mr. Devestation

Jerry Seeing To An Injured Bill Dundee

June 11, 1989: Louisville, KY
& Bam Bam Bigelow w/Jackie Fargo beat Dutch
Mantell & Master of Pain w/Ronnie P. Gossett

June 12, 1989: Memphis, TN
& Bam Bam Bigelow w/Jackie Fargo beat Dutch
Mantell & Master of Pain w/Ronnie P. Gossett

The Beast From The East: Bam Bam Bigelow

June 16, 1989: Dallas, TX
went to a draw with Eric Embry

June 19, 1989: Memphis, TN
beat the Master of Pain(c) w/Ronnie P. Gossett
-USWA Unified World Title Match

June 21, 1989: Henderson, KY
(c) beat Dutch Mantell
-USWA Unified World Title Match

June 24, 1989: Memphis, TN - TV Taping
& Nightmare Freddie beat Keith Eric & Keith
Roberson

June 24, 1989: Jonesboro, AR
(c) lost via DQ to Black Bart
-USWA Unified World Title Match

June 25, 1989: Jackson, TN
(c) lost via DQ to Black Bart
-USWA Unified World Title Match

June 26, 1989: Memphis, TN
(c) beat the Master of Pain w/Ronnie P. Gossett
-USWA Unified World Title Match

w/Plowboy Frasier & Bam Bam Bigelow beat
Master of Pain, Dutch Mantell & Ronnie P.
Gossett

June 28, 1989: Henderson, KY
(c) beat Master of Pain w/Ronnie P. Gossett
-USWA Unified World Title Match

June 30, 1989: Dallas, TX
(c) went to a No Contest with Chris Adams
-USWA Unified World Title Match

July 3, 1989: Memphis, TN
(c) beat Kerry Von Erich w/Ronnie P. Gossett
-USWA Unified World Title Match

July 8, 1989: Memphis, TN - TV Taping
won via DQ over Ronnie P. Gossett
- Boxing Match

July 8, 1989: Nashville, TN
(c) won via DQ over Iceman King Parsons

July 9, 1989: Jonesboro, AR
lost to Brickhouse Brown

w/Jeff Jarrett & Freddy won via DQ over Dutch
Mantel, Master of Pain & Ronnie P. Gossett

July 10, 1989: Memphis, TN
& Bam Bam Bigelow beat Dutch Mantel & Master
of Pain w/Ronnie P. Gossett

July 12, 1989: Henderson, KY
& Bam Bam Bigelow beat Iceman King Parsons
& Brickhouse Brown

July 15, 1989: Nashville, TN
& Bam Bam Bigelow beat Iceman King Parsons
& Brickhouse Brown

July 16, 1989: Jonesboro, AR
& Bill Dundee lost to Brickhouse Brown &
Iceman King Parsons

July 17, 1989: Memphis, TN
(c) Double Count Out with Bam Bam Bigelow
-USWA Unified World Title Match

July 19, 1989: Henderson, KY
& Nightmare Freddie won by DQ over
Brickhouse Brown & Iceman King Parsons

July 21, 1989: Dallas, TX
(c) won via DQ over Kerry Von Erich
-USWA Unified World Title Match

July 24, 1989: Memphis, TN
(c) won via DQ over Al Perez
-USWA Unified World Title Match

July 28, 1989: Dallas, TX
(c) went to a draw with Mil Mascaras
-USWA Unified World Title Match

Mil Mascaras VS. Jerry Lawler

July 31, 1989: Memphis, TN
(c) won via DQ over Bam Bam Bigelow
- USWA Unified World Title Match

Aug 2, 1989: Henderson, KY
(c) won via DQ over Bam Bam Bigelow
- USWA Unified World Title Match

Aug 4, 1989: Jonesboro, AR
& Plowboy Frazier won via DQ over Chris
Champion & Mark Starr
Aug 7, 1989: Memphis, TN
(c) beat Bam Bam Bigelow
- USWA Unified World Title Match
- Coward wave sthe Flag match

Aug 14, 1989: Memphis, TN
(c) beat Buddy Landell
- USWA Unified World Title Match

Aug 16, 1989: Henderson, KY
(c) beat the Super Destroyer
- USWA Unified World Title Match

Aug 19, 1989: Memphis, TN - TV Taping
& Spike Huber won via DQ over Chris Champion
& Mark Starr(c)
- CWA World Tag Title Match

Aug 21, 1989: Memphis, TN
w/Frank Morrell & Jerry Calhoun lost to Black
Bart, Buddy Landel & Master of Pain
- Ronnie P. Gossett won the right to book card.

beat Doug Gilbert
- Loser Leaves Town
- Gossett is special ref.

Aug 26, 1989: Memphis, TN - Taping
& Jeff Jarrett won via DQ over Chris Champion &
Mark Starr(c)
- CWA World Tag Title Match

Aug 26, 1989: Jonesboro, AR
beat Chris Champion

Aug 28, 1989: Memphis, TN
beat Ronnie P. Gossett
- Lumberjack Strap Match

Aug 30, 1989: Owensboro, KY
beat Doug Gilbert
- Loser Leaves town match
- Ronnie P Gossett was the Referee

w/Frank Morrell & Paul Neighbors won via DQ
over Master of Pain, Buddy Landel & Black Bart

Aug 31, 1989: Nashville, TN
w/Frank Morrell & Paul Neighbors won via DQ
over Master of Pain, Buddy Landell & Black Bart

beat Doug Gilbert
- Loser Leaves town match
- Ronnie P Gossett was the Referee

Sep 1, 1989: Dallas, TX
lost to Eric Embry
- Non Title Match

Sep 2, 1989: Nashville, TN
beat Ronnie P Gossett
in a Lumberjack strap match

Sep 4, 1989: Memphis, TN
(c) beat Buddy Landell
-USWA Unified World Title Match
- Title vs. Landell's Limo

Sep 6, 1989: Owensboro, KY
beat Ronnie P. Gossett
- Lumberjack Match

Sep 8, 1989: Dallas, TX
(c) beat Eic Embry
-USWA Unified World Title Match

Sep 9, 1989: Nashville, TN
(c) beat Buddy Landell
-USWA Unified World Title Match
- Title vs. Landell's Limo

Sep 10, 1989: Jonesboro, AR
(c) won via DQ over Buddy Landell
-USWA Unified World Title Match

Sep 11, 1989: Memphis, TN
& Kerry Von Erich beat Buddy Landell & Spike Huber
Sep 14, 1989: Jackson, TN
& Kerry Von Erich beat Chris Champion & Mark Starr w/Ronnie P. Gossett

Sep 16, 1989: Cherry Hill, NJ
& Larry Sharpe beat Boy Gone Bad & Sonny Austin

Sep 18, 1989: Memphis, TN
(c) lost via DQ to Kerry Von Erich
-USWA Unified World Title Match

Sep 20, 1989: Owensboro, KY
& Kerry Von Erich beat Buddy Landell & Spike Huber

Sep 22, 1989: Dallas, TX
beat Eic Embry
- Lumberjack Match

Sep 30, 1989: Memphis, TN TV results
won via DQ over Buddy Landell
Oct 2, 1989: Memphis, TN
(c) won via DQ over Dirty White Boy
- USWA Unified World Title Match
- Dirty White Boy is Tony Anthony

Oct 4, 1989: Owensboro, KY
(c) beat Buddy Landell
-USWA Unified World Title Match

Oct 7, 1989: Memphis, TN - TV Taping
& Dustin Rhodes & Nightmare Freddie beat Mike Davis, Kevin Dillinger & Spike Huber

Oct 9, 1989: Memphis, TN
(c) lost via DQ to Soultaker
- USWA Unified World Title Match
- Soultaker is Charles Wright, aka The Godfather from WWE, and a WWE HOF're as well.

& Dustin Rhodes lost to Buddy Landell & Dirty White Boy

Oct 11, 1989: Owensboro, KY
(c) vs   Bill Dundee
or   Ricky Morton   or   Robert Gibson
or   Dustin Rhodes   or   Dutch Mantell
- USWA Unified World Title Match
- Fans decide who Lawler defends title against.

Sep 22, 1989: Dallas, TX
won via DQ over Uncle Elmer
- Uncle Elmer is Plowboy Frazier

Oct 14, 1989: Memphis, TN - TV Taping
& Dutch Mantell won via DQ over Dirty White boy & Mike Davis

Oct 14, 1989: Nashville, TN
(c) won via DQ over Soultaker
- USWA World Title Match

& Dustin Rhodes lost to Buddy Landell & Dirty White Boy

Oct 16, 1989: Memphis, TN
(c) won via DQ over Soultaker
- USWA World Title Match

Oct 18, 1989: Evansville, IN
& Dustin Rhodes won via DQ over Buddy Landell & Dirty White Boy

(c) won via DQ over Soultaker
- USWA World Title Match

Oct 20, 1989: Dallas, TX
(c) beat Uncle Elmer
- USWA World Title Match

Oct 21, 1989: Nashville, TN
(c) won via DQ over Soultaker
- USWA World Title Match

Oct 23, 1989: Memphis, TN
(c) lost to Soultaker
-USWA World Title Match

Oct 27, 1989: Palmetto, FL
lost via DQ to Bam Bam Bigelow

Oct 28, 1989: Jonesboro, AR
lost to Soultaker(c)
-USWA World Title Match

Oct 30, 1989: Memphis, TN
lost via DQ to Soultaker(c)
-USWA World Title Match

Nov 3, 1989: Dallas, TX
(c)beat Terry Gordy
-USWA World Title Match

Nov 4, 1989: Nashville, TN
lost via DQ to Soultaker(c)
- USWA World Title Match

Nov 6, 1989: Memphis, TN
beat the Soultaker(c)
- USWA World Title Match
- Steel Cage Match

beat Dirty Rhodes KIX-106 Radio DJ

Nov 3, 1989: Dallas, TX
(c)beat Kerry Von Erich
-USWA World Title Match

Nov 11, 1989: Nashville, TN
beat the Soultaker(c)
- USWA World Title Match
- Steel Cage Match

Nov 13, 1989: Memphis, TN
(c) beat Dutch Mantel
- USWA World Title Match

* Jerry Lawler makes a heel turn.

Nov 17, 1989: Cleveland, OH
won via Count Out over Kamala
won via DQ over Manny Fernandez

Nov 19, 1989: Memphis, TN
lost to Dutch Mantel
- Texas Death Match
- Non Title Match

Nov 22, 1989: Evansville, IN
(c) won via DQ over Dutch Mantell
- USWA World Title Match

Master of Pain & Dutch Mantell Arrive.

Nov 23, 1989: Jackson, TN
(c) won via DQ over Dutch Mantell
- USWA World Title Match
- Thanksgiving Evening Show

Nov 27, 1989: Memphis, TN
(c) beat Bill Dundee
- USWA World Title Match

Nov 29, 1989: Evansville, IN
(c) won via DQ over Dutch Mantell
- USWA World Title Match

Nov 30, 1989: Nashville, TN
(c) won via DQ over Dutch Mantell
- USWA World Title Match

Oct 27, 1989: Palmetto, FL
(c) lost via DQ to Junkyard Dog
- USWA World Title Match

Dec 4, 1989: Memphis, TN
& the Soultaker went to a No Contest with
Dutch Mantell & the Master of Pain

Dec 6, 1989: Evansville, IN
lost to Dutch Mantel
- Texas Death Match
- Non Title Match

Jerry Lawler Going After Dutch Mantell

Dec 11, 1989: Memphis, TN
(c) beat Ricky Morton
- USWA World Title Match

Dec 13, 1989: Evansville, IN
& the Soultaker went to a No Contest with
Dutch Mantell & the Master of Pain

Dec 15, 1989: Dallas, TX
beat Kerry Von Erich(c)
- Texas Heavyweight Title Match
- Lawler wins Texas Title

Dec 23, 1989: Memphis, TN - TV Taping
beat Ken Raper

Dec 23, 1989: Evansville, IN
(c) lost via DQ to Bill Dundee
- USWA World Unified Title Match

* **Dec 23, 1989 also saw wrestler Jerry Bryant pass away after a battle with Lou Gehrig's. Bryant started wrestling in 1975 and stayed in Memphis his entire career. His most successful Memphis run had been just a few years prior as Lew Winston's tag partner in Memphis Vice. Bryant graduated from Treadwell High School in Memphis and had been friends with Jerry Lawler for many years.**

Jerry Bryant & Jerry Lawler

Dec 30, 1989: Memphis, TN
(c) lost to King Cobra
- USWA World Unified Title Match

1990

Chapter 21

Jan 1, 1990: Memphis, TN
lost via DQ to King Cobra(c)
- USWA Unified World Title Match

Jerry Lawler Is Not Happy

Jan 5, 1990: Dallas, TX
(c) lost to Kerry Von Erich
- Texas Title Match

Jan 8, 1990: Memphis, TN
beat King Cobra(c)
- USWA Unified World Title Match

Jan 15, 1990: Memphis, TN
w/Soultaker & Dirty White Boy beat Dutch
Mantell, King Cobra & Chris Champion

Jan 19, 1990: Dallas, TX
beat Terrance Garvin

Jan 26, 1990: Dallas, TX
& Billy Travis lost to Jeff Jarrett & Kerry Von
Erich

Jan 27, 1990: Branford, TN
lost via DQ to Rooster Cogburn

Feb 2, 1990: Dallas, TX
& Billy Travis lost to Jeff Jarrett & Bill Dundee

Feb 5, 1990: Memphis, TN
& Soultaker lost to Jeff Jarrett & Kerry Von Erich

Feb 7, 1990: Evansville, IN
& Soul Taker beat Junk Yard Dog & King Cobra

Feb 9, 1990: Dallas, TX
& Billy Travis beat Jeff Jarrett & Bill Dundee

Feb 12, 1990: Memphis, TN
& Soultaker lost to King Cobra & Junk Yard Dog

(c)beat Plowboy Frazier
- USWA Unified World Title Match

Feb 16, 1990: Dallas, TX
w/Terrance Garvin & Billy Travis won via DQ
over Kerry Von Erich, Bill Dundee & Jeff Jarrett

Feb 17, 1990: Nashville, TN
& Billy Travis lost to Jeff Jarrett & Bill Dundee

Feb 19, 1990: Memphis, TN
(c) won via DQ over Junk Yard Dog
- USWA Unified World Title Match

Feb 24, 1990: Jonesboro, AR - evening
(c) lost via DQ to Kerry Von Erich
- USWA Unified World Title Match

Feb 26, 1990: Memphis, TN
(c) lost to Jimmy Valiant
- USWA Unified World Title Match

Mar 2, 1990: Dallas, TX
beat Jimmy Valiant(c)
- USWA Unified World Title Match

Mar 5, 1990: Memphis, TN
lost to Jimmy Valiant(c)
- USWA Unified World Title Match

Mar 12, 1990: Memphis, TN
beat Jimmy Valiant(c)
- USWA Unified World Title Match

Mar 19, 1990: Memphis, TN
(c) beat Mike Awesome
- USWA Unified World Title Match

beat Chris Champion
- Added Lights Out Match

Mar 24, 1990: Palmetto, FL - TV Taping
beat Robbie Idol

(c) won via Count Out over Steve Keirn
- USWA Unified World Title Match

Mar 26, 1990: Memphis, TN
& Ronnie Gossett won via DQ over Mike
Awesome & Chris Champion

Mar 29, 1990: Nashville, TN
(c) beat Mike Awesome
- USWA Unified World Title Match

(c) beat Chris Champion
- USWA Unified World Title Match

Mar 31, 1990: Philadelphia, PA
(c) lost via DQ to Kerry Von Erich
- USWA Unified World Title Match

Jerry Lawler In Control Of Kerry Von Erich.

Apr 2, 1990: Memphis, TN
(c) won via DQ over Jimmy Valiant
- USWA Unified World Title Match

Apr 6, 1990: Dallas, TX
(c) beat Mike Awesome
- USWA Unified World Title Match

Apr 7, 1990: Middleton, TN
(c) beat Mike Awesome
- USWA Unified World Title Match

Apr 9, 1990: Memphis, TN
(c) won via DQ over Jimmy Valiant
- USWA Unified World Title Match

Apr 16, 1990: Memphis, TN
(c) beat Mike Awesome
- USWA Unified World Title Match

w/Jeff Gaylord, Sweet Daddy Falcone, & Ronnie
P. Gossett lost to Bill Dundee, Mike Awesome &
Chris Champion
- Texas Tornado Tough Guy Contest

Apr 20, 1990: Dallas, TX
(c) won via DQ over Jeff Jarrett
- USWA Unified World Title Match

Apr 21, 1990: Nashville, TN
(c) beat Mike Awesome
- USWA Unified World Title Match

w/Jeff Gaylord, Sweet Daddy Falcone, & Ronnie
P. Gossett lost to Bill Dundee, Mike Awesome &
Chris Champion
- Texas Tornado Tough Guy Contest

Apr 23, 1990: Memphis, TN
(c) won via DQ over Nitron
- USWA Unified World Title Match
Apr 28, 1990: Jonesboro, AR
(c) lost to Jimmy Valiant
- USWA Unified World Title Match

Apr 30, 1990: Memphis, TN
lost to Jimmy Valiant(c)
- USWA Unified World Title Match

May 4, 1990: Dallas, TX
lost to Kerry Von Erich
- Non Title Match

beat Matt Bourne
- Non Title Match

May 5, 1990: Memphis, TN - TV Taping
beat Jimmy Valiant(c)
- USWA Unified World Title Match

May 5, 1990: Nashville, TN
beat Jimmy Valiant(c)
- USWA Unified World Title Match

May 7, 1990: Memphis, TN
(c) beat Jimmy Valiant
- USWA Unified World Title Match

May 10, 1990: Evansville, IN
beat Jimmy Valiant(c)
- USWA Unified World Title Match

May 11, 1990: Dallas, TX
beat Jeff Gaylord

May 12, 1990: Nashville, TN
(c) beat Jimmy Valiant
- USWA Unified World Title Match

May 14, 1990: Memphis, TN
(c) beat Jimmy Valiant
- Stretcher Match
- USWA Unified World Title Match

May 18, 1990:
Jerry Lawler made an appearance on the nationally syndicated show, "People Magazine on TV".

May 21, 1990: Memphis, TN
(c) beat Kerry Von Erich
- USWA Unified World Title Match

May 23, 1990: Nashville, TN
Jerry Lawler made an appearance on the Nashville, TN show "Talk of The Town"

May 28, 1990: Memphis, TN
(c) beat the Snowman
- USWA Unified World Title Match
- Snowman was Eddie Crawford

June 1, 1990: Dallas, TX
lost to Bill Dundee
- Non Title Match

It Always Goes Back To Lawler VS. Dundee

June 4, 1990: Memphis, TN
(c) beat the Snowman
- USWA Unified World Title Match

June 9, 1990: Philadelphia, PA
won via DQ over Austin Idol

June 11, 1990: Memphis, TN
(c) beat the Snowman
- USWA Unified World Title Match

June 18, 1990: Memphis, TN
(c) lost to the Snowman
- USWA Unified World Title Match
- Special Ref: Leon Spinks
- Spinks knocks out Lawler

June 19, 1990: Dallas, TX
draw with Eric Embry

June 21, 1990: Louisville, KY
(c) lost to the Snowman
- USWA Unified World Title Match
- Special Ref: Leon Spinks
- Spinks knocks out Lawler

June 22, 1990: Jonesboro, AR
beat Joey Maggs
beat King Cobra
beat the Snowman
lost to Bill Dundee

June 25, 1990: Memphis, TN
won via DQ over Leon Spinks

July 1, 1990: Dallas, TX
lost to Bill Dundee

July 2, 1990: Memphis, TN
lost to the Snowman(c)
- USWA Unified World Title Match

July 7, 1990: Nashville, TN
lost to the Snowman(c)
- USWA Unified World Title Match

July 8, 1990: Dallas, TX
beat Bill Dundee

July 9, 1990: Memphis, TN
lost to the Snowman(c)
- USWA Unified World Title Match

& Bill Dundee lost via DQ to John Tatum & Dirty White Boy w/Dirty White Girl

* Jerry Lawler turns back into a babyface and the fans welcome him back.

July 14, 1990: Nashville, TN
lost to the Snowman(c)
- USWA Unified World Title Match
- 2 refs

July 15, 1990: Jackson, TN
That afternoon Jerry Lawler (& Lawler's Army Softball team) played 3 exhibition games at Tobe Bailey Field in Jackson against the Jackson Police Dept Association for their fundraiser.

lost to the Snowman(c)
- USWA Unified World Title Match

July 16, 1990: Memphis, TN
& Bill Dundee beat Eddie Gilbert & Dirty White Boy w/Dirty White Girl

July 20, 1990: Bradford, TN
vs. ?

July 23, 1990: Memphis, TN
w/Bill Dundee & Tessa beat Eddie Gilbert, Dirty White Boy & Dirty White Girl
- Texas Death Match
- Dirty White Girl is Kim Anthony

July 30, 1990: Memphis, TN
w/Bill Dundee & Tessa lost to Eddie Gilbert, Dirty White Boy & Dirty White Girl
- Texas Death Match

Aug 3, 1990: Dallas, TX
& Jeff Jarrett lost via DQ to Sweet Daddy Falcone & Gary Young

Aug 6, 1990: Memphis, TN
w/Bill Dundee & Austin Idol lost to Eddie Gilbert, John Tatum & Dirty White Boy w/Dirty White Girl
- Stretcher Match

Aug 7, 1990: Millington, TN
w/Bill Dundee & Jeff Jarrett vs. Eddie Gilbert, John Tatum & Dirty White Boy w/Dirty White Girl

Aug 11, 1990: Nashville, TN
w/Jeff Jarrett & Bill Dundee lost to Eddie Gilbert, John Tatum & Dirty White Boy w/Dirty White Girl
- Stretcher Match

Aug 13, 1990: Memphis, TN
w/Bill Dundee & Austin Idol lost to Eddie Gilbert, Doug Gilbert & Dirty White Boy w/Dirty White Girl
- Steel Cage Match

Aug 18, 1990: Nashville, TN
w/Jeff Jarrett & Bill Dundee lost to Eddie Gilbert, John Tatum & Dirty White Boy w/Dirty White Girl
- Steel Cage Match

Aug 20, 1990: Memphis, TN
w/Bill Dundee & Austin Idol beat Eddie Gilbert, Doug Gilbert & Dirty White Boy w/Dirty White Girl

Aug 24, 1990: Dallas, TX
& Jeff Jarrett lost to Gary Young & John Tatum

Aug 27, 1990: Memphis, TN
w/Bill Dundee & Austin Idol lost to Eddie Gilbert, Doug Gilbert & Dirty White Boy w/Dirty White Girl

Aug 31, 1990: Dallas, TX
& Bill Dundee lost to Gary Young & John Tatum

Sep 3, 1990: Memphis, TN
& Brickhouse Brown lost via DQ to Eddie & Doug Gilbert

Sep 10, 1990: Memphis, TN
beat Eddie Gilbert
- Ambulance Match

Sep 14, 1990: Philadelphia, PA
won via DQ over Terry Funk

Sep 16, 1990: Louisville, KY
beat Eddie Gilbert
- Ambulance Match

Eddie Gilbert VS. Jerry Lawler

Sep 17, 1990: Memphis, TN
beat Eddie Gilbert

Sep 18, 1990: Louisville, KY
won via DQ Eddie Gilbert

Sep 24, 1990: Memphis, TN
beat Eddie Gilbert
- Coal Miner's Glove Match

w/Bill Dundee, Jeff Jarrett, Brickhouse Brown & Jeff Gaylord beat Don Harris, Brian Lee, Doug Gilbert, Eddie Gilbert & Dirty White Boy w/Dirty White Girl

* Sometime during September 1990, Kevin Von Erich and World Class left the USWA. Regardless of the fact that Jerry Jarrett owned 60% of World Class. Kevin sued Jerry Jarrett saying he was not getting enough revenue from the operations. When Jerry Jarrett & Jerry Lawler took over World Class back in 1989, the territory was in financial shambles. As Jarrett had been known to do, he paid all the debt off from the revenue collected in ticket sales. Kevin & Kerry Von Erich did not like the money going towards their previous debts. Jarrett gave up the company instead of fighting it in court. There was nothing to win. When he won the court case, the promotion would have been right back in dire straits from the Von Erich's mismanagement and he would have had to still be partners with them. Jarrett and Lawler decided to wash their hands of World Class. By the beginning of 1991, the Von Erich-run World Class promotion had gone bankrupt and was closed.

Oct 1, 1990: Memphis, TN
beat Bill Dundee
beat Jeff Jarrett
beat Eddie Gilbert
- Lawler wins and is #1 contender
- Round Robin Tournament to decide #1 contender for USWA Unified World Title

* The Snowman (Eddie Crawford) was stripped of the USWA Unified World Title by the Jarrett promotion for no showing bookings. Crawford and Eddie Marlin confronted each other on the Sat morning Memphis show one weekend after Crawford was fired. Marlin accused Crawford of trading the Unified belt for drugs. This was not true. Crawford was holding out because he felt he was due more money than he had been paid. The belt was sold to a collector after the fact, but never to a drug dealer.

Oct 6, 1990: Clarksdale, MS
Jerry Lawler was at the opening of Take Two Video rental store.

Oct 8, 1990: Memphis, TN
USWA Unified World Title Tournament
Rd 2: won via DQ over Mark Callous
Quarter-finals: beat Dick Slater in the
Semi-finals: beat Terry Funk
Finals: beat Eddie Gilbert

Oct 13, 1990: Cleveland, OH
(c) beat Eddie Gilbert
- USWA Unified World Title Match

Oct 15, 1990: Memphis, TN
& Bill Dundee lost via DQ to Eddie Gilbert & Austin Idol

Oct 20, 1990: Nashville, TN
(c) drew with Bill Dundee
- USWA Unified World Title Match

Jerry Stepping Into The Ring As Champ.

Oct 22, 1990: Memphis, TN
beat MC Jammer

w/Bill Dundee & Jamie Dundee beat Sheik Abdul
Hussein, Sheik Fabiano & the Samuri

Oct 29, 1990: Memphis, TN
(c) beat Jeff Gaylord
- USWA Unified World Title Match

lost to Eddie Gilbert

Nov 3, 1990: Nashville, TN
(c) beat Jeff Gaylord
- USWA Unified World Title Match

Nov 5, 1990: Memphis, TN
(c) lost to Terry Funk
- USWA Unified World Title Match

Nov 6, 1990: Louisville, KY
(c) won via DQ over Jeff Gaylord
- USWA Unified World Title Match

Nov 9, 1990: Drexil Hill, PA
vs. Eddie Gilbert

Nov 10, 1990: Bensalem, PA
vs. Terry Funk

Nov 12, 1990: Memphis, TN
w/Bill Dundee & Jamie Dundee beat Sheik Abdul
Hussein, Sheik Fabiano & the Samuri

won via DQ over Eddie Gilbert
- Added Match

Nov 17, 1990: Nashville, TN
beat Jeff Gaylord

& Bill Dundee beat Lou Fabiano & sheik Abdul
Hussain

won via DQ over Eddie Gilbert
- Barbed Wire Match

Nov 19, 1990: Memphis, TN
w/Bill Dundee & Jeff Jarrett beat Sheik Abdul
Hussein, Sheik Fabiano & the Samuri
- Hospital Elimination Match

Nov 24, 1990: Memphis, TN
Jerry Lawler took part in the opening festivities
of the Salvation Army Angel Tree program at
Oak Court Mall.

Nov 26, 1990: Memphis, TN
won via Count Out over Black Magic

w/Jeff Jarrett & Bill Dundee beat Eddie Gilbert,
Doug Gilbert & Dirty White Boy w/Dirty White
Girl

Jeff Jarrett & Jerry Lawler

Nov 27, 1990: Louisville, KY
w/Jeff Jarrett, Bill Dundee & Eddie Marlin beat
Downtown Bruno, Doug Gilbert, Joey Maggs &
Dirty White Boy w/Dirty White Girl

won via DQ over Eddie Gilbert
- Barbed Wire Match

Dec 3, 1990: Memphis, TN
w/Jeff Jarrett, Bill Dundee & Eddie Marlin beat
Downtown Bruno, Doug Gilbert, Joey Maggs &
Dirty White Boy w/Dirty White Girl

went to a No Contest with Eddie Gilbert
- Barbed Wire Match

Dec 5, 1990: Evansville, IN
beat Doug Gilbert

went to a Double Count Out with Eddie Gilbert

Dec 8, 1990: Nashville, TN
w/Jeff Jarrett, Bill Dundee, Cody Michaels &
Eddie Marlin vs. Eddie & Doug Gilbert, Joey
Maggs, Sam Lowe & Dirty White Boy w/Dirty
White Girl

Dec 10, 1990: Memphis, TN
& Fabs (Steve Keirn & Stan Lane) lost via DQ to
Eddie Gilbert, Doug Gilbert & Dirty White Boy.

Dec 26, 1990: Memphis, TN
20-Man Battle Royal: won by Jerry Lawler

& Bam Bam Bigelow went to Double DQ with
Austin Idol & Eddie Gilbert

Dec 28, 1990: Dallas, TX
won via DQ over Terry Funk(c)
USWA Unified World Title Match

Dec 29, 1990: Nashville, TN
beat Terrance Garvin
- Bounty Match

w/Jeff Jarrett & Bill Dundee beat Eddie Gilbert,
Doug Gilbert & Dirty White Boy w/ Dirty White
Girl
- Explosive Match

* Pro Wrestling Illustrated 1990 Awards

1990 Inspirational Wrestler of the year:
2nd Runner Up: Jerry Lawler

1991
Chapter 22

Jan 2, 1991: Memphis, TN
beat Black Magic

& Bam Bam Bigelow beat Willie B Hurt & Don Bass

Jan 5, 1991: Nashville, TN
& Bill Dundee beat Doug Gilbert & Tony Anthony w/Kimberly
-Cage Match

Jan 7, 1991: Memphis, TN
& Bill Dundee beat Brian Lee & Alan Martin

w/Stan Lane, Steve Keirn & Jim Cornette beat Doug Gilbert, Stan Lowe, Joey Maggs & Tony Anthony w/Kimberly

Jan 14, 1991: Memphis, TN
& Bill Dundee lost to the Fabs(c) w/Jim Cornette
- USWA World Tag Title Match

Jan 19, 1991: Nashville, TN
& Bill Dundee won via DQ over the Fabulous Ones (Stan Lane & Steve Keirn)(c) w/Jim Cornette
- USWA World Tag Title Match

Jan 20, 1991: Memphis, TN
& Bill Dundee lost via DQ to the Fabs(c) w/Jim Cornette
- USWA World Tag Title Match

Jan 26, 1991: Memphis, TN - TV Taping
beat Terrence Garvin w/Uptown Bruno

Jan 28, 1991: Memphis, TN
& Jeff Jarrett No Contest with the Fabs(c) w/Jim Cornette
- USWA World Tag Title Match
- Belts held up

Feb 2, 1991: Nashville, TN
& Bill Dundee won via DQ over the Fabs(c) w/Jim Cornette
- USWA World Tag Title Match

Feb 4, 1991: Memphis, TN
& Jeff Jarrett beat the Fabs w/Jim Cornette
- USWA World Tag Title Match
- Special Ref: Jackie Fargo
- Belts held up from previous week.

The King & Jeff Jarrett VS. The Fabulous Ones w/Cornette. Special Ref: Jackie Fargo

Feb 9, 1991: Nashville, TN
vs. Eddie Gilbert

Feb 11, 1991: Memphis, TN
beat Eddie Gilbert via DQ

Feb 16, 1991: Nashville, TN
beat Eddie Gilbert

Feb 18, 1991: Memphis, TN
& Jeff Jarrett(c) beat Eddie Gilbert & Eric Embry
- USWA World Tag Title Match
- Embry & Prichard turn on Gilbert after the match.

Feb 25, 1991: Memphis, TN
& Eddie Gilbert lost to Tom Prichard & Eric Embry

Mar 2, 1991: Philadelphia, PA
won via DQ over Terry Funk
- USWA Unified World Title Match

Mar 4, 1991: Memphis, TN
Eddie Gilbert & Jeff Jarrett w/Jerry Lawler beat Eric Embry & Tom Prichard w/Tojo Yamamoto

beat Steve Austin

* Same Steve Austin who would eventually become HOF'er Stone Cold Steve Austin for the WWF/WWE.

Mar 9, 1991: Nashville, TN
beat Steve Austin

Mar 11, 1991: Memphis, TN
beat Terry Funk(c)
- USWA Unified World Title Match

Ladies & Gentlemen... The KING!

Mar 18, 1991: Memphis, TN
w/Eddie Gilbert, Jeff Jarrett, & Jackie Fargo beat Eric Embry, Tom Prichard, Psycho, Killer & Tojo Yamamoto

* **This was the first card held at the Pipkin Building at the Fairgrounds. Jerry Jarrett & Jerry Lawler were having a war with the new manager of the Mid-South Coliseum, Beth Wade. Wade was brought on as manager of the MSC in June 1990. She immediately increased cost of several items that Jarrett & Lawler were not happy about. There was a new $2 parking charge, a $1.25 ticket surcharge as well as a new $1,500 security fee every Monday night the promotion had to pay. Lawler claimed Wade made it very clear she did not like Wrestling in the Coliseum, nor the element and type of fans it bought in.**

Mar 25, 1991: Memphis, TN
& Steve Keirn went to a No Contest with Eric Embry & Tom Prichard w/Tojo Yamamoto

Mar 30, 1991: Nashville, TN
& Steve Keirn went to a No Contest with Eric Embry & Tom Prichard w/Tojo Yamamoto

Apr 1, 1991: Memphis, TN
lost to Eric Embry & Tojo Yamamoto
- 2 on 1 Handicap Match

Apr 6, 1991: Nashville, TN
won via DQ over Eric Embry(c) w/Tojo Yamamoto
- Texas Title Match

& Steve Keirn beat Eric Embry & Tom Prichard w/Tojo Yamamoto
- Anything goes Match

Apr 8, 1991: Memphis, TN
Double DQ with Eric Embry w/Tojo Yamamoto

Apr 13, 1991: Nashville, TN
(c) vs. Eric Embry(c) w/Tojo Yamamoto
USWA Title vs. Texas Title
- Steel Cage Match

Apr 26, 1991: Dallas, TX
beat Eric Embry

* **Even though World Class had left the USWA and actually gone out of business by this time, Jerry Jarrett & Jerry Lawler would still test the waters and occasionally run shows in Dallas, TX because of the large wrestling fan base there.**

May 4, 1991: Cleveland, OH
beat Kamala

May 18, 1991: Philadelphia, PA
(c) won via DQ over the HonkyTonk Man
- USWA Unified World Title Match
- HonkyTonk was Wayne Farris, Lawler's cousin

June 10, 1991: Memphis, TN
(c) beat the Texas Ranger
- USWA Unified World Title Match

June 17, 1991: Memphis, TN
(c) beat Leatherface
- USWA Unified World Title Match
- Leathrface was longtime Memphis enhancement guy, Ken Raper in a mask.

June 24, 1991: Memphis, TN
(c) went to a Double Count Out with Eric Embry
 w/Tojo Yamamoto
- USWA Unified World Title Match

June 29, 1991: Nashville, TN
(c) vs. Eric Embry w/Tojo Yamamoto
- USWA Unified World Title Match

July 1, 1991: Memphis, TN
& Jackie Fargo beat Eric Embry & Leatherface
w/Tojo Yamamoto

July 6, 1991: Nashville, TN
& Bill Dundee won via DQ over Eric Embry &
Leatherface w/Tojo Yamamoto

July 8, 1991: Memphis, TN
(c) beat Eric Embry w/Tojo Yamamoto
- USWA Unified World Title Match

July 13, 1991: Nashville, TN
won via DQ over Eric Embry w/Tojo Yamamoto
- Lumberjack Match

July 15, 1991: Memphis, TN
(c) beat Leatherface
- USWA Unified World Title Match

July 22, 1991: Memphis, TN
(c) beat Awesome Kong
- USWA Unified World Title Match
- Awesome Kong was Dwayne McCullough

July 29, 1991: Memphis, TN
(c) lost to Awesome Kong w/Reggie B. Fine
- USWA Unified World Title Match

July 30, 1991: Nashville, TN
(c) beat Leatherface
- USWA Unified World Title Match

Aug 3, 1991: Nashville, TN
lost to Awesome Kong(c) w/Reggie B. Fine
 Unified title

Aug 5, 1991: Memphis, TN
beat Eric Embry

beat Leatherface
- Lawler unmaked Leatherface as Ken Raper

Aug 12, 1991: Memphis, TN
beat Awesome Kong(c) w/Reggie B. Fine
- USWA Unified World Title Match

Aug 13, 1991: Louisville, KY
(c) beat Leatherface
- USWA Unified World Title Match

Aug 17, 1991: Blackwood, NJ
& Mark Curtis lost to Stan Lane & Jim Cornette

Aug 19, 1991: Memphis, TN
(c) won via DQ over the Dragon Master
w/Christopher Love
- USWA Unified World Title Match
- Dragon Master was Gary Masters
- Christopher Love was Bert Prentice

The King, Wearing A Retro Shirt.

Aug 26, 1991: Memphis, TN
(c) lost to the Dragon Master w/Christopher
Love
- USWA Unified World Title Match

Aug 27, 1991: Louisville, KY
(c) lost to the Dragon Master w/Christopher
Love
- USWA Unified World Title Match

Aug 31, 1991: Nashville, TN
(c) lost the Dragon Master w/Christopher Love
- USWA Unified World Title Match

Sep 2, 1991: Memphis, TN
beat the Dragon Master(c) w/Christopher Love
- USWA Unified World Title Match

The King

Sep 7, 1991: Nashville, TN
beat the Dragon Master(c) w/Christopher Love
- USWA Unified World Title Match

Sep 9, 1991: Memphis, TN
& Tony Anthony won via DQ overr Eric Embry &
PY Chu Hi
- Py Chu Hi is Phil Hickerson

Sep 16, 1991: Memphis, TN
& Tony Anthony beat Eric Embry & PY Chu Hi

Sep 28, 1991: Memphis, TN
w/Tony Anthony & Bill Dundee beat Tim White,
Randy Rhodes & the Scorpion

Sep 30, 1991: Memphis, TN
(c) No Contest with Koko Ware
- USWA Unified World Title Match

Oct 7, 1991: Memphis, TN
won via DQ over Eddie Gilbert
- Title vs Title
- USWA Unified World vs Global TV Title

Oct 14, 1991: Memphis, TN
(c) won via DQ over Billy Travis
- USWA Unified World Title Match

Oct 15, 1991: Louisville, KY
(c) beat Billy Travis
- USWA Unified World Title Match

Oct 21, 1991: Memphis, TN
(c) won via Count Out over Billy Travis
- USWA Unified World Title Match

Oct 22, 1991: Louisville, KY
(c) beat Billy Travis
- USWA Unified World Title Match

Oct 28, 1991: Memphis, TN
(c) beat Billy Travis's Revenge- The Big O
- USWA Unified World Title Match

Oct 29, 1991: Louisville, KY
(c) beat Billy Travis
- USWA Unified World Title Match
Nov 4, 1991: Memphis, TN
(c) won via DQ Jeff Gaylord
- USWA Unified World Title Match

Nov 11, 1991: Memphis, TN
& Bill Dundee went to a Double DQ with Jeff
Gaylord & the Big O

Nov 12, 1991: Louisville, KY
(c) beat Jeff Gaylord
- USWA Unified World Title Match

Nov 18, 1991: Memphis, TN
Tag Team Tournament
Quarterfinals
& Jeff Jarrett beat Doug Masters & Bart Sawyer

Semi-Finals
& Jeff Jarrett beat Jimmy Valiant & Tom Prichard

Finals
& Jeff Jarrett beat Billy Travis & Gravedigger

Nov 25, 1991: Memphis, TN
(c) lost to Kamala
- USWA Unified World Title Match

w/Jeff Jarrett, Tom Prichard & Spirit of America
beat Kamala, Eric Embry, Tony Falk &
Gravedigger
- Spirit of America is Randy Lewis

Dec 2, 1991: Memphis, TN
beat Kamala(c)
- USWA Unified World Title Match

Dec 7, 1991: Memphis, TN - TV Taping
(c) double Count Out with Kamala
- USWA Unified World Title Match

The King

Dec 9, 1991: Memphis, TN
(c) lost to Kamala
- USWA Unified World Title Match

Dec 16, 1991: Memphis, TN
beat the Sandman

Dec 28, 1991: Memphis, TN
Double elimination 3-Man Tournament
beat Jeff Gaylord
beat Sandman
lost to Jeff Gaylord
Jeff Gaylord beat Sandman
Finals: beat Jef Gaylord

Dec 29, 1991: Louisville, KY
beat the Sandman

* Pro Wrestling Illustrated 1991 Awards

1991 Inspirational Wrestler of the year:
1st Runner Up: Jerry Lawler

1992

Chapter 23

Jan 6, 1992: Memphis, TN
lost via DQ to Kamala(c)
- USWA Unified World Title Match

Jan 7, 1992: Louisville, KY
Double elimination 3-Man Tournament
beat Jeff Gaylord
beat Sandman
lost to Jeff Gaylord
Jeff Gaylord beat Sandman
Finals: beat Jef Gaylord

Jan 10, 1992: Drexil Hill, PA
vs. Bob Backland

Jan 11, 1992: Clementon, NJ
lost via DQ to Kamala(c)
- USWA Unified World Title Match

Jan 20, 1992: Memphis, TN
& Jeff Jarrett No Contest with the Moondogs
Spot & Spike(c) w/Richard Lee
- USWA World Tag Title Match

Jan 25, 1992: Memphis, TN
& Jeff Jarrett lost to Moondogs (Spot & Spike)(c)
w/Richard Lee
- USWA World Tag Title Match

Jan 31, 1992: Kennett, MO
& Jeff Jarrett won via DQ over the Moondogs
(Spot & Spike)(c) w/Richard Lee
- USWA World Tag Title Match

Feb 1, 1992: Nashville, TN
& Jeff Jarrett lost to Moondogs (Spot & Spike)(c)
w/Richard Lee
- USWA World Tag Title Match

Feb 2, 1992: Memphis, TN
& Austin Idol lost via DQ to Moondogs (Spot &
Spike)(c) w/Richard Lee
- USWA World Tag Title Match

Feb 10, 1992: Memphis, TN
w/Jeff Jarrett & Austin Idol lost to Moondogs
Spot & Spike & the Big Black Dog w/Richard
Lee

Jerry Is Ready For The Moondogs

Feb 11, 1992: Louisville, KY
& Jeff Jarrett lost to Moondogs (Spot & Spike)(c)
w/Richard Lee
- USWA World Tag Title Match

Feb 16, 1992: Memphis, TN
won via DQ over the Big Black Dog

& Jeff Jarrett won via DQ over Moondogs (Spot
& Spike)(c) w/Richard Lee
- USWA World Tag Title Match

Feb 24, 1992: Memphis, TN
w/Jeff Jarrett & Junk Yard Dog beat Moondogs
(Spot & Spike) & the Big Black Dog w/Richard
Lee

Feb 25, 1992: Louisville, KY
won via Count Out over the Big Black Dog

Mar 2, 1992: Memphis, TN
& Koko B Ware lost to Moondogs Spot &
Spike(c) w/Richard Lee
- USWA World Tag Title Match

Mar 3, 1992: Louisville, KY
w/Koko Ware & Tom Prichard lost to the
Moondogs (Spot & Spike) & the Big Black Dog
w/Richard Lee

Mar 9, 1992: Memphis, TN
w/Koko B Ware & Kamala won via DQ over
Moondogs (Spot & Spike) & Richard Lee

Mar 10, 1992: Louisville, KY
& Leatherface lost to Moondogs Spot & Spike(c)
w/Richard Lee
- USWA World Tag Title Match

Mar 16, 1992: Memphis, TN
w/Tom Prichard, Kamala & Jimmy Valiant
Double DQ with the Moondogs (Spot & Spike),
the Big Black Dog & Richard Lee

Mar 17, 1992: Louisville, KY
w/Jimmy Valiant & Tom Prichard won via DQ
over Moondogs (Spot & Spike), the Big Black
Dog & Richard Lee

Mar 23, 1992: Memphis, TN
& Jeff Jarrett won via DQ over Moondogs (Spot
& Spike)(c) w/Richard Lee
- USWA World Tag Title Match
- Lumberjack Match

Mar 24, 1992: Louisville, KY
w/Jeff Jarrett & Jimmy Valiant lost to Moondogs
(Spot & Spike) & the Big Black Dog w/Richard
Lee

Mar 28, 1992: Jonesboro, AR
& Jeff Jarrett Double DQ with the Moondogs
(Spot & Spike)(c) w/Richard Lee
- USWA World Tag Title Match
- Steel Cage Match

Mar 30, 1992: Memphis, TN
w/Jeff Jarrett & Leatherface lost to Moondogs
(Spot & Spike) & Richard Lee

Mar 31, 1992: Louisville, KY
& Jeff Jarrett went to a Double Count Out with
Moondog Spot & Black Dog w/Richard Lee

April 4, 1992: Nashville, TN
& Jeff Jarrett beat Moondog Spot & Black Dog
w/Richard Lee

Apr 6, 1992: Memphis, TN
& Jeff Jarrett Won A Tag Team Battle Royal

& Jeff Jarrett lost to Moondogs (Spike & Cujo)(c)
w/Richard Lee
- USWA World Tag Title Match

Richard Lee & His Moondogs (Spike & Cujo)

Apr 13, 1992: Memphis, TN
w/Jeff Jarrett & Eric Embry beat Moondogs
(Spot, Spike & Cujo) & Richard Lee
- No DQ Match

Apr 20, 1992: Memphis, TN
w/Jeff Jarrett & Charlie Trapper beat Moondogs
(Spot & Spike) & Richard Lee

Apr 27, 1992: Memphis, TN
w/Charlie Trapper, Jeff Jarrett & Big Black Dog
lost to Richard Lee, Moondogs (Cujo, Spike &
Spot)

May 4, 1992: Memphis, TN
beat Kamala(c)
- USWA Unified World Title Match

May 11, 1992: Memphis, TN
& Jeff Jarrett Double DQ with Moondogs (Spot &
Spike)(c) w/Richard Lee
- USWA World Tag Title Match

May 18, 1992: Memphis, TN
lost via DQ to Eddie Gilbert(c)
- Global North American Title Match

w/Jeff Jarrett & Eric Embry beat Moondogs
(Spot, Spike & Cujo) w/Richard Lee

May 25, 1992: Memphis, TN
(c) beat Steven Dane
- USWA Unified World Title Match

May 30, 1992: Memphis, TN
(c) won via DQ Marty Jannetty
- USWA Unified World Title Match

June 8, 1992: Memphis, TN
(c) beat Eddie Gilbert(c)
USWA Unified World Title vs. Global North
American Title - Unification Match

Jerry Beats Eddie Gilbert To Unify The
Global Belt With The Unified Title.

June 15, 1992: Memphis, TN
(c) lost to Eddie Gilbert
- USWA Unified World Title Match
- Title vs. Gilbert retiring

w/Jeff Jarrett & the Hornet beat Richard Lee &
the Moondogs (Spot & Cujo)

June 22, 1992: Memphis, TN
beat Dennis Caralluzo & Mike Doggendorf
Handicap Match
won via DQ over Mike Samples

June 29, 1992: Memphis, TN
& Jeff Jarrett beat Moondogs (Spot & Cujo)(c)
w/Richard Lee
- USWA World Tag Title Match
- Steel Cage Match
- Special Ref: Jackie Fargo

*** On July 1, 1992 Stan "Plowboy" Frazier
passed away from complications from
diabetes (kidney failure). Stan was one of
Jerry's favorite tag team partners during
the 1970s & 1980s. The duo was highly
successful.**

Plowboy Frazier Standing Beside Andre
the Giant.

July 6, 1992: Memphis, TN
& Jeff Jarrett(c) lost to Moondogs (Spot & Cujo)
w/Richard Lee
- USWA World Tag Title Match

July 13, 1992: Memphis, TN
w/Jeff Jarrett & Jackie Fargo beat Moondogs
(Spot & Cujo) & Richard Lee

July 20, 1992: Memphis, TN
& Jeff Jarrett beat Moondogs (Spot & Cujo)(c)
w/Richard Lee
- USWA World Tag Title Match

July 27, 1992: Memphis, TN
& Jeff Jarrett(c) beat Moondogs (Spot & Cujo)
w/Richard Lee
- USWA World Tag Title Match
- Titles vs. Richard Lee' hair(lost)

Aug 3, 1992: Memphis, TN
& Jeff Jarrett(c) beat Moondogs (Spot & Cujo)
w/Richard Lee
- USWA World Tag Title Match
- Titles vs. Moondog Fifi's hair(lost)
- Moondog Fifi was Diane Von Hoffman

Aug 10, 1992: Memphis, TN
& Jeff Jarrett(c) lost to Moondogs (Spot & Cujo)
w/Richard Lee
- USWA World Tag Title Match

Aug 17, 1992: Memphis, TN
& Jeff Jarrett beat Moondogs (Spot & Cujo)(c)
w/Richard Lee
- USWA World Tag Title Match

Aug 24, 1992: Memphis, TN
& Jeff Jarrett(c) beat Moondogs (Spot & Cujo)
w/Richard Lee
- USWA World Tag Title Match

Aug 27, 1992: Louisville, KY
beat the Dragon Master

Aug 30, 1992: Williamstown, NJ
went to a Double DQ with Eddie Gilbert

Aug 31, 1992: Memphis, TN
& Jeff Jarrett(c) beat Pat Tanaka & Kato
- USWA World Tag Title Match

Sep 7, 1992: Memphis, TN
& Jeff Jarrett(c) beat Eddie & Doug Gilbert
- USWA World Tag Title Match

Sep 14, 1992: Memphis, TN
& Jeff Jarrett(c) beat Mr. Hughes & Tracey
Smothers
- USWA World Tag Title Match

won via Count Out Mr. Hughes (Curtis Hughes)

Sep 21, 1992: Memphis, TN
w/Jeff Jarrett & Eddie Marlin lost to Mike
Samples, Richard Lee & Bert Prentice

& Jeff Jarrett(c) lost via DQ to Mr. Hughes & Jeff
Gaylord
- USWA World Tag Title Match

Oct 3, 1992: Memphis, TN - TV Taping
& Jeff Jarrett lost to Moondogs (Spot & Spike)
w/Richard Lee
- Jerry Lawler had car trouble and was not at
the match. Jarrett wrestled alone.
- USWA World Tag Title Match

Oct 5, 1992: Memphis, TN
& Jeff Jarrett lost via DQ to Moondogs (Spot &
Spike)(c) w/Richard Lee
- USWA World Tag Title Match
- Anything Goes Match

Oct 19, 1992: Memphis, TN
lost to Todd Champion(c)
- USWA Unified World Title Match

w/Jeff Jarrett & Junk Yard Dog beat Moondogs
(Spot & Spike) & the King Killer w/Richard Lee
- King Killer was Mike Miller

The King

Oct 26, 1992: Memphis, TN
lost via DQ to Todd Champion

w/Jeff Jarrett & Eddie Gilbert beat Moondogs
(Spot & Spike) & the King Killer w/Richard Lee

Nov 2, 1992: Memphis, TN
beat Todd Champion(c)
- USWA Unified World Title Match
- No DQ Match
- Special ref: Jeff Jarrett

Nov 9, 1992: Memphis, TN
(c) beat Todd Champion
- USWA Unified World Title Match
- Special Ref: Downtown Bruno

The King

Nov 16, 1992: Memphis, TN
w/Eddie & Doug Gilbert beat Moondogs (Spot & Spike) & Richard Lee
- Barbed Wire Match

Nov 23, 1992: Memphis, TN
w/Eddie & Doug Gilbert beat Moondog Spike, Curtis Thompson & Richard Lee

Dec 7, 1992: Memphis, TN
(c) lost to Koko B Ware
- USWA Unified World Title Match

Dec 14, 1992: Memphis, TN
beat Koko B Ware(c)
- USWA Unified World Title Match

Dec 21, 1992: Memphis, TN
& Moondogs (Spot & Spike) beat Mike Miller, Ron & Don Harris

(c) beat the Christmas Creature
- Christmas Creature was Glen Jacobs, would eventually become Kane for the WWE
- USWA Unified World Title Match

Dec 28, 1992: Memphis, TN
(c) beat the Christmas Creature
- USWA Unified World Title Match
- Title vs. Mask
- Unmasked as Glen Jacobs

* Pro Wrestling Illustrated 1992 Awards

1992 Feud of the Year
Winner: Jerry Lawler & Jeff Jarrett vs. the Moondogs

1993

Chapter 24

Jan 4, 1993: Memphis, TN
beat Mike Samples via DQ

Double DQ with Mike Miller

Jan 11, 1993: Memphis, TN
beat Mike Miller

Jan 16, 1993: Nashville, TN
beat Mike Miller

Jan 18, 1993: Memphis, TN
& Jeff Jarrett won via DQ over Ron & Don Harris

w/Jeff Jarrett, Moondog Spot & Tony DeNucci lost to Brian Christopher, Mike Miller, Ron & Don Harris

Jan 23, 1993: Memphis, TN - TV Taping
& Jeff Jarrett beat Ken Raper & Ken Wayne

Jan 24, 1993: Sacramento, CA - Royal Rumble
Competed in the Royal Rumble

* Because of Jerry Jarrett's job with the WWF, Jerry Lawler was brought in to the WWF

Jan 25, 1993: Memphis, TN
Semi-finals: & Jeff Jarrett won via DQ over Brian Christopher & Mike Miller

Finals: & Jeff Jarrett lost to Ron & Don Harris
- USWA World Tag Title Tournament

Jan 30, 1993: Nashville, TN
Semi-finals: & Jeff Jarrett won via DQ over Brian Christopher & Mike Miller

Finals: & Jeff Jarrett lost to Ron & Don Harris
- USWA World Tag Title Tournament

Feb 1, 1993: Memphis, TN
(c) beat on Mr. Perfect via reverse decision
- USWA Unified World Title Match
- Mr. Perfect was Curt Hennig

Feb 6, 1993: Nashville, TN
& Jeff Jarrett beat Jeff Gaylord & Doink the Clown

Feb 8, 1993: Memphis, TN
& Jeff Jarrett beat Jeff Gaylord & Doink the Clown

Feb 9, 1993: Louisville, KY
& Jeff Jarrett beat Jeff Gaylord & Doink the Clown

Feb 13, 1993: Nashville, TN
(c) won via DQ over Lex Luger
- USWA Unified World Title Match

Feb 15, 1993: Memphis, TN
(c) beat Brian Christopher
- USWA Unified World Title Match

Feb 18, 1993: Kerry Von Erich passed away on this day after shooting himself in the chest.

Kerry Von Erich
Feb 3, 1960- Feb 18, 1993

Feb 20, 1993: Nashville, TN
(c) won via DQ over Lex Luger
- USWA Unified World Title Match

Feb 22, 1993: Memphis, TN
& Jeff Jarrett lost via DQ to Lex Luger & Brian Christopher

Feb 25, 1993: Memphis, TN
(c) beat Jeff Gaylord
- USWA Unified World Title Match

The King

Feb 26, 1993: Long Island, NY
beat the Big Boss Man

Feb 27, 1993: Auburn Hils, MI
lost via Count Out to Randy Savage

Feb 28, 1993: Cincinnati, OH
lost to Randy Savage via Count Out

Feb 28, 1993: Dayton, OH - evening
lost via Count Out to Randy Savage

Mar 1, 1993: Memphis, TN
w/Jeff Jarrett & Giant Gonzalez beat Brian Christopher, Ron & Don Harris

Mar 5, 1993: Memphis, TN
(c) beat Jeff Gaylord
- USWA Unified World Title Match

Mar 6, 1993: Nashville, TN
(c) Double DQ with Randy Savage
- USWA Unified World Title Match

Mar 8, 1993: Memphis, TN
(c) Double DQ with Randy Savage
- USWA Unified World Title Match

Mar 9, 1993: Louisville, KY
(c) won via DQ over Randy Savage
- USWA Unified World Title Match

Mar 14, 1993: Leitchfield, KY
(c) won via DQ over Randy Savage
- USWA Unified World Title Match

Mar 15, 1993: Memphis, TN
(c) beat the Russian Brute
- USWA Unified World Title Match

w/Jeff Jarrett & Danny Davis lost to Brian Christopher & Harlem Knights (Nelson & Bobby Knight)

Jerry Relaxing On His Couch.

Mar 21, 1993: Boston, MA
beat Tito Santana

Mar 21, 1993: New York, NY - evening
beat Tito Santana

Mar 22 New York, NY - RAW TV
beat Jim Powers

Mar 23, 1993: Louisville, KY
w/Jeff Jarrett & Danny Davis beat Brian
Christopher & Harlem Knights

Mar 29, 1993: Memphis, TN
& the Big Boss Man lost via DQ to the Harlem
Knights

Mar 30, 1993: Louisville, KY
(c) won via DQ over Shawn Michaels(c)
- USWA Unified World Title vs. WWF Inter-
Continental Title

Apr 3, 1993: Nashville, TN
(c) beat Scotty Flamingo
- USWA Unified World Title Match
- Scotty Flamingo was Scott Levy. He would go
on to become Raven for ECW, WCW, TNA &
WWF.

& Jeff Jarrett lost to Harlem Knights

Apr 5, 1993: Memphis, TN
(c) won via DQ over Scotty Flamingo
- USWA Unified World Title Match

The King

Apr 10, 1993: Nashville, TN

(c) won via DQ over Scotty Flamingo
- USWA Unified World Title Match

Apr 12, 1993: Memphis, TN
(c) beat Nelson Knight
- USWA Unified World Title Match
- Knight was Nelson Frazier, would go on to
become Mabel, King Mabel & Viscera in the
WWF.

w/Jeff Jarrett, Richard Lee, Moondogs Spot &
Splat lost to Nelson & Bobby Knight, Scott
Flamingo, Mike Samples & Brian Christopher

Apr 13, 1993: Louisville, KY
(c) won via DQ over Scotty Flamingo
- USWA Unified World Title Match

Apr 15, 1993: Memphis, TN
(c) vs. Randy Savage
- USWA Unified World Title Match

Apr 16, 1993: Jonesboro, AR
(c) won via DQ over Randy Savage
- USWA Unified World Title Match

Apr 17, 1993: Nashville, TN
(c) won via DQ over Randy Savage
- USWA Unified World Title Match

w/Jeff Jarrett, the Moondogs & Richard Lee beat
Brian Christopher, Scotty Flamingo, the Harlem
Knights & Mike Samples

Apr 19, 1994: Memphis, TN
(c) won via DQ over Randy Savage
- USWA Unified World Title Match
- Steel Cage match

Apr 26, 1993: Memphis, TN
& Miss Texas beat Scotty Flamingo & Sherri
Martel

Apr 30, 1993: Covington, KY
(c) won via DQ over Brian Christopher
- USWA Unified World Title Match

May 3, 1993: Memphis, TN
(c) lost to Papa Shango
- USWA Unified World Title Match
- Papa Shango is Charles Wright, previously the
Soultaker in Memphis. Would become the
Godfather in the WWF/WWE and a WWE HOF'er.

May 8, 1993: Nashville, TN
Double DQ with Papa Shango(c)
- USWA Unified World Title Match

May 10, 1993: Memphis, TN
Double DQ with Papa Shango(c)
- USWA Unified World Title Match

May 15, 1993: Nashville, TN
Double DQ with Papa Shango(c)
- USWA Unified World Title Match

May 17, 1993: Memphis, TN
& Koko B Ware lost to Rex King & Steve Doll
- USWA World Tag Title Match

& Koko B Ware Won A Tag Team Battle Royal

May 24, 1993: Memphis, TN
& Koko B Ware lost via DQ to Rex King & Steve Doll
- USWA World Tag Title Match

May 28, 1993: Covington, KY
& Koko B Ware lost via DQ to Rex King & Steve Doll
- USWA World Tag Title Match

May 29, 1993: Nashville, TN
& Koko B Ware lost via DQ to Rex King & Steve Doll
- USWA World Tag Title Match

May 31, 1993: Memphis, TN
Round 1: beat CW Bergstrom
Quarterfinals: beat Rock n" Roll Phantom
Semifinals: beat Danny Davis
Finals: beat Steve Doll
- #1 Contenders tournament

June 5, 1993: Nashville, TN
Round 1: beat CW Bergstrom
Semifinals: beat Rex King
Finals: beat Steve Doll
- #1 Contenders tournament

June 7, 1993: New York, NY - RAW TV
lost via DQ to Mr. Perfect

beat Mark Thunder

June 12, 1993: Memphis, TN - TV Taping
& Jeff Jarrett defeated Rex King and Steve Doll

June 12, 1993: Nashville, TN
& Jeff Jarrett lost via DQ to Rex King & Steve Doll
- USWA World Tag Title Match

June 14, 1993: Memphis, TN
lost via DQ to Papa Shango(c)
- USWA Unified World Title Match

June 18, 1993: Louisville, KY
won via DQ over Papa Shango(c)
- USWA Unified World Title Match

June 19, 1993: Nashville, TN
won via DQ over Papa Shango(c)
- USWA Unified World Title Match

June 21, 1993: Memphis, TN
lost via DQ to Owen Hart(c)
- USWA Unified World Title Match

beat ref Paul Neighbors

June 28, 1993: Memphis, TN
lost via DQ to Owen Hart(c)
- USWA Unified World Title Match

Owen Hart: USWA World Unified Champ

July 5, 1993: Memphis, TN
beat Owen Hart(c)
- USWA Unified World Title Match

July 7, 1993: Salisbury, MD Wrestling Challenge
beat Owen Hart

July 10, 1993: Memphis, TN - TV Taping
(c) No Contest with Brian Christopher
- USWA Unified World Title Match

July 12, 1993: Memphis, TN
(c) won via DQ over Vampire Warrior
- USWA Unified World Title Match

July 17, 1993: West Palm Beach, FL
lost to Razor Ramon

July 18, 1993: Tampa, FL
lost to Razor Ramon

July 24, 1993: Memphis, TN - TV Taping
beat Leon Downs

July 26, 1993: Memphis, TN
(c) beat Vampire Warrior
- USWA Unified World Title Match

July 31, 1993: Pittsburgh, PA
won via DQ over Randy Savage

Aug 1, 1993: Richfield, OH
won via DQ over Randy Savage

Aug 2, 1993: Memphis, TN
(c) Double DQ w/Bret Hart
- USWA Unified World Title Match

Aug 9, 1993: Memphis, TN
(c) won via DQ over Mr. Perfect
- USWA Unified World Title Match

Aug 13, 1993: New York, NY
won via DQ over Randy Savage

Aug 14, 1993: Memphis, TN - TV Taping
& Jeff Jarrett went to a TV Time Limit Draw
with Vampire Warrior & Brian Christopher

Aug 16, 1993: Memphis, TN
& Jeff Jarrett lost to Bret & Owen Hart

Aug 23, 1993: Memphis, TN
beat Paul Neighbors
-Stretcher Match

Aug 29, 1993: Memphis, TN
(c) beat Bret Hart
- USWA Unified World Title Match
- Steel Cage match

Aug 30, 1993: Auburn Hills, MI - Summerslam
won via DQ over Bret Hart

Sep 4, 1993: Nashville, TN
(c) won via DQ over Giant Gonzalez
- USWA Unified World Title Match

Sep 6, 1993: Memphis, TN
(c) won via DQ Giant Gonzalez
- USWA Unified World Title Match

Sep 11, 1993: Memphis, TN
beat Lee Vincent

Sep 13, 1993: Memphis, TN
(c) lost to Tatanka
- USWA Unified World Title Match

Sep 18, 1993: Nashville, TN
won via DQ over Tatanka(c)
- USWA Unified World Title Match

Sep 20, 1993: Memphis, TN
w/Jeff Jarrett, Moondogs (Spot & Spike) beat
Tatanka, Tommy Rich, Dog Catcher #1 & 2
- USWA Unified World Title Elimination Match
- Lawler pinned Tatanka and was last man

Jerry Lawler Is World Unified Champ Again!

Sep 22, 1993: Evansville, IN
(c) won via DQ over Tatanka
- USWA Unified World Title Match

Sep 28, 1993: Worcester, MA
lost to Randy Savage

lost to Bret Hart

Sep 29, 1993: Portland, ME
lost to Bret Hart

Oct 4, 1993: Memphis, TN
(c) won via DQ over Randy Savage
- USWA Unified World Title Match

The King

Oct 11, 1993: Memphis, TN
(c) lost to Randy Savage
- USWA Unified World Title Match

Oct 18, 1993: Memphis, TN
beat Doink the Clown

w/Jeff Jarrett & Brian Christopher beat Doink
the Clown, Shawn Michaels & Koko B Ware
Oct 19, 1993: Glens Falls, NY
lost to Bret Hart
- Steel Cage Match

Oct 20, 1993: Burlington, VT
lost to Bret Hart
- Steel Cage Match

Oct 22, 1993: Pittsburgh, PA
lost to Bret Hart
- Steel Cage Match

Oct 23, 1993: Baltimore, MD
lost to Bret Hart

Oct 25, 1995 Memphis, TN
USWA World Tag Title Tournament
Rd. One: & Red Knight beat Doomsday & Reggie
B Fine
Semifinals: & Red Knight beat the Moondogs
Finals: & Red Knight lost to Jeff Jarrett & Brian
Christopher

Oct 28, 1993: Detroit, MI
lost to Bret Hart
- Steel Cage match

Oct 29, 1993: Long island, NY
lost via DQ to Bret Hart

Oct 30, 1993: Rochester, NY
lost to Bret Hart

Oct 31, 1993: Toronto, Ontario
lost to Bret Hart
- Steel Cage Match

Nov 1, 1993: Peterborough, Ontario
lost to Bret Hart
- Steel Cage Match

Nov 5, 1993: Indianapolis, IN
lost to Bret Hart
Steel Cage Match

Nov 6, 1993: Richfield, OH
lost to Bret Hart
- Steel Cage Match

Nov 7, 1993: Loch Sheldrake, NY
lost to Bret Hart
- Steel Cage Match

Nov 8, 1993: Bushkill, PA - RAW TV #39
lost to Bret Hart

Nov 9, 1993: Carbondale, PA
lost to the Undertaker

Nov 10, 1993: Delhi, NY - TV Taping
won via DQ over Owen Hart

Nov 15, 1993: Memphis, TN
& Brian Christopher won via Count Out over Rex
Hargrove & Koko B Ware

Nov 20, 1993: Memphis, TN
& Brian Christopher won by Count Out over PG-
13(JC-Ice/Jamie Dundee & Wolfie-D)

Nov 22, 1993: Memphis, TN
& Brian Christopher defeated Rex Hargrove and
Koko B. Ware

Nov 23, 1993: Baltimore, MD
lost to Bret Hart

Nov 27, 1993: Memphis, TN - TV Taping
won via DQ over Reggie B. Fine

Nov 29, 1993: Memphis, TN
won via DQ over Brian Lee(c)
- SMW Title Match

& Brian Christopher beat Rex Hargrove & Reggie
B Fine

Dec 1, 1993: Evansville, IN
& Brian Christopher beat Mike Samples & the
Warlock

Dec 4, 1993: Nashville, TN
& Brian Christopher beat Buddy Landell &
Reggie B. Fine

Dec 6, 1997: Memphis, TN
beat the Warlock

& Brian Christopher lost via DQ to Reggie B.
Fine & Doug Gilbert

Dec 7, 1993: Louisville, KY
& Brian Christopher beat Buddy Landell &
Reggie B. Fine

Dec 11, 1993: Nashville, TN
& Brian Christopher beat Doug Gilbert & Mad
Dog Lynch

Dec 11, 1993: Memphis, TN
w/Brian Christopher & Little Eagle No Contest
PG-13 & Midget-D

Dec 13, 1993: Memphis, TN
& Brian Christopher lost to Eddie & Doug Gilbert

Dec 18, 1993: Memphis, TN - TV Taping
won via Count Out over Reggie B. Fine

Dec 20, 1993: Memphis, TN
beat Jeff Jarrett(c)
- USWA Unified World Title Match

Dec 27, 1993: Memphis, TN
& Brian Christopher lost via DQ to Eddie & Doug
Gilbert

Dec 30, 1993: Nashville, TN
& Brian Christopher lost via DQ to Eddie & Doug
Gilbert

* Pro Wrestling Illustrated 1993 Awards

1993 Feud of the Year
Winner: Jerry Lawler vs. Bret Hart

1993 Most Hated
Winner: Jerry Lawler

1994

Chapter 25

Jan 1, 1994: Memphis, TN - TV Taping
& Brian Christopher won via DQ over Doug &
Eddie Gilbert

Jan 3, 1994: Memphis, TN
(c) won via DQ over Eddie Gilbert
- USWA Unified World Title Match

w/Brian Christopher, Ricky Morton & Robert
Gibson lost to Killer Kyle, Buddy Landell, Doug &
Eddie Gilbert

Jan 1, 1994: Memphis, TN - TV Taping
& Brian Christopher beat Reggie B. Fine & Ali
Ben Khan

Jan 10, 1994: Memphis, TN
& Brian Christopher won via DQ over Tommy
Rich & Doug Gilbert
- Special Ref: Steve Keirn

Jan 15, 1994:
& Brian Christopher lost to Doug & Eddie Gilbert
- Falls Count Anywhere

Jan 16, 1994: Clinchco, VA
& Brian Christopher beat Doug & Eddie Gilbert
- Stretcher Match

Jan 17, 1994: Memphis, TN
(c) won via Count Out over Skull Von Crush
- USWA Unified World Title Match

& Brian Christopher beat Doug & Eddie Gilbert
- Lumberjack Match

Jan 24, 1994: Memphis, TN
& Brian Christopher lost to Doug & Eddie Gilbert
- Texas Death Match

Jan 29, 1994: Memphis, TN - TV Taping
& Brian Christopher won a tag match,
opponents unknown.

Jan 29, 1994: Nashville, TN
& Brian Christopher lost to Doug Gilbert &
Wolfie-D

Jan 31, 1994: Memphis, TN
(c) lost to Eddie Gilbert
- USWA Unified World Title Match

Feb 5, 1994: Clementon, NJ
No Contest with Abdullah the Butcher

Feb 7, 1994: Memphis, TN
beat to Eddie Gilbert(c)
- USWA Unified World Title Match

& Brian Christopher won via DQ over the
Moondogs (Spot & Rex) w/Richard Lee

The King

Feb 14, 1994: Memphis, TN
(c) lost via count out to Eddie Gilbert
- USWA Unified World Title Match
- Count Out Rule Waived So Gilbert Won Title

& Brian Christopher No Contest with the
Moondogs (Spot & Rex) w/Richard Lee

Feb 19, 1994: Memphis, TN - TV Taping
beat Eddie Gilbert
- Lawler's Crown vs. Eddie's Grandmother's Van

Feb 19, 1994: Woodbury, NJ
beat Doink the Clown

Feb 21, 1994: Memphis, TN
lost via DQ to Eddie Gilbert(c)
- USWA Unified World Title Match

& /Brian Christopher beat the Moondogs (Spot & Rex) w/Richard Lee

Feb 26, 1994: Memphis, TN
& Brian Christopher beat Ghetto Blaster & Lucifer

The King Backstage @ the MSC

Mar 7, 1994: Memphis, TN
w/Brian Christopher & Austin Idol won via DQ over Terry Funk, Doug & Eddie Gilbert

beat Moondog Spot, Brian Christopher, Terry Funk, Jimmy Valiant, Koko B Ware, Doug & Eddie Gilbert & Austin Idol
- 10-Man Elimination Match

Mar 12, 1994: Memphis, TN - TV Taping
& Brian Christopher went to a No Contest with the Moondogs (Spot & Rex) w/Richard Lee

Mar 14, 1994: Memphis, TN
won via DQ over Tommy Rich

w/Brian Christopher & the Dream Machine beat Tommy Rich, Doug & Eddie Gilbert
- Rage In A Cage Match

Mar 25, 1994: Senatobia, MS
beat Eddie Gilbert(c)
- USWA Unified World Title

Mar 26, 1994: Woodbury, NJ
lost to Chris Benoit

Mar 28, 1994: Memphis, TN
(c) Double DQ with the Dream Machine
- USWA Unified World Title

& Brian Christopher lost to Doug Gilbert & Tommy Rich
- PIle Driver Match

Apr 4, 1994: Memphis, TN
(c) beat Adam Bomb
- USWA Unified World Title

w/Brian Christopher & Jimmy Valiant beat Doug Gilbert, Tommy Rich & the Dream Machine
- "I Quit" Match

Apr 8, 1994: Nashville, TN
(c) beat Adam Bomb
- USWA Unified World Title

Apr 9, 1994: Memphis, TN
(c) beat Adam Bomb
- USWA Unified World Title

Apr 18, 1994: Memphis, TN
lost to the Dream Machine
- Non-Title Match

Apr 23, 1994: Woodbury, NJ
beat Johnny Gunn

Apr 25, 1994: Memphis, TN
(c) beat the Dream Machine
- USWA Unified World Title

Apr 30, 1994: Red Lion, PA
lost to Doink the Clown

May 2, 1994: Memphis, TN
(c) beat the Dream Machine
- USWA Unified World Title
- Taped Fist Match

May 6, 1994: Blytheville, AR
lost to Dream Machine
- Non-Title Match

May 9, 1994: Memphis, TN
& Eddie Gilbert went to a No Contest with Jeff Jarrett & the Dream Machine

The King

May 16, 1994: Memphis, TN
& Jeff Jarrett won via DQ over Eddie Gilbert & the Dream Machine

May 24, 1994: Canton, OH Wrestling challenge TV Taping
beat John Paul

May 29, 1994: Memphis, TN
Lost to Eddie Gilbert

& Brian Christopher lost to Bam Bam Bigelow & the Dream Machine

June 6, 1994: Memphis, TN
(c) won via DQ over Bam Bam Bigelow
- USWA Unified World Title

June 13, 1994: Memphis, TN
& Brian Christopher beat Tony Falk, Eddie Gilbert & Scott Bowden
- 3 on 2 Texas Tornado Death Match

June 17, 1994: Covington, TN
beat Doug Gilbert

June 19, 1994: Baltimore, MD - King Of The Ring
lost to Roddy Piper

June 27, 1994: Memphis, TN
& Brian Christopher vs. Tommy Rich, Doug Gilbert, Dream Machine & Phil Hickerson
- 4 on 2 Handicap Match

July 4, 1994: Memphis, TN
(c) won via DQ over Tommy Rich
- USWA Unified World Title

& Brian Christopher & Moondog Spot lost to Tommy Rich, Eddie Gilbert & the Dream Machine
- Steel Cage Handcuff Elimination
- Last 2 men left were Lawler & Rich. Rich handcuffed Lawler to cage to win.

Jul 7, 1994: Landover, MD
lost to Randy Savage
July 8, 1994: East Rutherford, NJ
lost to Randy Savage

July 9, 1994: Uniondale, NY
lost to Randy Savage

July 11, 1994: Memphis, TN
lost to Tommy Rich
- Barbed Wire Match

July 16, 1994: Memphis, TN - TV Taping
(c) lost via forfeit to Sid Vicious
- USWA Unified World Title

* Lawler was not able to make it back to Memphis in time for the match, therefore he had to forfeit the World Title to Sid.

July 18, 1994: Memphis, TN
beat Tommy Rich

July 22, 1994: Miami, FL
beat Duke Drosie

July 23, 1994: Tampa, FL
won via DQ over Duke Drosie

July 25, 1994: Memphis, TN
beat Tommy Rich

July 28, 1994: San Diego, CA
won via DQ over Duke Drosie

July 29, 1994: Los Angeles, CA
won via DQ over Duke Drosie

July 30, 1994: Oakland, CA
won via DQ over Duke Drosie

Aug 1, 1994: Youngstown, OH - TV Taping
won via DQ over Duke Drosie

Aug 3, 1994: Cincinnati, OH
lost to Razor Ramon

Aug 4, 1994: Richfield, OH
lost to Razor Ramon

Aug 5, 1994: Pittsburgh, PA
beat duke Drosie via DQ

Aug 6, 1994: Philadelphia, PA
beat Duke Drosie via DQ

Aug 8, 1994: Memphis, TN
& King Kong Bundy lost to Sid Vicious & Spike
Huber

Aug 15, 1994: Lowell, MA - RAW TV Taping
lost via Count Out to Duke Drosie

Aug 20, 1994: Nashville, TN
& Buddy Landell beat Doug Gilbert & Tommy
Rich
& Jeff Gaylord lost to Sid Vicious & Spellbinder

Aug 22, 1994: Memphis, TN
w/Austin Idol & Jeff Gaylord lost via DQ to Sid
Vicious, Spellbinder & Spike Huber

Aug 25, 1994: Omaha, NE
won via DQ over Duke Drosie

Aug 26, 1994: Des Moines, IA
won via DQ over Duke Drosie

**Aug 30, 1994: Milwaukee, WI - Wrestling
Challenge - Taping**
beat Ben Jordan
won via DQ over Duke Drosie

**Aug 31, 1994: Green Bay, WI - Superstars
TV Taping**
won via DQ over Duke Drosie

Sep 5, 1994: Memphis, TN
lost to Sid Vicious(c)
- USWA Unified World Title

Sid Vicious: USWA World Unified Champ

Sep 12, 1994: Memphis, TN
lost to Sid Vicious(c)
- USWA Unified World Title
- Piledriver vs. Power Bomb Match

Sep 19, 1994: Memphis, TN
lost via DQ to Sid Vicious
- USWA Unified World Title

Sep 28, 1994: White Plains, NY
lost to the Undertaker
- Casket Match

Oct 3, 1994: Memphis, TN
drew with Tommy Rich,
- Rich won coin toss to advance Rich won Title
- 1st Round of USWA Unified Title Tournament
- USWA Title, Not USWA Unified World Title

& Brian Christopher lost to Sid Vicious & Doug
Gilbert

Oct 8, 1994: Johnson City, TN
drew with Tommy Rich
- Rich won coin toss to advance, Rich won Title
- 1st Round of USWA Unified Title Tournament
- USWA Title, Not USWA Unified World Title

& Brian Christopher beat Sid Vicious & Doug Gilbert
Stretcher Match

The King

Oct 10, 1994: Memphis, TN
& Randy Hales beat Scott Bowden & Tommy Rich

Oct 19, 1994: Albany, NY - Wrestling Challenge - TV Taping
beat Gary Scott
beat Sparky Plug

Oct 24, 1994: Memphis, TN
& Brian Christopher lost via DQ to Tommy Rich & Doug Gilbert

Oct 27, 1994: East Rutherford, NJ
beat Doink the Clown

Oct 28, 1994: Uniondale, NY
beat Doink the Clown

Oct 29, 1994: New York, NY - Madison Square Garden
w/Quessy beat Doink & Dink the Clowns

Nov 8, 1994: Bushkill, PA - Wrestling Superstars - TV Taping
beat Doink the Clown

Nov 10, 1994: St. Louis, MO
beat Doink the Clown

Nov 11, 1994: Chicago, IL
beat Doink the Clown

Nov 12, 1994: Boston, MA
beat Doink the Clown

Nov 14, 1994: Memphis, TN
W/Brian Christopher & Bill Dundee beat Doug Gilbert, Tommy Rich & Scott Bowden

Nov 19, 1994: Cherry Hill, NJ
lost via DQ to the Dirty White Boy
- NWA World Title Tournament

Nov 21, 1994: Memphis, TN
W/Brian Christopher & Bill Dundee beat Doug Gilbert, Tommy Rich, the Dream Machine

Nov 23, 1994: San Antonio, TX - Survivor Series 1994
w/Quessy, Sleezy & Cheesey beat Doink, Dink, Wink & Pink the Clowns in An Elimination Match

Nov 26, 1996: Memphis, TN - TV Taping
beat Ederick Hines

Nov 29, 1994: Poughkeepsie, NY
lost to Lex Luger

Dec 5, 1994: Memphis, TN
lost to Spellbinder via DQ

w/Frank Morrell, Bill Dundee & Brian Christopher
No Contest with Don Bass, Scott Bowden, Doug Gilbert & Tommy Rich

Dec 13, 1994: Liberty, NY - Wrestling Challenge - TV Taping
beat 1-2-3 Kid

Dec 19, 1994: Memphis, TN
& Brian Christopher beat Sid Vicious & Spellbinder
- Piledriver vs. Power Bomb Match

Dec 26, 1994: Memphis, TN
& Brian Christopher lost via DQ to Sid Vicious &
Spellbinder

* Pro Wrestling Illustrated 1994 Awards

1994 Most Hated
3rd Runner Up: Jerry Lawler

1995

Chapter 26

Jan 2, 1995: Memphis, TN
beat Spellbinder

Spellbinder & Bert Prentice

Jan 9, 1995: Houston, TX - RAW Taping
During the King's Court segment, William Shatner gives Jerry Lawler a monkey flip. Bret Hart comes out to run Jerry off before he can attach Shatner.

Jan 16, 1995: Memphis, TN
beat Bill Dundee
lost via DQ to Brian Christopher

Jan 22, 1995: Tampa, FL - Royal Rumble 95
Vince McMahon & Jerry Lawler on commentary

Jan 24, 1995: West Palm Beach, Fl - WWF TV Taping
20-Man Battle Royal

Jan 28, 1995: Knoxville, TN
beat Dirty White Boy(c)
- SMW Title Match
- SMW Super Saturday Night Fever

Jan 30, 1995: Memphis, TN
beat Brian Christopher & Bill Dundee
- 3-Way Match

Feb 6, 1995: Memphis, TN
beat Sid Vicious(c)
- USWA Unified World Title Match
- No DQ Match

Feb 13, 1995: Memphis, TN
(c) beat Bill Dundee
- USWA Unified World Title Match

& Sid Vicious beat Big Daddy Cyrus & Crusher Bones

Feb 18, 1995: Eddie Gilbert passes away on this day of a heart attack while on a wrestling tour of Puerto Rico.

"Hot Stuff" Eddie Gilbert
Aug 14, 1961 - Feb 18, 1995

* Eddie's passing was a hard one for a lot of fans. He was not that old and was

always looked as one of the next generation to keep the legacy of Memphis Wrestling alive. It was not meant to be.

Feb 25, 1995: Memphis, TN - TV Taping
(c) lost to Bill Dundee
- USWA Unified World Title Match

The King

Feb 25, 1995: Johnson City, TN
(c) lost via DQ to the Dirty White Boy
- SMW Title Match

Feb 26, 1995: Knoxville, TN
(c) lost to Bobby Blaze
- SMW Title Match

Feb 27, 1995: Memphis, TN
& Bill Dundee won via DQ over Big Daddy Cyrus & Crusher Bones

Mar 6, 1995: Memphis, TN
Bill Dundee wins
- Double Elimination Gauntlet Match

* Individual Match Results
BC beat JL
JL beat BD
BD beat BC
BC won via DQ JL - Lawler eliminated w/2 losses
BD beat BC - Christopher eliminated w/2 losses

Mar 13, 1995: Stockton, CA - RAW TV Taping
w/Bull Nakana won via Count Out over Bret Hart

Mar 14, 1995: Fresno, CA
lost to 1-2-3 Kid

Mar 19, 1995: New York, NY - Madison Square Garden
& Owen Hart lost to Bret Hart & Razor Ramon

Mar 20, 1995: Detroit, MI
& Owen Hart lost to Davey Boy Smith & Bret Hart

Mar 20, 1995: Boston, MA - Evening
& Owen Hart lost to Davey Boy Smith & Bret Hart

Mar 24, 1995: San Antonio, TX
lost to Davey Boy Smith

Mar 25, 1995: Landover, MD
& Owen Hart lost to Davey Boy Smith & Bret Hart

Mar 27, 1995: Memphis, TN
w/Wolfie D, Bill Dundee & Mable beat Tommy Rich, Spellbinder, Gorgeous George III & Doug Gilbert

Apr 2, 1995: Hartford, CT Wrestlemania XI
Vince McMahon & Jerry Lawler on commentary

Apr 4, 1995: Glens Falls, NY
beat Adam Bomb

Apr 10, 1995: Memphis, TN
beat Bill Dundee

Apr 17, 1995: Memphis, TN
lost via DQ to Mable

May 1, 1995: Memphis, TN
beat Razor Ramon(c)
- USWA Unified World Title Match

& Psycho Sid won via Count Out over Brian Lee & Razor Ramon

May 7, 1995: Memphis, TN - TV Taping
beat Gorgeous George III

May 8, 1995: Memphis, TN
& Psycho Sid beat Brian Lee & Ron Harris

May 12, 1995: Providence, RI
lost to Bret Hart
Kiss My Foot Match

May 13, 1995: Boston, MA
& Hakushi lost to Bret Hart & Davey Boy Smith

May 14, 1995: Syracuse, NY - In Your House
beat Bret Hart

May 16, 1995: Danbury, CT - Wrestling Superstars TV Taping
beat Aldo Montoya

May 19, 1995: Montreal, Quebec
lost to via reversed decision Jean Pierre Lafitte

May 22, 1995: Memphis, TN
& Doug Gilbert lost to Brian Lee & Jimmy Harris
- Gilbert turned on Lawler

May 29, 1995: Memphis, TN
(c) won via DQ over Tommy Rich
- USWA Unified World Title Match

w/Bill Dundee, Brian Christopher, JC Ice & Wolfie D beat Max Muscle, Jimmy Harris, Brian Lee, Tommy Rich & Doug Gilbert
- Coward Waves The Flag Match

June 6, 1995: Wheeling, WV
lost to Shawn Michaels

June 10, 1995: Memphis, TN- Memphis Memories II
& Jimmy Valiant beat Phil Hickerson & Joe Leduc

& Jimmy Valiant lost to Tommy Rich & Doug Gilbert
- Best of Memphis Tag Team Tournament

June 19, 1995: Memphis, TN
& Bill Dundee lost to Doug Gilbert & Brian Lee
- Loser Gets Tarred & Feathered
- Dundee was loser

June 25, 1995: Memphis, TN - TV Taping
& Bill Dundee beat Fred James & Romeo Rodriguez

June 25, 1995: Philadelphia, PA - King of the Ring
lost to Bret Hart
-Kiss MY Foot Match

July 3, 1995: Memphis, TN
(c) beat Brian Lee
- USWA Unified World Title Match

w/Brian Christopher, Bill Dundee & Sid Vicious beat Doug Gilbert, Billy Jack Haynes, Brian Lee, Jim Harris & Brandon Baxter
- Handicap Stretcher Match

The King

July 10, 1995: Memphis, TN
w/Bill Dundee & Sid Vicious beat Brandon Baxter, Jim Harris & Brian Lee
- Handcuff Elimination Match

July 17, 1995: Memphis, TN
(c) won via DQ over Buddy Landell
- USWA Unified World Title Match

July 18, 1995: Louisville, KY
& Jimmy Valiant beat Brandon Baxter, Jim Harris & Brian Lee

July 23, 1995: WWE In Your House #2
Vince McMahon & Jerry Lawler on commentary

July 25, 1995: Louisville, KY
(c) won via DQ over Buddy Landell
- USWA Unified World Title Match

July 26, 1995: St. Louis, MO
& Hakushi lost to Bret Hart & Shawn Michaels

July 31, 1995: Memphis, TN
won via DQ over Billy Jack Haynes
- USWA Unified World Title vs. USWA Title

Aug 5, 1995: Memphis, TN
& Bill Dundee beat Gorgeous George III & the
Gambler

The King

Aug 6, 1995: Louisville, KY
(c) won via DQ over Tracey Smothers
- USWA Unified World Title Match

Aug 7, 1995: Memphis, TN
(c) beat Buddy Landell
- USWA Unified World Title Match

w/Bill Dundee, JC Ice, Wolfie D, Tommy Rich,
Doug Gilbert & Billy Jack Haynes beat Jimmy
Del Ray, Tom Prichard, Pat Tanaka, Buddy
Landell, Gorgeous George III, Robert Gibson &
Tracey Smothers
- 14-Man Tag Team Rage In The Cage Match

Aug 14, 1995: Worcester, MA - RAW Taping
lost via DQ to Shawn Michaels
- Inter-Continental Title Match

Aug 21, 1995: Memphis, TN

(c) beat Tracey Smothers
- USWA Unified World Title Match

**Aug 27, 1995: Pittsburgh, PA - Summer
Slam 95**
Vince McMahon, Jerry Lawler & Dox Hendrix on
commentary

Bret Hart w/George Steele won via DQ over
Issac Yankem DDS w/Jerry Lawler

Sep 4, 1995: Memphis, TN
& Sid Vicious lost via DQ to Jesse James
Armstrong & Brian Lee

Sep 11, 1995: Memphis, TN
(c) beat Jesse James Armstrong
- USWA Unified World Title Match

**Sep 24, 1995: Saginaw, MI - In Your House
#3**
Vince McMahon, Jim Ross & Jerry Lawler on
commentary

**Sep 25, 1995: Grand Rapids, MI - RAW
Taping**
Bret Hart beats Pierre Lafitte. Hart then attacks
Jerry Lawler who is commentating at ringside.

Oct 5, 1995: Boston, MA
Bret Hart w/George Steele won via submission
over Issac Yankem DDS w/Jerry Lawler
-Steele runs off Lawler early in the match

**Oct 23, 1995: Brandon, Manitoba - RAW
Taping**
& Isaac Yankem DDS won via DQ over Hakushi
& Bret Hart

**Oct 24, 1995: Regina, Saskatchewan -
Wrestling Superstars Taping**
& Isaac Yankem DDS lost to Billy & Bart
Gunn(c)
- WWF World Tag Title Match

Nov 6, 1995: Memphis, TN
(c) lost to Ahmed Johnson
- USWA Unified World Title Match

Nov 14, 1995: Louisville, KY
(c) lost to Ahmed Johnson
- USWA Unified World Title Match

Nov 19, 1995: Landover, MD - Survivor Series
w/Isaac Yankem, Mabel & Triple H lost to Henry Godwin, Savio Vega, Fatu & the Undertaker

Nov 22, 1995: Memphis, TN
won via DQ over Ahmed Johnson(c)
- USWA Unified World Title Match

The King

Nov 27, 1995: Memphis, TN
won via DQ over Brad Armstrong(c)
- SMW Title Match

Dec 11, 1995: Salisbury, MD - RAW Taping
Ahmed Johnson won via DQ over Issac Yankem DDS when Jerry Lawler attacked Johnson during the match.

Dec 17, 1995: Hershey, PA - WWF In Your House PPV
Vince McMahon & Jerry Lawler on commentary

Dec 18, 1995: Newark, DE - RAW Taping
Undertaker vs. Issac Yankem match. Jerry Lawler was at ringside doing his normal commentary and decided to try to steal the remains of the Undertaker's urn. Taker then turned towards Lawler and scared him, causing the King to run to the backstage area.

Dec 26, 1995: Louisville, KY
beat Tommy Rich(c)
- SMW Title Match

Dec 27, 1995: Memphis, TN
beat Brad Armstrong(c)
- SMW Title Match

* Pro Wrestling Illustrated 1995 Awards

1995 Most Hated
Winner: Jerry Lawler

1996

Chapter 27

Jan 3, 1996: Memphis TN
lost to Tex Slazenger(c)
- USWA Title Match
- USWA Title, not the USWA Unified World Title

Jan 5, 1996: Long Island, NY
& Isaac Yankem DDS lost to the Smoking Gunns(c)
- WWF World Tag Title Match

Jan 6, 1996: New Haven, CT
& Isaac Yankem DDS lost to the Smoking Gunns(c)
- WWF World Tag Title Match

Jan 10, 1996: Memphis, TN
beat Tex Slazenger(c)
USWA Title Match

Jan 13, 1996: Memphis, TN
(c) lost to Tommy Rich
USWA Title Match

Jan 15, 1996: Memphis, TN
& Tex Slazenger lost to Tommy Rich & Doug Gilbert

Jan 21, 1996: Fresno, CA - Royal Rumble
Competed in Royal Rumble

Feb 3, 1996: Cherry Hill, NJ
lost to Doug Gilbert

Feb 14, 1996: Memphis, TN
& Jeff Jarrett won via DQ over Bret Hart & the Undertaker
- Undertaker chokeslammed Ref Bill Rush for DQ

Feb 16, 1996: Nashville, TN
lost to Bret Hart(c)
- WWF World Title Match
- Steel Cage Match

Feb 17, 1996: Memphis, TN
lost to Bret Hart(c)
- WWF World Title Match
- Steel Cage Match

The King

Feb 18, 1996: Louisville, KY - WWF In Your House #6
Vince McMahon & Jerry Lawler on commentary

Feb 24, 1996: Memphis, TN
& Brian Christopher won via DQ over Bodydonnas (Zip &Skip) w/Sunny

Feb 28, 1996: Memphis
beat Bill Dundee

Mar 4, 1996: Memphis, TN
USWA Unified World Title Tournament
Rd 1: beat Brian Christopher
Semi-finals: beat Giant Warrior
Finals: beat Mabel
- Wins USWA World Title

Mar 6 Memphis, TN
& Brian Christopher beat the Headbangers

Mar 8 Truman, AR
vs. Bill Dundee

Mar 10, 1996: Corpus Christi, TX - WWF Superstars Taping
beat Al Jackson

Mar 18, 1996: Memphis, TN
(c) won via DQ over Mankind
- USWA Unified World Title Match
- Mankind was Cactus Jack, Mick Foley

The King

Mar 23, 1996: Memphis, TN - TV Taping
won via DQ over Reggie B. Fine

Mar 25, 1996: Memphis, TN
& Brian Christopher lost to Men On Mission
(King Mabel & Sir Mo)

Mar 31, 1996: Anaheim, CA - Wrestlemania XII
Vince McMahon & Jerry Lawler on commentary

Apr 1, 1996: San Bernardino, CA - RAW Taping
lost to Shawn Michaels(c)
- WWE World Heavyweight Title Match
- Michaels' 1st defense of WWE World Title.

Apr 2, 1996: San Diego, CA - WWF Superstars Taping
beat Greg Davis

Apr 8, 1996: Memphis, TN
(c) lost via DQ to Tommy Rich
USWA Unified World Title Match

w/Brian Christopher & Moondog Spot lost to
Mabel, Mo & Reggie B. Fine

Apr 15, 1996: Memphis, TN
(c) went to a draw with Jeff Jarrett
USWA Unified World Title Match

Apr 20, 1996: Memphis, TN - TV Taping
(c) lost to Jeff Jarrett
- Unified World Title Match

Apr 22, 1996: Memphis, TN
won via DQ over Tony Falk

Apr 28, 1996: Omaha, NE - WWF In Your House PPV
Vince McMahon & Jerry Lawler on commentary

May 6, 1996: Memphis, TN
lost to Brian Christopher

May 9, 1996: Erie, PA
beat Razor Ramon
- Special Ref: Mr. Perfect

May 10, 1996: Hamilton, Ontario
beat Razor Ramon
- Special Ref: Mr. Perfect

May 11, 1996: Syracuse, NY
beat Razor Ramon
- Special Ref: Mr. Perfect

May 12, 1996: Binghamton, NY
beat Razor Ramon
- Special Ref: Mr. Perfect

May 18, 1996: Memphis, TN
& Bill Dundee beat the Cyberpunks(c)
- USWA World Tag Title Match
- Cyperpunks were JC Ice & Wolfie D

May 20, 1996: Memphis, TN
beat King Mabel(c)
- USWA Unified World Title Match

May 26, 1996: Florence, NC - WWF In Your House PPV
Vince McMahon & Jerry Lawler on commentary

lost to Ahmed Johnson

May 27, 1996: Fayetteville, NC
lost to Shawn Michaels(c)
- WWF World Title Match

May 28, 1996: North Charleston, SC
beat Marty Garner

June 1, 1996: Memphis, TN
(c) lost to Brian Christopher
- USWA Unified World Title Match

The King

June 10, 1996: Memphis, TN
lost via DQ to CyberPunk Fire
- Mask vs $5,000

June 17, 1996: Memphis, TN
beat CyberPunk Fire

* Final regular card for Jerry Jarrett/Jerry Lawler at the Mid-South Coliseum. End of an era. Memphis Wrestling officially moved to the Mid-South Coliseum in June 1971. The fans always loved the "Roundhouse" but with the dwindling tickets sales, it could not sustain Memphis Wrestling being able to afford the cost incurred with renting the building two to four times a month.

June 23 Milwaukee, WI - King of the Ring
lost to the Ultimate Warrior

July 1, 1996: Memphis, TN
& Bill Dundee beat Flex Kavana & Bart Sawyer(c)
- USWA WorldTag Title Match
- Flex Kavana was Dewayne Johnson, otherwise known as the Rock. One of pro wrestling and now Hollywood's biggest stars.

July 8, 1996: Memphis, TN
& Bill Dundee(c) lost to Flex Kavana & Bart Sawyer
- USWA World Tag Title Match

July 21, 1996: Vancouver, BC - WWF In Your House PPV
Vince McMahon, Jim Ross & Jerry Lawler on commentary

lost to Phinneas Goodwinn
July 22, 1996: Seattle, WA - RAW Taping
beat Aldo Montoya Raw

July 23, 1996: Yakima, WA - WWF Superstars Taping
lost to Aldo Montoya

Aug 2, 1996: Montreal, Quebec
lost to Aldo Montoya

Aug 17, 1996: West Helena, AR
beat Jeff Jarrett(c)
- USWA World Unified Title

Aug 18, 1996: Cleveland, OH - SummerSlam
beat Jake Roberts

Aug 19, 1996: Wheeling, W
lost to Marc Mero

Aug 20, 1996: Columbus, OH
& Mankind lost to the Undertaker & Jake Roberts

Aug 30, 1996: Memphis, TN
(c) lost to Sid Vicious
- USWA World Unified Title

Sep 2, 1996: Memphis, TN
beat Sid Vicious(c)
- USWA Unified World Title Match

Sep 5, 1996: Austin, TX
lost to Barry Windham

Sep 6, 1996: Houston, TX
lost to Barry Windham

Sep 7, 1996: Dallas, TX
lost to Barry Windham

Sep 8, 1996: Oklahoma City, OK
lost to Barry Windham

Sep 8, 1996: Tulsa, OK
lost to Barry Windham

Sep 12, 1996: Miami, FL
lost to Barry Windham

Sep 13, 1996: Huntington, WV
beat Barry Windham

Sep 14, 1996: Louisville, KY
beat Barry Windham
Sep 21, 1996: Baltimore, MD
lost via Count Out to Mark Henry

Sep 22, 1996: Philadelphia, PA - WWF In Your House
lost via submission to Mark Henry

Sep 23, 1996: Hershey, PA - RAW Taping
lost to Jake Roberts

Sep 26, 1996: Union City, TN
(c) lost via DQ to Mark Henry
- USWA Unified World Title Match

Sep 28, 1996: Memphis, TN
& Scott Bowden lost to Mark Henry & Brian Christopher

Oct 4, 1996: Jonesboro, AR
(c) lost to the Colorado Kid
- USWA World Unified Title
- Colorado Kid was Mike Rapada

Oct 20, 1996: Indianapolis, IN - WWF In Your House
Vince McMahon, Jim Ross & Jerry Lawler on commentary

Nov 16, 1996: Memphis, TN
beat the Colorado Kid(c)
- USWA World Unified Title

Nov 17, 1996: New York, NY - Madison Square Garden - Survivor Series
Vince McMahon, Jim Ross & Jerry Lawler on commentary

w/Triple H, Goldust & Crush lost to Jake Roberts, Rocky Maivia, Barry Windham & Marc Mero

The King

Dec 15, 1996: West Palm Beach, FL - WWF In Your House
Vince McMahon & Jerry Lawler on commentary

Dec 30, 1996: Albany, NY - RAW Taping
beat Tony Devito
won via Count Out over Goldust
& Triple H won via DQ over Goldust & Marc Mero

* Pro Wrestling Illustrated 1996 Awards

1996 Most Hated
2nd Runner Up: Jerry Lawler

Check Out Mark James' Entire Line Of Books At
www.markjamesbooks.com

Memphis Wrestling History Presents 1978

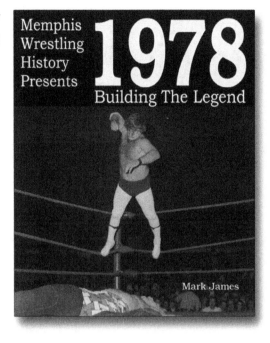

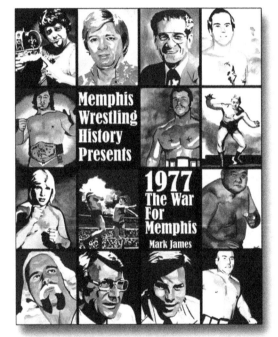

Memphis Wrestling History Presents 1977

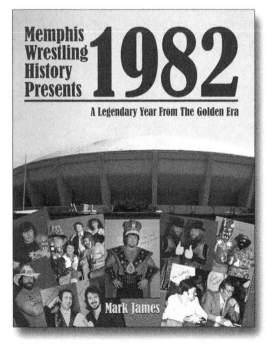

Memphis Wrestling History Presents 1982

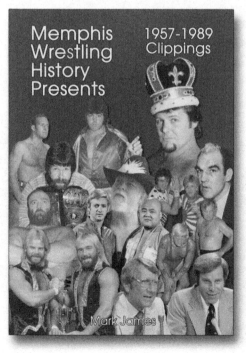
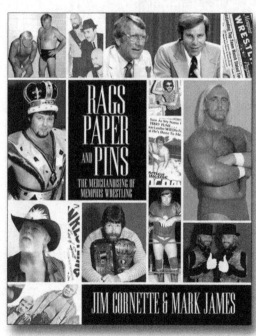

Check Out Mark James' Entire Line Of Books At
www.markjamesbooks.com

Memphis Wrestling History Presents:
1992-1993 Programs & Booking Sheets

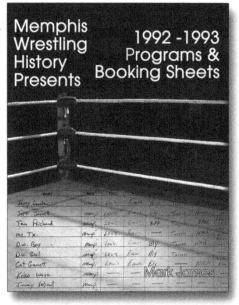

Memphis Wrestling History Presents:
Tennessee Athletic Commission

Memphis Filings 1977-1980

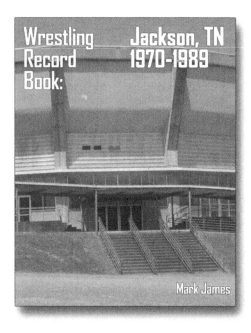

Check Out Mark James' Entire Line Of Books At
www.markjamesbooks.com

Wrestling Record Book: Atlanta, GA 1960-1984

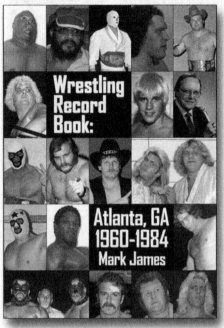

Wrestling Record Book: Mid-South/UWF 1979-87

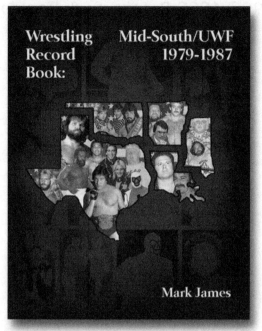

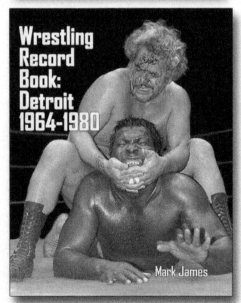

Wrestling Record Book: Detroit 1965-1980

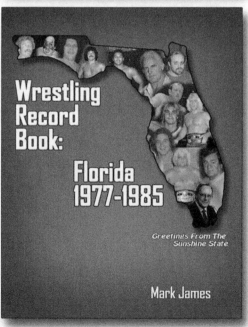

Wrestling Record Book: Florida 1977-1985

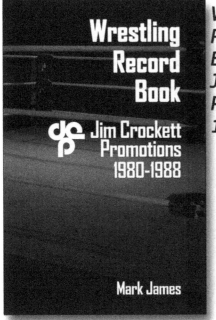

Wrestling Record Book: Jim Crockett Promotions 1980-1988

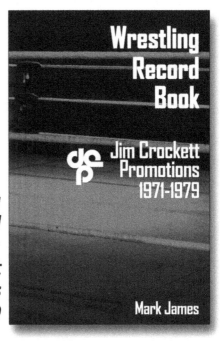

Wrestling Record Book: Jim Crockett Promotions 1971-1979

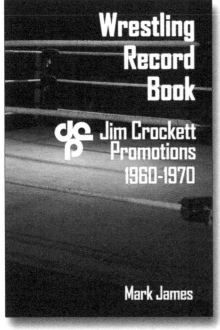

Wrestling Record Book: Jim Crockett Promotions 1960-1970

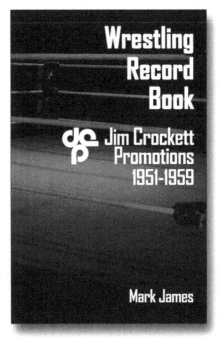

Wrestling Record Book: Jim Crockett Promotions 1951-1959

Check Out Mark James' Entire Line Of Books At
www.markjamesbooks.com

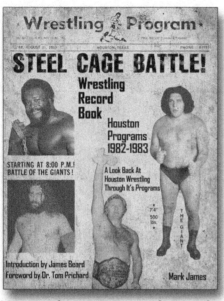

Wrestling
Record
Book

Nashville
Programs
1951-1952

Wrestling Record Book:
Houston Programs 1982-1983

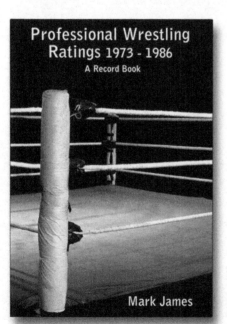

Professional Wrestling Ratings
1973-1986: A Record Book

Memphis
Wrestling
History:
1970-85

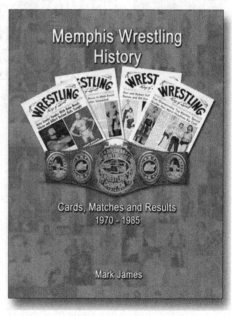

Check Out Mark James' Entire Line Of Books At
www.markjamesbooks.com

AWA Record Book: The 1960s
by George Schire & Mark James

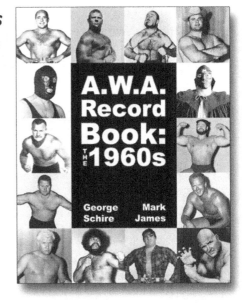

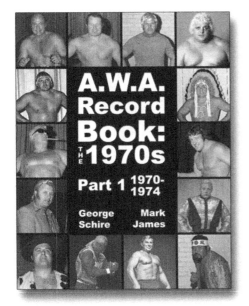

AWA Record Book:
The 1970s Part 1 1970-74
by George Schire & Mark James

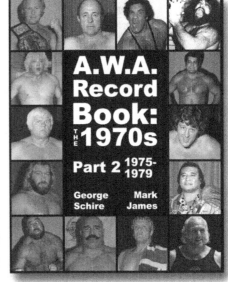

AWA Record Book:
The 1970s Part 2 1975-79
by George Schire & Mark James

Check Out Mark James' Entire Line Of Books At
www.markjamesbooks.com

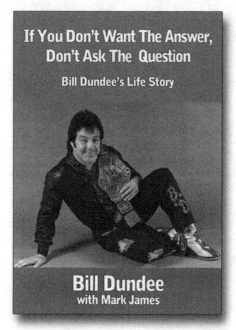

*If You Don't Want The Answer,
Don't Ask The Question*

Bill Dundee's Autobiography

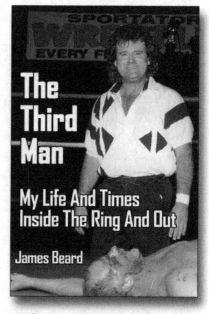

The Third Man
My Life And Times
Inside The Ring And Out

Referee James Beard

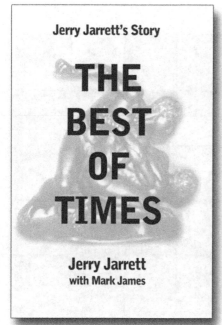

The Best Of Times
Jerry Jarrett's Autobiography

Check Out Mark James' Entire Line Of Books At
www.markjamesbooks.com

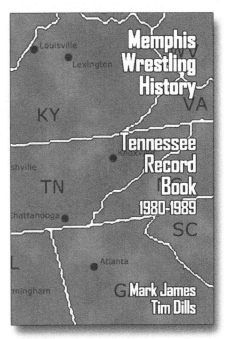

Memphis Wrestling History: Tennesse Record Book 1980-1989

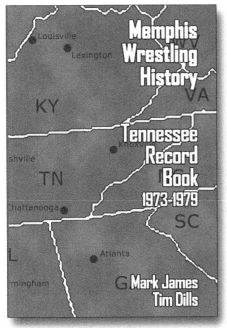

Memphis Wrestling History: Tennesse Record Book 1973-1979

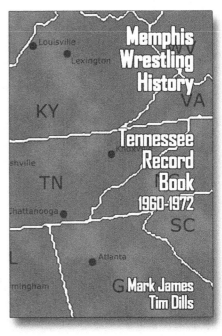

Memphis Wrestling History: Tennesse Record Book 1960-1972

Check Out Mark James' Entire Line Of Books At
www.markjamesbooks.com

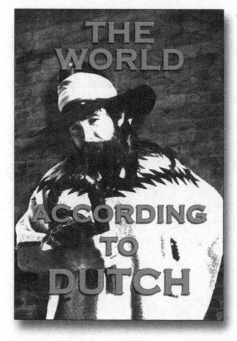

The World According To Dutch
Great Wrestling Stories From Dutch Mantell

Dad You Don't Work, You Wrestle
George South's Autobiography

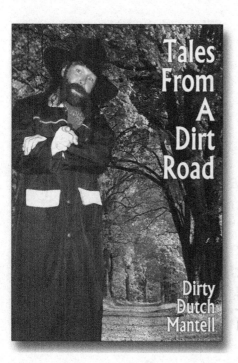

Tales From A Dirt Road
More Wrestling Stories From Dutch Mantell

Check Out Mark James' Entire Line Of Books At
www.markjamesbooks.com

The Wrestling News Vol 1: 1972-1973
Issues 1-16

by Brian Bukantis & Mark James

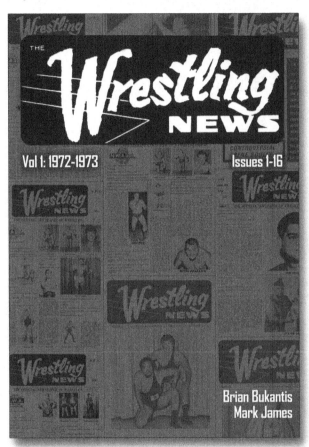

Check Out Mark James' Entire Line Of Books At
www.markjamesbooks.com

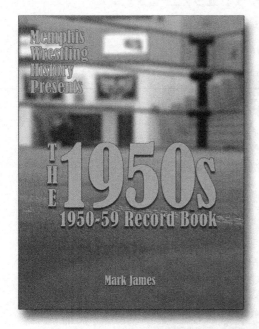

Memphis Wrestling History Presents The 1950s

Memphis Wrestling History Presents The 1960s

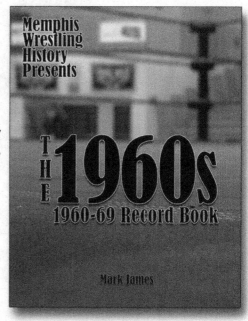

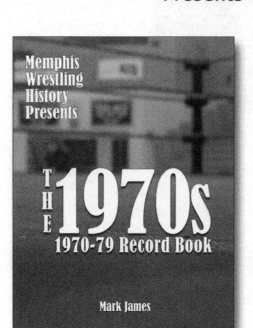

Memphis Wrestling History Presents The 1970s

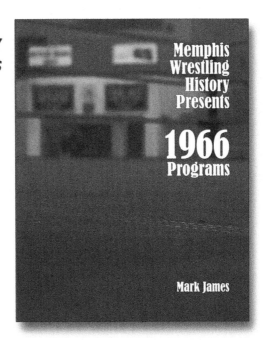
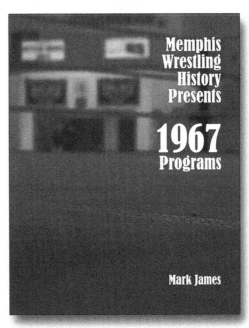

21468306R00150

Made in the USA
Middletown, DE
13 December 2018